Tolley's
Limited Liability Partnerships
Handbook

by

Simon Young, MA (Cantab), MBA

of

Veitch Penny, solicitors

Members of the LexisNexis Group worldwide

United Kingdom	Butterworths Tolley, a Division of Reed Elsevier (UK) Ltd, 2 Addiscombe Road, CROYDON CR9 5AF
Argentina	Abeledo Perrot, Jurisprudencia Argentina and Depalma, BUENOS AIRES
Australia	Butterworths, a Division of Reed International Books Australia Pty Ltd, CHATSWOOD New South Wales
Austria	ARD Betriebsdienst and Verlag Orac, VIENNA
Canada	Butterworths Canada Ltd, MARKHAM, Ontario
Chile	Publitecsa and Conosur Ltda, SANTIAGO DE CHILE
Czech Republic	Orac sro, PRAGUE
France	Editions du Juris-Classeur SA, PARIS
Hong Kong	Butterworths Asia (Hong Kong), HONG KONG
Hungary	Hvg Orac, BUDAPEST
India	Butterworths India, NEW DELHI
Ireland	Butterworths (Ireland) Ltd, DUBLIN
Italy	Giuffrè, Milan
Malaysia	Malayan Law Journal Sdn Bhd, KUALA LUMPUR
New Zealand	Butterworths of New Zealand, WELLINGTON
Poland	Wydawnictwa Prawnicze PWN, WARSAW
Singapore	Butterworths Asia, SINGAPORE
South Africa	Butterworths Publishers (Pty) Ltd, DURBAN
Switzerland	Stämpfli Verlag AG, BERNE
USA	LexisNexis, DAYTON, Ohio

A CIP Catalogue record for this book is available from the British Library.

ISBN 0 75451 181-2

Typeset by Kerrypress Ltd, Luton, Bedfordshire
Printed and Bound in Great Britain by the Cromwell Press, Trowbridge, Witshire

Visit Butterworths LexisNexis *direct* at www.butterworths.com

Contents

Contents

Acknowledgements

This book arose from a breach on my part of the classic motto of 'Never volunteer for anything'! Having read a single column inch report on the LLP Bill, as it then was, I was foolish enough to agree, at a meeting of the Law Society Management Section Executive, to write an article on the subject for the Section's newsletter. Little did I realise that it would proceed to take over my life!

Thanks are due firstly to Maureen Miller of the Law Society for fostering that initial interest and encouraging that first article, as well as for much subsequent support. Steven Durno, also of the Law Society, who has coordinated the Society's efforts in respect of the legislation, has again been unfailingly and promptly helpful on a number of occasions.

In giving presentations across the country on the subject, I have been helped in the development of my ideas by a number of fellow speakers, and particular thanks are due to Nick Carter-Pegg of BDO Stoy Hayward, Trevor Frid of Ernst & Young, and Stephen Peters of Tenon Recovery.

Whether they will believe it or not, I am also most grateful to the team at Tolley – Stephen Barc, Jacquie Bird and Irene Kaplan – for making it all happen. Without their constant encouragement (I think that's the word I want!) quite simply I would never have made myself do it, and I am very glad I have.

My partners at Veitch Penny have been consistent in their support and in their indulgence for my occasional disappearances from the office with mutterings of conferences and deadlines. Thanks also to our Marketing Manager Karen Jenkins for arranging a number of presentations for me on the subject.

Most of all though, my thanks go to the group of friends who have put up with me so much over the gestation period of this book and the other works on the subject which preceded it, and have never protested (to me, at least!) at my constant nattering about a subject which is scarcely the normal subject of dinner table conversation. To all of them – Diane Heggadon, Alan Keen, Adam Morgan, Ian Penny and Ray & Sue Sweeney – my warm and sincere thanks.

Simon Young
17 October 2001

1 – The Background and Legislative Development

This introductory chapter looks at the development of the law of partnership and the ways in which it has spread into other types of business vehicles. It goes on to consider some difficulties with modern partnership practice, and identifies the needs which gave rise to the concept of limited liability partnerships.

The progress of the legislation which has created these new entities is reviewed, and in the process a number of the themes which will pervade the discussion of them throughout the book are considered. Lastly, the chapter considers in outline possible future changes in partnership law generally, and their relevance for those considering limited liability partnerships as the business vehicle of choice.

The spread of partnership law   1.1

This book concerns itself largely with the *Limited Liability Partnerships Act 2000 (LLPA 2000)*, the latest concluded variation in the spread of partnership law across the landscape of British business law. It helps to be able to see this development in the context of the overall development of the law defining the business vehicles which have been available to entrepreneurs over the last two centuries, all of which have derived from partnerships in one way and another, from the inception of joint stock companies, which begat limited companies, through limited partnerships, to the confusingly similarly named but very different limited liability partnerships ('LLPs').

It should also be recognised that the movement for development of partnership law is still continuing, as proposals are presently being made for radical changes to the law relating to those partnerships where the concept of unlimited personal liability is to be retained.

In the beginning was the partnership   1.2

It is perhaps trite to say that, before anyone thought of doing anything else, the only way in which two or more people could operate a business venture was as a partnership. The OED records the use of the term as far back as 1700. What is perhaps remarkable is that the concept has survived largely unchanged in its fundamentals for 300 years, namely that a group of people could combine, with unlimited liability, to operate a business which had no identity of its own separate from the members of that group as combined individuals.

The last major attempt at statutory control was the *Partnership Act 1890* (*PA 1890*), and it was notable that during the recent progress of the *LLPA 2000* through various Parliamentary stages, whilst the concept underlying it received almost universal support, there were many attempts to incorporate the affectionately viewed mechanism and subsequently developed case law of the *PA 1890*, on the basis of 'If it isn't broke, don't fix it'.

The Companies Acts   1.3

However, the *LLPA 2000* should not be thought of as the first time that the concept of a partnership has been used to spin off a new business vehicle into common use. It was the need for partnerships to be able to change to cope with the demands of the Industrial Revolution that led to the passing of the Joint Stock Companies Acts in the middle of the 19th Century, and they in turn were the forebears of the positive rash of Companies Acts which continues up to the present day.

Even now there are cross-overs between the concepts, as with the restriction on numbers of partners in a firm which appears in company legislation, as in 1.5 below.

Limited partnerships   1.4

The next development was the formation of limited partnerships, in accordance with the *Limited Partnerships Act 1907* (*LPA 1907*).

Here, the idea was to allow participation in the business by one or more 'limited' partners, whose role was simply to provide capital but not otherwise to participate in or be liable for the running of the business, which was to be left to the 'general' partner(s). The key to this remaining in the partnership sphere rather than that of a company was, and indeed still is, that the general partners retained unlimited personal liability. These have in practice been of specialist use only, largely in the investment field.

The restrictions of partnerships 1.5

A constant theme of the development of the business world throughout the 20th Century, and the latter half in particular, has been the relentless growth of the professional services sector. The President of the Institute of Chartered Accountants in England and Wales once said 'The work now shared amongst hundreds of members of the [accountancy] profession will pass to a few big international firms', and that was in 1926!

It is perhaps not surprising therefore that the concept of a partnership being a small group working together has in many cases long since ceased to be relevant. It has done so in the face of legal restriction, since statute has restricted the size of partnerships, the latest version of which is *section 716* of the *Companies Act 1985*, which still limits a partnership's membership to 20, unless the partnership carries on a profession which is exempted either by the Act itself (such as chartered accountants and solicitors) or by one of a series of regulations passed under it (such as registered architects or chartered surveyors).

For those City professional service firms who now number even their UK partners in hundreds, the attempt to retain the personal concept of partnership has therefore long been something of an irrelevance.

The rise of personal liability 1.6

Going hand-in-hand with the increase in the size of professional service firms has been an increase in the frequency and size of claims against them, and the consequent risk of an uninsured and uninsurable wipe-out of the partners' personal assets, perhaps even years after their retirement or death. The risk of negligence claims spread beyond previously considered bounds, and caused a measure of panic in the professional ranks. So too did the increase in willingness amongst business institutions to see their professional advisers, or anyone against whom they could construct a duty of care, as an insured Aunt Sally to recompense them against their own failings.

The classic example was mortgage lenders who, in the early to middle parts of the 1990s, blamed everyone and everything in sight, except of course their own lending policies when 'market share' was what mattered most to them, for losses suffered in the property recession of the late 1980s. It is therefore no surprise that there is (necessarily anecdotal) evidence of firms where prospective partners refused to join because the risks were unacceptable, or where partners sought to vest all their assets in their spouses.

Introducing the concept of limited liability partnerships 1.7

Whereas the concept of previous types of business vehicle were home-grown, that of the limited liability partnership is an import. Bearing in mind that the spread of the litigious approach which gives rise to their perceived need is often considered as migrating here from the US, it is perhaps no surprise that that is where the idea originated. Dr Kern Alexander, in an address to the Institute of Advanced Legal Studies, in June 2001, traced the development of the LLP in the US, from the first statute in Texas in 1991, through to the stage where 49 states have such laws. The earliest of these tend to shield partners only from vicarious liability for the negligence of others within the partnership, but not for normal trading debts. Later statutes, including those based upon the *Uniform Partnership Act* (as last revised in 1996) which has been applied in over 40 states, protect against personal liability for business and contractual debts as well.

The status of LLP is only a variation of the existing partnership entity, arrived at by vote and then registered at state level. The vote is reversible. There is no creation of a separate, incorporated, entity, and for that reason tax transparency (see 1.12 below) applies, and has come to be accepted internationally (e.g. in the Canadian tax authorities' treatment of US LLPs which has moved to transparency from their previous approach of treating LLPs as incorporated bodies). As the partnership does not become incorporated, there is no requirement under these statutes for disclosure of partners' financial positions. Some states impose minimum capital and/or insurance requirements.

Bringing the concept to the UK 1.8

The concept of LLPs, in UK terms, was first seized upon by the largest firms of accountants. One reason they fought shy of incorporation, through their US arms, was fear of US-style litigation. As they did not initially find support from the UK Government for the idea of UK LLPs, they turned their attention to the possibility of offshore incorporation, and even got so far as to commission the drafting of legislation in Jersey.

At that stage the Government woke up to the possible loss of revenue and international commercial prestige if the major firms carried out their threat to move their bases offshore, and began to espouse the idea of limitation of liability.

The consultation process 1.9

In 1996 the Common Law Team of the Law Commission looked at the possibility of replacing joint and several liability within professional partnerships by a system of proportional liability. This was followed the next year by a consultation paper issued by the DTI itself, entitled *Limited Liability Partnerships: A New Form of Business Association for Professions*. (It is worth noting that at this stage both the DTI and the Law Commission were limiting their consideration to professional partnerships.)

A positive response to the DTI consultation paper led to the publication of a draft Bill and regulations in September 1998, and after further consultation a revised version was published in July 1999.

Progress through Parliament   1.10

The Bill was introduced in the House of Lords in November 1999. One important change from earlier thoughts was that the Government now believed that the new opportunity should be available, not just to professional partnerships, but to any business. The explanatory notes, which accompanied the Bill, gave as the reasons for promoting the Bill concerns arising from:

- increased frequency and size of professional negligence claims;
- depersonalising increases of numbers of partners within firms;
- increasing specialisation of partnerships;
- merging of different professions within a firm; and
- personal risks when claims exceed assets/insurance.

The principle of the Bill received all-party support, but did not attract universal approbation. In the Lords, Lord Phillips of Sudbury, himself a practising solicitor, described the Bill as providing 'your two-man cowboy building outfit with a uniquely flexible and light-framed means of screwing the public'. In the Commons, Austin Mitchell MP categorised the supporters of the Bill as painting the 'tear-jerking spectacle of those in accountancy partnerships living in terror in case their yachts, farms, pubs and holiday retreats are suddenly confiscated'. They were however lone voices crying in the wilderness, and the Bill received Royal Assent on 20 July 2000.

The partnership ethos   1.11

Whilst the principle of the Bill was generally accepted, it was not the case that the details had as smooth a passage. The main battleground, which emerged on many occasions and in many guises, was whether the new animal should (as in the US model) look more like a partnership, or a limited company. The Government favoured the latter, but others tried hard to preserve both the ethos of the inter-personal relationships of partnerships, and the framework of the *Partnership Act 1890* which they saw as embodying that ethos. Those opponents were partially successful, in that in February 2000 a further consultation paper was published proposing a default code (based on selected provisions of the *PA 1890*) to govern by regulation some aspects of the governance of LLPs and the relationships between members. Responses being favourable, these provisions were later incorporated by regulation.

The success was however only partial, and the Government did not relent on two central issues: namely the refusal to legislate for a duty of good faith between the members of an LLP as individuals; and the specific disapplication of all partnership law in respect of LLPs to the extent that it is not expressly embodied in the *LLPA 2000* or regulations made under it (or any later statutory provision).

The role of the Inland Revenue   1.12

It was recognised by the Government that many professions had for some years had the opportunity, if they disliked partnership status, to incorporate under the Companies Acts, but that few had chosen to do so either for cultural or, very often, for fiscal reasons. Imposing on LLPs a tax regime similar to that of limited companies was therefore likely to mean a low take-up rate. An important theme of the legislation has therefore been that LLPs will in effect be taxed as if they were still partnerships, so that it is the individual members rather than the LLP itself which will be taxable. (There are however still concerns as to the use of LLPs for tax avoidance purposes, and Inland Revenue investigations into that sphere are continuing.)

Further, the transfer from partnership to LLP status is intended to be tax neutral. The jargon adopted is that the approach is one of 'transparency', i.e. that the Revenue will look through the corporate entity to the reality of the underlying membership.

The protection of the public   1.13

Protecting the public was the other main battleground in the passage of the legislation. The Government was adamant that the price to be paid for limitation of liability was that the public should be protected by the publication of information about the LLP's finances akin to that required of limited companies.

Opponents argued that this would place unduly onerous duties of disclosure on the members of LLPs, and place them at a disadvantage in relation to those who chose to remain as partnerships, or (in the case of the 'global' firms) to utilise LLPs operating under the looser US requirements. Their cries were not heard, and there remain duties of disclosure based on company-style provisions. For the most part however they are duties of disclosure of the members' aggregate financial position, rather than that of individuals' positions, as the underlying idea is that a member of the public thinking of doing business with an LLP needs to know how the overall business is doing, and how much the totality of its membership has backed their faith in the business by investing their own capital in it, rather than how its rewards or that capital is divided amongst the members.

The main regulations   1.14

As will be seen, the *LLPA 2000* achieves much of its effect through regulations made under it. The main ones are the *Limited Liability Partnerships Regulations 2001 (SI 2001/1090)* ('the *Regulations*'). To say that they are not easy to understand is an understatement indeed. The problem is that they do not work as 'stand-alone' regulations, but rather (for the most part) by extremely lengthy schedules which apply, disapply, amend, supplement or replace detailed provisions of the *Companies Act 1985 (CA 1985)*, the *Insolvency Act 1986 (IA 1986)* and sundry other statutes.

There was much opposition to the incorporation of so much of the effect of the new law being in secondary legislation, as opposed to being on the face of the *LLPA 2000* itself and accordingly needing full Parliamentary scrutiny for any amendment. However the only concession the Government was prepared to make was to say that any amendments to the *Regulations* could only be made under the affirmative resolution procedure, rather than by Ministerial decision alone.

Brief mention should also be made that there is, in *LLPA 2000, s 14*, the (as yet unexercised) power to make regulations for 'oversea' LLPs, described in *s 14(3)* as bodies incorporated or otherwise established outside Great Britain and having such connection with Great Britain, and such other features, as regulations may prescribe.

Other regulations   1.15

There are also the *Limited Liability Partnerships (Fees) (No 2) Regulations 2001 (SI 2001/969)*. All fees quoted in this book are as prescribed by those regulations and the Schedule to them.

All forms are as prescribed by the *Limited Liability Partnerships (Forms) Regulations 2001 (SI 2001/927)*, except for the forms required by specific provisions of the *LLPA 2000* (Forms LLP 2, LLP 3, LLP 8, LLP 287, LLP 287a, LLP 288a, LLP 288b, and LLP 288c) which were approved separately by the Registrar of Companies by a Notice of Approval dated 5 March 2001.

A comprehensible version   1.16

Any reader anxious to check detailed provisions would do well to read Douglas Armour's book *Limited Liability Partnerships: The New Legislation* which sets out in full the *LLPA 2000* and the *Regulations*, as well as the relevant sections of the *Companies Act 1985*, the *Insolvency Act 1986* and the *Company Directors Disqualification Act 1986* as modified by the *Regulations* in their application to LLPs.

Commencement   1.17

The whole of *LLPA 2000* came into force on 6 April 2001. Similarly, so did the various sets of regulations referred to above. The first LLPs were incorporated on the commencement day, the proud possessor of number OC300001 being Ernst & Young LLP.

Application of the Act   1.18

The *LLPA 2000* applies to LLPs and their formation in England, Wales and Scotland. The provisions for Scottish LLPs (to which the *Regulations* broadly apply, but in respect of which there are also separate regulations) are outside the scope of this work.

The *LLPA 2000* does not apply (with the exception of the sections relating to taxation of LLPs) to Northern Ireland. There is also provision for oversea LLPs, i.e. those incorporated or established abroad but having some connection with Great Britain.

The future of partnership law   1.19

As mentioned above at 1.2 and 1.4 above, the last significant changes in partnership law, before the *LLPA 2000*, were in 1890 and 1907 respectively. It does not appear likely, however, that we will need to wait as long for the next change.

In September 2000, the Law Commission and the Scottish Law Commission jointly published an extensive consultation paper entitled simply *Partnership Law (the Commissions' proposals)*. (They also announced the intention to publish a further such paper dealing with limited partnerships, under the *LPA 1907*.) That consultation paper is itself the result of nearly three years' work and preliminary consultation, following a request for the subject to be considered which was made to the two Commissions in November 1997 by the DTI, so it can be considered that there is political impetus behind the investigation, and that some reform may be expected.

Areas for potential reform   1.20

The Commissions' proposals (see 1.19 above) list ten main areas for consideration, as follows:

- partnerships should have a separate legal personality (as do LLPs) either as a result of voluntary registration or (as they would prefer) of the application of such a new principle to all partnerships;

- a partnership should not necessarily be dissolved when a partner joins or leaves;

- an outgoing partner should not have an implied right to force winding up on his departure;

- those partnerships having legal personality should, on dissolution, continue in existence during an orderly winding up, like a company;

- partners would only be agents of each other if the partnership did not have separate legal personality;

- a partnership with legal personality should have primary liability for the firm's debts, albeit that partners' personal liability would continue to exist as a secondary liability;

- partnerships with legal personality should be able to hold property of any kind in their own names;

- a duty of good faith as between partners should continue, and indeed should be supplemented by a duty to act with reasonable care and skill;

- a partnership with legal personality could both sue and be sued in its own name, with individual partners being sued in the same action and, to facilitate the latter, partners would be obliged to furnish details of all (including former) partners who might be liable;

- a system of registration is proposed; and

- additional obligations as to disclosure of partners' details under the *Business Names Act 1985* is contemplated.

The impact of the proposals on potential LLPs   1.21

It is not in one sense within the scope of this book to deal in detail with the proposals set out in 1.20 above. Nonetheless anyone considering a move from the current status of partnership to that of LLP would do well to contemplate what the consequences would be for them if the proposals did go through. For instance, if the important thing for them is to have a business with a separate legal personality, then they might choose to wait and see whether this is automatically conferred by future legislation. On the other hand, if the desired aim is to avoid joint and several personal liability, then they need to know that this does not appear likely to form part of general revisions in future, and that they might as well seek LLP status now, under the *LLPA 2000*.

For that reason the Commissions' proposals will be referred to at various points throughout this book, where it is felt they help to shed light on aspects of the decision as to whether forming a limited liability partnership is desirable.

Company law reform   1.22

Another area where there is considerable effort going into the formulation of law reform which is likely to have some impact upon LLPs is the comprehensive review of company law being undertaken by the DTI. At the time of writing, this has encompassed a number of consultation papers.

The final report of the Company Law Steering Group's review, *Modern Company Law for a Competitive Economy*, was published in July 2001, and is referred to in various places below, especially in Chapter 10.

Future types of business vehicles   1.23

If the Commissions' proposals are considered likely to be at least partially implemented, then it looks as if any business, depending on its circumstances, will need to select its status from a bewildering array of business vehicles, as follows:

- sole trader;

- old-style partnership;
- new-style partnership with separate legal personality;
- limited partnership (under *LPA 1907*);
- limited liability partnership (under *LLPA 2000*);
- limited company; and
- public limited company.

2 – What is an LLP?

> This chapter considers in broad terms the concepts applicable to an LLP.
>
> In particular, it places the LLP, as a body corporate, in the spectrum of business vehicles, and looks at the consequences of the corporate identity. It considers the prerequisites for the formation and continuity of an LLP. The contrast between the laws applicable to LLPs and partnerships are considered in general.

The definition of an LLP   2.1

Since LLPs are entirely creatures of statute, it follows that the first task of the *LLPA 2000* is to define what its subject matter is.

The first statement (*LLPA 2000, s 1(1)*) is that an LLP is a new form of legal entity. Although that seems at first sight a simplistic statement, it is worth bearing in mind when considering the construction of the legislation, since there is always going to be the temptation to consider an LLP as a sub-species of one of the types of legal entity with which we are familiar, i.e. a limited company or a partnership. It is not – it is a stand-alone concept which, save insofar as other statutory provisions are specifically applied to it, must be viewed under its own code.

An LLP's corporate personality   2.2

The *LLPA 2000* goes on (in *s 1(2)*) to state that an LLP is a body corporate, and lest there be any doubt it spells out the fact that that means it has legal personality separate from that of its members.

Indeed the very term 'members', which is used throughout the legislation, has presumably been introduced to distinguish the position of the individuals involved in an LLP from that of 'partners' in a partnership, and to reinforce the separate nature of an LLP. In this sense the LLP is much more like a limited company than a partnership (though that distinction may reduce or disappear if the proposals of the Law Commission and Scottish Law Commission for giving separate legal personality to all or some normal partnerships (see 1.19 above) eventually find their way onto the statute book). The ways in which this separate personality affects the position of an LLP will pervade the rest of this book, but amongst the most significant are its ability to join in other business ventures as shareholder/member/partner, to own land in its own right, to sue and be sued and to grant floating charges.

The moment of creation   2.3

LLPA 2000, s 1(2) goes on to state that an LLP is formed by being incorporated under the Act. Therefore of course no LLP could be formed under UK law before the commencement of the *LLPA 2000* on 6 April 2001. (That is not to say that no business using the suffix 'LLP' could be trading in the UK before that date – the major law firm 'Clifford Chance LLP' practised as such for some time beforehand, being the UK arm of an LLP registered under the law of New York.)

It is the fact of incorporation which gives birth to the LLP, not the decision to form an LLP or even the documentation, in the shape of a limited liability partners' agreement (to use the term adopted by the legislation – somewhat curiously since it otherwise refers to 'members') which records and details that decision. Again, though this is a simple concept, it has its practical aspects, since the moment of creation will be dependent on an event beyond the control of the members, i.e. the dating by the Registrar of Companies of the LLP's certificate of incorporation. Results of this timing difficulty are that the dangers of pre-incorporation contracts will need to be guarded against where possible, and that efforts should also be made to avoid the situation where a period of time after incorporation exists during which the LLP has no provisions in place for its internal governance other than those specified in the *Regulations*.

Unlimited capacity   2.4

An LLP has unlimited capacity (*LLPA 2000, s 1(3)*). There are therefore no restrictions placed on its operations at all, and it can do anything any other legal person – natural or incorporated – can do. There is no equivalent either of the distinction between public and private limited companies, or of the doctrine that a limited company may risk operating ultra vires if it carries out activities beyond the scope of the objects clauses contained in its memorandum of association.

As will be seen, there is no obligation for an LLP to define, in its initial documentation, what its business purposes are – merely that it is intended to be a business entity. It is therefore quite at liberty wholly to alter the nature of its business at any time without any external sanction.

Unlimited maximum size   2.5

There is no restriction on the number of members which an LLP may have. That may seem not worthy of noting, for there will be many who no longer appreciate that, in theory at least, partnerships are still restricted in size.

Section 716 of the *Companies Act 1985* provides that partnerships shall not have more than 20 partners, unless the partnerships are of such a type as to attract an exemption, either under the Act itself (e.g. chartered account-ants and solicitors) or under any of the 16 sets of regulations so far passed to give exemptions to other professions (e.g. registered architects, chartered surveyors, etc.). However, that section is not one of those included in *SI 2001/1090, Sch 2* as a provision of the *Companies Act 1985* applicable to LLPs by virtue of *SI 2001/1090, reg 4*. (A DTI Consultation Paper, *Removing the 20 Partner Limit* (URN 01/752), was published in April 2001, and responses are currently being considered by the Government.)

Minimum size   2.6

The minimum number of members required to form an LLP is two (*LLPA 2000, s 2(1)(a)*). The idea is that that remains a constant minimum throughout the existence of the LLP (though see 2.9 below as to the possible usage of LLPs by what are in reality sole traders).

It is not however an absolute, i.e. the LLP as an entity does not cease to exist the moment the qualification fails to be met, e.g. by reason of the death of one of the only two members. Rather, it becomes a reason for someone to apply to have the LLP wound up (*IA 1986, s 122(1)(c)* as modified). It might also be a reason for the Registrar to investigate the possibility of striking it off the register as having ceased to operate (*CA 1985, s 652* as modified). In the meantime, the LLP continues to exist and can continue to trade. If however it does so for more than a six months period of grace, then the surviving member becomes jointly and severally liable with the LLP for debts incurred thereafter (*CA 1985, s 24* as modified). A prudent survivor will therefore arrange that within the six months period he/she either introduces a new member or ceases to trade, if they want to avoid personal liability.

Duration and continuity   2.7

Like a limited company, an LLP does not die naturally, though it can be killed off. Thus its existence is not even terminated by the death of its last surviving member, or by the cessation of a specific reason for which it was brought into life, e.g. the completion of a joint venture. It has to be brought to an end by a positive act, being either the conclusion of a winding up or a striking off.

The idea is that, like a company, the continuity of existence until that act, e.g. during the conduct of a winding up, allows for an orderly disposal of the LLP's affairs. This distinguishes it from a partnership at will under the *Partnership Act 1890*, which may cease to exist at a moment's notice, by reason of a unilateral act, and thus needs to be wound up under the provisions of that Act since it has no continued existence after that moment. (Such an act would usually be the service by an individual partner of a notice to dissolve the partnership. No such power is conferred on a member of an LLP. The problems that such notices can cause are recognised in the Law Commission/Scottish Law Commission joint proposals as one of the main reasons for altering the personality of normal partnerships.)

Disapplication of partnership law   2.8

To emphasise the fact referred to at 2.1 above, to the effect that an LLP is of a unique nature, *LLPA 2000, s 1(5)* specifically states that, except as it or any other statute may specifically require, the law relating to partnerships does not apply to LLPs. It should be noted that that goes further than saying that no statutory provisions shall apply unless otherwise specified: the wording would seem to be apt to exclude case law as well. It would seem therefore that not only will none of the provisions of *PA 1890* be applicable but, even where the wording of selected parts of them have sneaked back onto the scene by being re-embodied in the *Regulations* as default provisions, the case law on the interpretation of them as provisions of *PA 1890* may not be capable of usage in construing the new *Regulations*.

It will be interesting to see how far the courts are prepared to take this disapplication when interpretative questions come before them.

The requirements for incorporation   2.9

As noted above at 2.3, an LLP exists by virtue of incorporation. *LLPA 2000, s 2(1)(a)* provides that a prerequisite for incorporation is the completion of the necessary documentation by 'two or more persons associated for carrying on a lawful business with a view to profit'.

'Person' in this sense means legal person, and so those who are associating can be individuals, limited companies, other LLPs or any combination of them. (They cannot at present be partnerships *per se*, though this would change if the Law Commission/Scottish Law Commission joint proposals for giving separate legal personality to partnerships were to be introduced.)

Association – reality or illusion?   2.10

'Associated' in *LLPA 2000, s 2(1)(a)* (see 2.9 above) is nowhere defined, and should therefore presumably be given its natural, and fairly loose, meaning. The way(s) of association are not therefore seemingly limited. It does not therefore require, for instance, that all members must intend to be active in the operation of the business, and the equivalent of a sleeping partner is quite feasible.

Further, no minimum investment is needed. A sole trader or practitioner may well therefore seek the protection of limited liability by persuading another to lend his name to the exercise, making a minimal capital contribution, keeping out of the running of the business, and receiving a token reward; since that other would seem to be at minimal risk of personal liability even if the business fails. Even a supplier diligent enough to inspect the accounts will not necessarily be aware of this, as disclosure requirements almost exclusively relate to aggregate figures in respect of members' interests, and the agreement between members is not a public document.

The requirement of a lawful business   2.11

The second limb of the above requirement (see 2.9) is that the association must be for the purpose of carrying on a 'lawful business'. The word 'business' is defined simply (in *LLPA 2000, s 18*) as including every trade, profession and occupation. Thus the availability of LLP status is not in any way limited to professional service firms, as some supporters in Parliament had suggested. It is just as available for a firm of plumbers as it is for a firm of accountants. The take-up rate may nonetheless be higher in the professions, because of the greater perception of vulnerability to negligence claims, but that will be solely a matter of choice.

The term does however appear to connote the carrying-on of an actual activity, so that merely an association with a view to profit will not be enough. For instance, it is thought that merely combining to hold investments for members' own benefit would not qualify, though no doubt holding them for others' benefit, as an investment manager, would. Unfortunately, 'lawful' is not defined. It is hoped that it would not be construed so as to prevent the formation of an LLP to carry on a business which would become lawful on the granting of a licence or similar consent, such as a public house, but would not be able to seek that legal sanction until after incorporation.

The requirement for profit 2.12

The business to be carried on by the persons who have associated must be one which is to be carried on with a view to profit. Again, 'profit' is to be given its natural meaning. One class of venture, which is therefore effectively excluded from using LLP status, is that of a charitable or philanthropic enterprise. Such bodies are likely to have to remain either unincorporated associations, or else companies (usually limited by guarantee rather than shares). (It is however worth noting that the Charity Commission and the Company Law Steering Group are both backing the idea of a new vehicle, the 'Charitable Incorporated Organisation', which may supersede these concepts.)

Although there is nothing to say what the 'profit' is to be used for however, i.e. it is not required to be for the personal or exclusive benefit of the members, so ostensibly there would be nothing to prevent an LLP being utilised in the same way as trading companies operated by charities, this would not seem possible in practice, since such an operation needs to be 100 per cent owned by the charity, which would preclude its having the necessary two members.

Premature incorporation 2.13

When the *Limited Liability Partnerships Act 2000* came into force, there was a rush of registrations, some of which came from existing partnerships who avowedly had not yet decided whether they actually wanted to trade as LLPs, but who wanted to protect, by registration, their existing trading names. Some are believed to have used only nominee partners/members to represent the whole firm. As pointed out by the author and others, this gave rise to two concerns. Firstly, those firms had started the clock running for the purposes of the stamp duty exemption available to new LLPs (strictly limited to one year) (see 9.20 *et seq.* below), and those which used nominees had compounded the problems by not having identical lists of partners and members. Secondly, they must have made a declaration that they were 'associated for carrying on a lawful business', when in fact they had no such completed intention.

The moral is that formation should only follow a definite decision to proceed promptly to use the LLP as a trading vehicle. (A way round the problem for firms in the scenario in question would be to form a limited company with the desired name, since no such requirements as to trading apply thereto, and then if proceeding later with the LLP to change the name of the company immediately before incorporating the LLP.)

3 – The Process of Formation and Naming

This chapter looks at the processes required for the formation of an LLP in practical terms. One of the key choices necessary is the name of the LLP, and the restrictions on that choice are considered. Another is the location of the registered office. The forms and fees required are reviewed.

The incorporation document – general 3.1

The primary document required for formation of an LLP is the 'incorporation document'. The document itself must have been subscribed by the requisite 'two or more persons associated for carrying on a lawful business with a view to profit' (*LLPA 2000, s 2(1)(a)*) (see Chapter 2 above).

The document, or a copy authenticated in a manner approved by the Registrar, must be delivered to him. The form is Form LLP2 (there is no LLP1!). It includes (*LLPA 2000, s 2(1)(c)*) a statement that the requisite persons have indeed subscribed their names to the incorporation document. That statement is capable of being signed either by any one of the subscribing members, or by a solicitor engaged in the formation. Anyone making such a statement which they know to be false, or which they do not believe to be true, is committing an offence (*LLPA 2000, s 2(3)(4)*).

No agreement required 3.2

Before turning to the detail of the incorporation document, and the choices which that necessitates, it is worth pausing to emphasise that there is no requirement to file or produce any form of written members' agreement, or even evidence of a verbal agreement, since none needs to exist. This can produce a curious result when it comes to interpretation of the application of other statutes applied to the *LLPA 2000* by the *Regulations*. In the case of application of the *CA 1985*, or the *Company*

Directors Disqualification Act 1986, it is provided (by *SI 2001/1090, regs 4(1)(e)* and *4(2)(e)*) that reference to the memorandum of association of a company is to be interpreted as including reference to the incorporation document of an LLP. However, in the case of reference to the *Insolvency Act 1986*, reference to either the memorandum of association of a company, or to its articles, is specifically deemed (by *SI 2001/1090, reg 5(2)(e)*) to include reference to an LLP's limited liability partnership agreement (to the exclusion of the incorporation document) even though none may exist.

Further, even if such an agreement does exist, there is no need to file it or in any other way make it a public document. Thus the privacy of internal arrangements, which many see as a crucial advantage of partnerships over companies, is preserved for LLPs.

The incorporation document – requirements   3.3

There are only five pieces of information which need to appear on the incorporation document, and none of them is of a financial nature (*LLPA 2000, s 2(2)*). They are:

- the LLP's name;
- whether the LLP's registered office is to be situated in:
  - England and Wales,
  - Wales, or
  - Scotland;
- the address of the registered office;
- the names, addresses, and dates of birth of all initial members; and
- either:
  - that all members from time to time will be 'designated' members, or
  - which of the initial members are to be so designated.

(Note, however, the point as to Confidentiality Orders, relating to members' addresses, referred to at 6.31 below.)

The scheduled requirements   3.4

The *Schedule* to the *LLPA 2000*, which is given force by *LLPA 2000, s 1(6)*, contains detailed provisions about the requirements as to the naming of the LLP, and the siting etc. of the registered office. These requirements will therefore have to be taken into account in making the choices which must be made before completion of the incorporation documents.

The format of names – general 3.5

For any LLP whose registered office is situated in either England and Wales, or Scotland, there is a choice of three suffixes which must be used for the LLP's name (*LLPA 2000, Sch, para 2(1)*). They may either use the full phrase 'limited liability partnership', or one of the abbreviated forms 'LLP' or 'llp'. None of those terms may be used anywhere in the name other than at the end, so that whilst 'Fred Bloggs (Coventry) llp' would be permissible, 'Fred Bloggs llp (Coventry)' would not.

Guidelines on the naming of LLPs (*Limited Liability Partnerships: Company Formation and Names*, GBLLP1, May 2001) are available from Companies House (notes can be downloaded from www.companieshouse.gov.uk).

The format of names – Wales 3.6

For those LLPs which, in their incorporation document, wish to state that their registered office is in Wales, there is an option (*LLPA 2000, Sch, para 2(2)*) for their suffix to be expressed in the Welsh language equivalent of the above.

Thus the suffix must be either 'limited liability partnership', 'partneriaeth atebolrwydd cyfyngedig', or one of the abbreviated forms 'LLP', 'llp', 'PAC' or 'pac'. (The same limitations as to placing such an expression anywhere in the name other than the end will apply.)

The choice of name – avoiding existing names 3.7

The restrictions applying to the choice of name are intended to assimilate the requirements for LLPs' names with those of companies, and to avoid any confusion by similarity of names. Thus the Registrar's record-keeping requirements are extended (*LLPA 2000, Sch, para 1*, inserting a new *CA 1985, s 714(da)*) to include a register of all incorporated LLPs). The name of an LLP must not be the same as one appearing in any section of his registers as kept under *CA 1985, s 714(1)*.

When determining if a name is the same, there are certain specific factors which need (*LLPA 2000, Sch, para 8*) to be disregarded, namely:

- use of 'the' at the start of the name;

- the formatting of the name (font sizes, upper/lower case etc.);

- any distinction between 'and' and '&'; and

- use of various expressions, including 'company' and 'limited liability partnership' in various forms.

The effect of the last point in particular is that 'Fred Bloggs LLP' would be regarded as being the same as 'Fred Bloggs Limited', and so if the latter already exists, formation of an LLP with the former name would not be permissible.

The choice of name – other restrictions   3.8

As with a company, there are also other restrictions (*LLPA 2000, Sch, para 3*) on an LLP's ability to choose its name. It cannot select any name which would, in the opinion of the Secretary of State, be offensive; or by its very usage constitute a criminal offence; or be likely to be connected in any way with central or local government (unless specific approval is given).

In addition the name may not include without the Secretary of State's consent any word or expression requiring approval under regulations made pursuant to *section 29* of the *Companies Act 1985*. These tend to be terms which have association with royalty, or imply a broad base e.g. 'international', or have associations with a particular profession, e.g. 'dental' (*Companies and Business Names Regulations 1981 (SI 1981/1685)*, as modified).

Names that are 'too like' others   3.9

It is even possible for an LLP to be required to change its name, after it has been formed, and the initially chosen name has been approved by the Registrar.

If the name is 'too like' a name which appears (or should have appeared) in the register at the time of formation, the Secretary of State may direct the LLP that it must, within such period as he may specify, change its name (*LLPA 2000, Sch, para 4(2)*). Normally, that direction must be given to the LLP within one year of its incorporation. The period is extended to five years, however, if the Secretary of State believes either that misleading information has been given to secure the LLP's registration under a particular name, or that undertakings or assurances given in order to obtain such registration have not been fulfilled (*LLPA 2000, Sch, para 4(3)*).

Misleading names 3.10

Another possible cause for a direction from the Secretary of State to change a name is if it is believed by him that the LLP's registered name gives so misleading an indication of the nature of its activities as to be likely to cause harm to the public.

There is no time limit for when such a direction may be given. As above (see 3.9), it must give a period within which compliance must be effected (*LLPA 2000, Sch, para 4(4)*).

Application to set aside Secretary of State's direction 3.11

Any LLP in respect of which the Secretary of State issues such a direction as is referred to in 3.9 or 3.10 above has the right to apply, within three weeks of the direction, to the High Court to have the direction set aside.

The Court can either set the direction aside or confirm it. In the latter case it must set a period for compliance (*LLPA 2000, Sch, para 4(5),(6)*).

Failure to comply with direction 3.12

If an LLP fails to comply with any such direction as is mentioned in 3.9 or 3.10 above, within:

- the time limit specified therein; or

- any extension of the time limit granted by the Secretary of State (*LLPA 2000, Sch, para 4(7)*); or

- (if it has been confirmed by the Court as above on an application to set aside) within the time prescribed by the Court,

then an offence has been committed.

Those liable for that offence are both the LLP itself, and any designated member in default (*LLPA 2000, Sch, para 4(8)*). Anyone so convicted is liable to a fine (*LLPA 2000, Sch, para 4(9)*).

The registered office 3.13

LLPA 2000, Sch, para 9(1) requires that an LLP shall at all times have a registered office situate in one of the three possible locations referred to at

3.3 above, to which communications and notices may be addressed. Like a company, it does not have to be a trading address.

The initial registered office is that specified in the incorporation document (*LLPA 2000, Sch, para 9(2)*). This can be changed at any time, on the filing (normally by a designated member) of Form 287. Form 287a is appropriate if the new registered office is to be in Wales. Such a change will take effect on delivery of the above form. However, third parties have a 14–day period of grace within which they can still serve documents at the old address (*CA 1985, s 287*).

Incorporation fees   3.14

The fee payable on incorporation, under the *Fees Regulations*, is £95. That includes the provision of the LLP's certificate of incorporation.

Publication of the LLP's name   3.15

Each LLP must display its name outside every office or place of business it has, in conspicuous and legible fashion, and if it does not it, and every member in default, is liable to a fine and, potentially, a daily default fine (*CA 1985, s 348*, as modified). Further, again at peril of a fine for default, it must print its name legibly, by *CA 1985, s 249* as modified, on all:

- business letters;
- notices and official publications;
- cheques, bills of exchange, promissory notes, and endorsements;
- orders for money or goods;
- invoices, receipts, letters of credit and bills of parcels.

Consequences of default   3.16

There are two consequences of default in respect of the above provisions as to documents. One is, as mentioned, a fine, which may be imposed not only on a member, but also on any other person, who issues or authorises the issue of any document without the appropriate name on it. The second, and perhaps the more far-reaching, is that any member or other person who signs, or authorises the signature of, any cheque, order etc. which does not have the LLP's name on it is personally liable to the third party involved, e.g. the payee of the cheque or the supplier from which goods are ordered. That liability may be absolved if the LLP actually makes the required payment, but the substantial risk to the individual will persist until this is done. This may be of particular importance when the LLP is being established, when enthusiasm may suggest the use of documentation before the properly printed stock is received. This is a temptation to resist.

LLP seal 3.17

An LLP may choose to have a seal. If so, it is required by *CA 1985, s 350*, as modified, to have its name legibly shown on that seal, and failure to comply with this, or use of a seal purporting to be that of the LLP but which does not comply, will render the LLP or the member or other person using or authorising the improper seal liable to a fine.

Particulars in correspondence 3.18

Certain details must appear on all business letters and order forms of the LLP (*CA 1985, s 351* as modified). These are:

- the LLP's place of registration;
- its registered number;
- its registered office address;
- if its name ends in an abbreviation (i.e. 'LLP', 'llp', 'PAC', or 'pac') the fact that it is a limited liability partnership, or a partneriaeth atebolrwydd cyfygedig.

Failure to comply renders both the LLP, and any member or other person issuing or authorising the issue of a non-compliant document, liable to a fine.

Application of the Business Names Act 1985 3.19

The *Business Names Act 1985* is applied to LLPs by *paragraph 9* of and *Schedule 5* to the *Regulations*. It will take effect in relation to any LLP which uses a business name which is not its corporate name, without any addition. Its effect will vary according to whether the LLP has more than 20 members. If it has, it will suffice if it keeps at its principal place of business a list of the members' names, available for public inspection during normal business hours, and states on all its business letters, orders, receipts, invoices and payment demands that such a notice is available for inspection and where it is kept. If, however, the LLP has 20 or fewer members, it must on all such documents as are referred to above show its corporate name and the names of all members, as well as an address for service. Further, all LLPs to which the statute applies, regardless of size, must display a notice giving its corporate name, the names of all members, and the service address, in all places of business it has to which the public has access.

4 – Post Formation Administration

Change of name 4.1

Like a company, an LLP may change its name at any time (*LLPA 2000, Sch, para 4(1)*). Exactly the same obligations and restrictions apply to the choice of the new name as applied to it upon formation, and exactly the same powers are vested in the Secretary of State to direct a subsequent change of the new name.

There is no provision in the legislation requiring any special decision-taking process for the name change, so it can, unless the partnership agreement provides otherwise, be determined upon by simple majority. Upon change, a notice of the change, in Form LLP3, must be signed by a designated member, and delivered to the Registrar (*LLPA 2000, Sch, para 5*). A fee of £20 is payable. There is no time limit for delivery, because the change is ineffective until the Registrar has checked the register (i.e. the one kept under *CA 1985, s 714(1)*), entered the new name in it and issued a certificate of the change of name.

Effect of change of name 4.2

Such a change of name has no effect on the rights or duties of the LLP (*LLPA 2000, Sch, para 6(a)*).

There is no effect either upon any legal proceedings which may have been started by it or commenced against it, and any such proceedings simply continue against it in its new name (*LLPA 2000, Sch, para 6(b)*).

Change of registered office 4.3

Likewise, the members of an LLP can at any time resolve, by ordinary means, to change its registered office. Notice must be given to the Registrar in Form LLP 287, signed by a designated member (or, if appropriate, by any relevant insolvency practitioner who has assumed control of the LLP's affairs). No fee is payable. As with change of name, there is normally no time limit for filing the notice, since the change is not effective until registered.

As noted on the form (see also 3.13 above), for a period of 14 days from the date of registration, service of legal proceedings upon the LLP at its old registered office remains valid (*CA 1985, s 287*). A time period does however become relevant if the change is consequent upon an unavoidable failure by the LLP to perform any of the statutory obligations relevant to a registered office (e.g. to keep a register, index or other document there) or to mention the correct address in any correspondence. If it was not practicable to give prior notice of the change to the Registrar, but the LLP resumes performance of its duties at other premises as soon as practicable, and then gives notice to the Registrar within 14 days of that resumption, it shall not be treated as being in breach of duty. This would be apt to cover, for instance, a period during which an LLP suffered a fire at its premises, and there was a hiatus before it could resume elsewhere.

Steps to follow changes 4.4

Whenever an LLP effects either of the changes noted at 4.1 and 4.3 above, i.e. in respect of its name and registered office, it should act promptly in changing various items to reflect the new situation, and to comply with the relevant statutory requirements.

Thus the signage outside all offices will need to be changed, the correspondence and other stationery will need updating, and the common seal (if any) will need renewing (*CA 1985, s 348–351*).

Joining/leaving members 4.5

Upon any person either becoming a member of an LLP, or ceasing to be a member of an LLP, then notice of that change must be given to the Registrar within 14 days (*LLPA 2000, s 9(1)(a)*). No fee is payable.

The details required for new members are simply names, address and date of birth (*CA 1985, s 288*).

The notice, in Form LLP 288a (for appointments) or Form LLP 288b (for terminations) must be signed by a designated member (*LLPA 2000, s 9(3)(b)*). In the former case, it must also be signed by the incoming member whose details appear upon the form, to confirm his consent (*LLPA 2000, s 9(3)*). Form LLP 288a also provides for an indication as to whether the new member is or is not to be a designated member, though strictly speaking that latter element of notification is not necessary if the LLP is one where all members from time to time are designated members. Form LLP 288b makes no similar provision, since if a person ceases to be a member that automatically means he ceases to be a designated member (*LLPA 2000, s 8(6)*).

Changes in designated members 4.6

If a person is and is continuing to be a member, but either becomes a designated member when he was previously not one, or ceases to be a designated member, then again notice to the Registrar must be given within 14 days (*LLPA 2000, s 9(1)(a)*).

Beware of the fact that Companies House' own guidance note *Limited Liability Partnerships: Administration and Management* (GBLLP2, April 2001), inadvertently gives a period of 28 days for this purpose. They appear to have been confused by the fact that Form LLP 288c, to be used for the notice, is also used for changes of members' details, for which 28 days *is* the applicable period. No fee is payable.

Change of members' details 4.7

If any member changes his name or address, notice must be given to the Registrar. (See also 6.31 below as to Confidentiality Orders.)

Form LLP 288c is used, and must be signed by a designated member. No fee is payable. Here, the relevant period for filing is within 28 days of the change (*LLPA 2000, s 9(1)(b)*).

Enforcement of notice requirements 4.8

Failure to comply with any of the above requirements for notification of changes in relation to members at 4.5, 4.6 or 4.7 above, is an offence on the part of the LLP, and of every one of the designated members (*LLPA 2000, s 9(4)*). It is, however, a defence for any designated member who may be charged with such an offence to prove that he took all reasonable steps to ensure compliance (*LLPA 2000, s 9(5)*).

In practice, the difficult issues are likely to be changes in members' names (e.g. on marriage) and (more commonly) addresses. When a person becomes a member, or ceases to be one, it tends to be an event of relative significance, and minds will tend to be directed towards the consequent administrative issues. The same will hopefully apply when someone becomes or ceases to be a designated member, though this may be regarded as less significant for the business.

A change in a member's residential address does not however touch upon the business at all and, unless the member remembers to notify the appropriate administrator, may not even be communicated to the LLP at all. It, however, and potentially any designated member, will still be liable for breach of this statutory obligation. Prudence dictates therefore that there should be a positive obligation placed on members by the partnership agreement to report such changes, and that whoever is responsible for preparation of the annual return (see 4.9 below) should make positive enquiries of all members as to their current addresses. Anyone guilty of an offence under this section is liable to a fine (*LLPA 2000, s 9(6)*).

Annual returns   4.9

Annual returns are provided for by *sections 363 and 364* of the *Companies Act 1985*. Each LLP will have a 'return date'. This will normally be the anniversary of the date of incorporation (*CA 1985, s 363(1)(a)*). If, however, when making any return, the LLP opts to deliver its next return to a different date, then the anniversaries of that date will subsequently apply, until any similar future alteration (*CA 1985, s 363(1)(b)*).

The return, in Form LLP 363, will be sent as a 'shuttle' document by Companies House to the LLP, with the data previously recorded already filled in. This should be checked, and the form, with any necessary variations, should be signed by a designated member to certify its correctness. It must be delivered to Companies House within 28 days of the return date. A fee of £35 is payable.

Contents of returns   4.10

The return provides the following information (*CA 1985, s 364*):

- the registered office address;
- the names and addresses of all members;
- if some members only are designated, which those members are;
- the address of any place other than the registered office at which there may be kept any register of debenture holders, or any duplicate or part of such a register.

It also contains a space to opt for a date for the next return which is different from the anniversary of the return date of the return which is being completed.

Limitations on usefulness of the return   **4.11**

Any applicable changes in details relating to the situation of the registered office, or the members, should still be given on the appropriate form.

In other words, though the return is a useful reminder to administrators, and a good opportunity to catch up on omissions from the last year, it does not of itself take the place of the obligation to file notification of individual changes.

Failure to file returns   **4.12**

A failure to file such a return within 28 days of the return date is an offence (*CA 1985, s 363(3)*). It continues until such time as a valid return is delivered to the Registrar.

The offence is committed not only by the LLP, but also by every designated member, unless any such member can show that he took all reasonable steps to avoid the commission or continuation of the offence (*CA 1985, s 363(4)*). Any person committing such an offence is liable on summary conviction to a fine.

Ensuring internal compliance   **4.13**

Again, therefore, (because of the point made in 4.8 above) it behoves all designated members to ensure that the system for the filing of the return, and the lines of responsibility in this regard, are clearly delineated.

There is no requirement in the legislation for anyone to have a post equivalent to that of a company secretary, but this is a clear example of the need for someone within the LLP to know that they have tasks of an administrative or secretarial nature delegated to them, and preferably for someone else to be designated to check upon the performance of those duties. This may be clarified in the partnership agreement, or documented elsewhere, but it is advisable for it to be clearly and widely known who has such tasks.

5 – The Transfer of Business

This chapter deals with the processes involved in transferring the business of an existing business into an LLP, and looks at the documentation which will be required.

It refers to later chapters dealing with the tax effects of transfer. In considering transfers, it indicates factors which may tend to make transfer, and hence LLP status, attractive or otherwise, for businesses with particular features. The chapter also indicates factors which may affect individuals who either cease to be involved, or join initially at the time of conversion.

The concept of transfer   5.1

Matters covered under a transfer will include those which need to be considered when an existing business converts into an LLP, rather than when an LLP is used as the vehicle for an entirely new business. In practice there is unlikely to be a conversion from an existing limited company to an LLP, as the tax structures affecting the two are so different, and the Government, when bringing in the legislation, refused to make amendments in such a way as to make such a conversion attractive. It is not necessarily the case however that the conversion will automatically be from an existing partnership. It might well be from the business of a sole trader, if one or more new owners of the business were at that time being taken in.

The matters which need consideration will in many instances be familiar to professional advisers who are accustomed to dealing with transfers occurring upon incorporation of an existing business.

The extent of transfer   5.2

The first question which needs to be considered is whether it is the whole of the existing business which is to be transferred into the LLP, or merely a selected part or parts. There would, for instance, be nothing to stop a business hiving off into an LLP a part of the business which was perceived to be particularly risk-sensitive, but retaining as a partnership other areas for which they wished positively to avoid LLP status, e.g. to avoid public financial disclosure. Such a partial transfer will obviously be more complex than a total one, since there will be a need to define precisely what is or is not to pass into the LLP.

In most cases however, it is envisaged that the transfer will be of the whole business.

Cessation of the existing business 5.3

Another matter which will fall to be determined early on is what is to happen to the existing business. Upon the transfer being implemented, will the existing partnership fall to be dissolved immediately? Alternatively, will an interim period be allowed during which the partnership will continue to exist, albeit no longer as an active trading entity, whilst any transitional problems are allowed to work their course, so that it is only formally dissolved after a set period?

In broad terms, the simpler the business, the less there is likely to be a need for such a transitional stage.

Advantages of transitional provisions 5.4

Matters which might dispose a business to making such transitional arrangements (as mentioned in 5.3 above) would include the following circumstances:

- If it were decided (because perhaps of changes in profit-sharing arrangements) that rather than transferring the right to bill existing work-in-progress and the right to collect outstanding bills to the new LLP, it was to be the case that the old partnership should render interim bills for all work outstanding at the transfer date, and collect those from debtors direct.

- If there were a need for continuity whilst appointments (e.g. as auditors or insolvency practitioners) were to be transferred.

- If there were outstanding litigation in which the partners were involved.

- If there were need for arrangements to be made for freehold or leasehold property, in the names of the partners, which for some reason is not to be transferred into the beneficial ownership of the LLP.

Disadvantages of transitional provisions 5.5

One straightforward snag with transitional provisions (as mentioned in 5.3 above) is that they are likely to be more cumbersome to operate administratively than a clean break. There will be two businesses running in parallel, each having its own legal and accounting requirements.

Another drawback, which may have a particular impact for professional service firms, is that it is thought likely that the newly created LLP will not, in terms of its professional indemnity insurance, be able to be classed as the 'successor practice' to the transferring partnership. This is because the latter will still exist.

Dissolution agreement 5.6

Depending on the assessment of the need for transitional provisions (see 5.3 above), there may need to be a dissolution agreement, as well as the transfer of business agreement. If so, it will need to make clear that no new commitments can be entered into during this period except for the purpose of effecting an orderly winding up, so that there is no danger of a trading phoenix rising from the ashes.

There will need to be a degree of discretion as to unforeseen circumstances. The agreement will need to deal with such post-termination issues as would have been appropriate before transfer, e.g. matters arising on the death of a partner, or in respect of restrictive covenants entered into by members. There should be a long-stop date at which dissolution is deemed to occur come what may, and provision for earlier agreement as to dissolution if all transitional arrangements can be completed earlier than expected.

Transfer agreement 5.7

Precisely when the transfer is made will depend on individual circumstances. Businesses may find that they incorporate their LLP first and then, perhaps some months later (e.g. to suit their year end), effect the transfer. Alternatively they may wish to transfer as soon as the certificate of incorporation is received, so that they want all documentation in place and ready to bind all parties either the moment the LLP comes into legal existence or at a pre-determined date thereafter.

The latter circumstances are provided for by *LLPA 2000, s 5(2)*. This states that a pre-incorporation agreement, between the persons who subscribe their names to the incorporation document, may impose obligations upon the nascent LLP, even though it does not itself exist at the time of the agreement, so that the obligations come into effect at any time after its incorporation.

The effect of personnel changes   5.8

One apparent problem with the wording of *LLPA 2000, s 5(2)* is however the requirement that such an agreement (as is referred to in 5.7 above) be made 'between the persons who subscribe their names to the incorporation document'. It is arguable that by implication words to the effect of 'and no others' need to be read into the end of this phrase, since the statute does not refer to the possibility of any other signatories, and actually says that the agreement must be 'made . . . between' such persons, and not just be signed by them (which would allow the possibility of others).

The potential difficulty caused is if not all the partners in the old partnership wish to become members of the new LLP. To make the agreement effective from the partnership side, it may well need to have all partners as parties to it. If one or more of them is not also a subscriber to the incorporation document, does this then invalidate the agreement, since it does not comply with *section 5(2)*? It may seem that in practice the point will never be relevant, since those involved will only sign if they are happy in any event. What however if things do not in practice work out as intended, and there are unhappy individuals? Can they claim that the agreement was a nullity because it did not comply with *section 5(2)*? In order to avoid having to test the point in court, it may well be sensible to try to ensure that all partners do indeed become members of the LLP, even if it is known that they will be so only for a very limited period, and that means putting the transfer into place at a time other than the natural time for adding or removing members, i.e. the financial year end.

The scope of the transfer agreement   5.9

It is not of course possible to prescribe a 'one-size-fits-all' list of contents for a transfer agreement, as so much will depend on the individual circumstances. Matters which will however most often need to be dealt with are listed below, and each is developed in following paragraphs:

- obligations to former partners and their estates (see 5.10);

- obligations owed by former partners under restrictive covenants (see 5.11);

- valuation of assets (see 5.12);

- novation of continuing contracts (see 5.13);

- personal appointments (see 5.14);

- how work-in-progress is to be dealt with (see 5.15);

- assignment of book debts and liabilities (see 5.16);

- professional indemnity insurance (see 5.17 and 5.18);

- transfer of real property (see 5.19–5.24);

- banking matters (see 5.25);

- transfer of partners' financial balances (see 5.26);

- external finance agreements and rental arrangements (see 5.27);

- staff employment contracts and rights (see 5.28);

- VAT consequences of transfer (see 5.29);

- intellectual property ownership and obligations (see 5.30); and

- provision for goodwill (see 5.31).

Obligations to former partners **5.10**

Many partnerships will have outstanding obligations to former partners, or perhaps even to their families and estates. These may be straightforward and defined, e.g. where a former partner's capital account is being paid off over a set period, by known instalments. Others may be more complex, such as the provision of annuities for former partners and spouses, where the extent of the obligation is unlikely to be capable of definition, other than by obtaining an actuarial valuation or, more finitely, by purchasing an open market annuity to convert the firm's liability into capital terms. Further, these obligations may not yet be capped if, for instance, senior partners, who are to continue for a while as members of the LLP, have a legitimate expectation under existing arrangements of receiving such annuities upon their own retirements. Such payments may include sums categorised as 'goodwill'.

The transfer agreement will need to deal with all issues relating to future liability for such obligations, so that it is clear whether the LLP is to be obliged to take them on for the future, and to indemnify individual partners against any claims by the annuitant. The more difficult it is to quantify these obligations, the less the LLP is likely to wish to take these over, and the greater the scope for disagreement. The problem is exacerbated by the fact that the change to company-style accounting will mean that all such obligations need to appear at their true cost in the balance sheet of the LLP. If large, this may make the business appear to third parties to be unattractive. This is an area which is perceived as one of the most common disincentives to conversion, if the above problems cannot easily be resolved.

Worse still, the draft Statement of Recommended Practice ('SORP') for LLPs states that provision should be made not only for those annuities which are at least predictable and susceptible of actuarial conversion to a capital figure by reason of their being referable to established sums. However, it also provides that similar provision be made for those annuities which are in reality completely unpredictable because they are linked to future profit levels.

Not only therefore will actuarial calculations (an expensive exercise needing to be repeated annually) have to be based on guesswork as to how long a retired/retiring member may live, but also on guesswork as to how much profit the LLP will make during each succeeding year of his life! It seems to the author that this is accountancy gone mad, and it is fervently to be hoped that these provisions will be removed or substantially amended before the SORP is finalised.

Obligations of former partners   5.11

Often former partners will continue to owe obligations to the partnership they have left, either as a matter of general partnership law or, more usually, as a consequence of express obligations arising from the partnership agreement and/or a retirement agreement. Commonly, these would be duties of confidentiality, and the obligation to observe restrictive covenants.

The original documents will need to be checked to see whether the benefit of such obligations can be passed to the LLP. if so, then they will need to be assigned, and the transfer agreement should provide for how that is to be done. If not, then the LLP may need to agree to indemnify the partners who benefit from the covenants against the cost of enforcement action, in return for their agreement to take such action and to hold the proceeds in trust for the LLP. One difficulty which may occur, depending on the construction of the clause in question, is whether, if the partnership which has the benefit of the covenant ceases to trade or exist, there can be any loss from any breach of the covenant in any event. If such covenants (which will be of limited duration) are of especial value to the business, it may be necessary to wait until they have expired before transfer becomes practical.

Valuation of assets   5.12

It may well be the case in many instances that valuation of assets is not a major issue. This is because the closing balances for the valuation of assets in the books of account of the partnership, arrived at by applying the same policies as previously (e.g. as to depreciation), will simply become the opening balances of the LLP, which will continue to apply the same policies.

However, in some circumstances it may be that the transfer agreement needs to treat the issue in greater detail. This could be the case if, for example, freehold properties are shown in the accounts of the partnership at their original cost, with no adjustment for their subsequent increase (or, if acquired in the late 1980s, perhaps decrease!) in value. There may also be matters for which no true value has ever needed to be ascribed, but now need to be provided for.

Novation of current contracts   5.13

Third parties with whom the partnership has had dealings, either as suppliers or as clients/customers, may not be bound to accept a change in the identity of the party with whom they have contracted. In other words the business may not be able to insist on novating their contracts, so as to substitute the LLP's obligations and rights for the partnership's.

In many cases the third party will agree, and the transfer agreement might have annexed to it a draft novation agreement for standard use; but it should also provide for the circumstances where this is not possible. In terms of suppliers to the business, where there are continuing contractual obligations, the agreement should provide for the continuing perform-ance of the obligations by the partnership in dissolution, upon its being indemnified by the LLP against the cost of such performance. Any resultant benefits should be held in trust for the LLP. Care will need to be taken to check that the making of such arrangements do not however constitute a breach of the third-party agreement.

With regard to clients and customers, again novation should be attempted, and new terms of engagement letters etc. should be sent for agreement where possible. However, in some cases it may be necessary for the partnership effectively to sub-contract the performance of the obligations to the LLP, in return for indemnifying it against the costs of so doing, and holding receipts for post-transfer work upon trust for the LLP.

Personal appointments   5.14

There may be some appointments which, though legally personal to the appointee, are in effect appointments of the business in which the appointee is a partner/member. An example would be appointments of insolvency practitioners, as liquidators, receivers, supervisors of voluntary arrangements etc.

Since they are personal, the appointments themselves will need no alteration, but the transfer agreement should provide for them to continue for the benefit of the LLP.

Treatment of work in progress 5.15

The issue of work in progress has been referred to a number of times above. The transfer agreement will need to indicate clearly how this is to be dealt with as between the partnerships and the LLP. Options will include the following:

- All work in progress is billed by the partnership, on an interim basis, as at the transfer date. This might be appropriate if the LLP was not going to be taking over the benefit of pre-transfer book debts or the burden of pre-transfer liabilities.

- All work in progress is billed, as at the transfer date, by the LLP, upon the basis that pre- and post-transfer work is apportioned on the first post-transfer bill delivered. Again, this would not be appropriate if the LLP was to take over all book debts and liabilities. In this instance, provision should be made for resolving any disputes as between the partnership in dissolution, and the LLP, as to the amounts to be billed (especially in cases of work which is for a fixed fee, or which is not to be identified on the basis of recorded time and hence needs somehow to be apportioned).

- The LLP takes over all rights to bill for and to receive monies for such work in progress as may have existed. This may well be applicable if the LLP is taking over all book debts and liabilities, and will be more attractive if there are not likely to be any outgoing or incoming members of the LLP over the period for which receipts are envisaged from the partnership's work.

Book debts and liabilities 5.16

The issue of book debts and liabilities follows on from that of work in progress (see 5.15 above). Essentially what needs to be resolved is whether the LLP simply steps into the shoes of the partnership and takes over the benefit of all debts owed to the partnership and the burden of all liabilities owed by it, without needing to separate or quantify them. In many instances this will be the simplest and preferred way forward. (Even so, it may be necessary for some specific exclusions to be provided for, e.g. professional indemnity claims.)

If the above method is adopted, the partnership will need to retain the right to inspect and copy the records which will be passed over to the LLP. If, however, perhaps because of differences in the make-up of the LLP from that of the partnership, this is not suitable, then the agreement may need to provide that the partnership, as part of its dissolution process, collects the debts due to it, and pays the monies that it owes. Again, the issue of who has possession of the books and records, and who has the right to inspect and copy them, needs to be dealt with.

An incidental reason why the destiny of book debts needs clearly to be dealt with, is that an LLP can create a charge over them, and any prospective chargee will no doubt wish to ensure that such debts have been properly vested in the chargor LLP in the first place.

Professional indemnity claims   5.17

Two types of professional negligence claims will need to be dealt with. The first, and easier, will be those claims which are already known of, and probably the subject of negotiations and/or litigation. They should already have been notified to the partnership's insurers, and the transfer agreement simply needs to deal with liability for the uninsured excess in respect of such claims.

More difficult will be those claims which have not yet emerged, and which may lie dormant for some years. To insurers, the LLP will probably be a successor practice to the partnership (though this should be checked with them) and so claims which arise in the normal course of events should be covered, so that again it is the issue of the uninsured element of any claims which the agreement needs to deal with.

Dealing with gaps in insurance cover   5.18

There may, however, be other instances of unexpected lack of insurance cover which need also to be resolved.

What if, for instance, negligence occurs in a matter being conducted across the bridge between the periods of the partnership and the LLP, where the LLP has different insurers from those of the partnership, and the matter should have been reported to insurers before the transfer but was not? It is possible that the partnership's insurers may refuse cover because the claim was not notified to them at the right time. The LLP's insurers may likewise disclaim because the claim or circumstances were not reported to them at the inception of cover.

Consideration will need to be given to whether the agreement should provide both a warranty from the partners that they have revealed all claims, or circumstances which might give rise to a claim, which are known to them; and an indemnity to the LLP against liability for any breach of that warranty. Clearly the future owners of the LLP may benefit from this; but may the founding members (who will be in command of the process of transfer) want to protect their personal positions by excluding such liability so far as they legally can? The fact that there is no real definition, of what constitutes 'circumstances' which mean that a potential claim should be reported, could give rise to some perfectly genuine disagreement in this area, and the transfer agreement should be clear as to the consequences of the various possible outcomes.

Transfer of real property   5.19

One of the distinguishing differences between partnerships and LLPs is that the latter, as a separate legal entity, can hold real property, whether freehold or leasehold, in its own right; whereas partnerships have always had to rely upon the holding of land by nominees or trustees.

Often, this issue has caused problems in practice, especially where land has been included in the partnership's books on tax accountants' advice, or at the behest of bankers to bolster the balance sheet, with no thought being given to whether it was really intended that the land should thus become a partnership asset, held upon similar shares to the rest of the partnership capital, rather than the often different trusts which may appear on the face of the conveyancing documentation. A classic instance of this is in family farming partnerships where land, put in the accounts at low historic cost, may apparently become an asset of a partnership which changes over the generations, and may have no written partnership agreement, without any consideration of underlying ownership issues. With an LLP being created, the chance arises to put this beyond doubt.

Keeping land out of the LLP   5.20

It will not always be desirable or possible to transfer property into the LLP.

For one thing, those partners who own the land may prefer to retain it as a private asset, marketable outside the scope of the LLP, especially if they have viewed it as a 'pension fund'. This will be less commonly so where it is formally held upon trust for the existing partnership, but even in such circumstances it might be desired to retain it personally if, for instance, expansion of the number of members was contemplated and the existing owners wished to retain the benefit of future increases in value. There might also be a wish to retain it if the land is disproportionately high in value to the remainder of the business's capital, and it is feared that the high consequent capital contributions required for new members to acquire equal shares in the LLP will prove off-putting to prospective members.

The impact of deferred gains   5.21

There will normally be no tax consequences inherent in the transfer of property into the LLP, in terms either of capital gains tax or stamp duty provided, in the case of the latter, that the transaction is completed within a year and that conditions as to underlying ownership are complied with.

One instance, however, where tax may prove a disincentive to transfer is if there are significant deferred gains already locked into the property, e.g. because roll-over relief has been obtained on the acquisition of the property. There is no problem if the LLP continues to flourish, or indeed if the property is subsequently disposed of in the normal course of events. A problem may however arise if the LLP ceases trading and goes into formal liquidation, since at that time the deferred liabilities revert to the transferring members, regardless of actual disposal of the asset (*Taxation of Chargeable Gains Act 1992, s 156A*, as imported by *LLPA 2000, s 10(4)*).

If significant gains have thus been rolled over into a property then it may be prudent to keep this outside the LLP, since then it will require an actual disposal to trigger the liability to tax if all goes wrong. If however it is decided nonetheless to transfer the property into the LLP, it may be desired to seek an indemnity from the LLP to the transferring partners against any such eventual liability, even though in the case of an insolvent liquidation it may be of little use since those indemnified would only rank as unsecured creditors. In any event, the Inland Revenue have indicated (*Tax Bulletin*, December 2000) that an LLP which either temporarily ceases trading, or which permanently ceases but winds up its affairs promptly and without the need for a liquidator's appointment, will not thus lose the advantages of transparency. (See 9.11 *et seq.* below for further details.)

Third-party consents   5.22

Even if it is desired to transfer land into the name of the LLP, it may not be possible to do so.

In many cases third-party consents will be needed, either from mortgagees or landlords. In cases where consent cannot be refused unreasonably, it is suggested that it would normally be unreasonable to refuse consent to a transfer to the LLP, subject to a requirement to give personal guarantees. In such cases, the documentation (comprising the property transfer or assignment, the necessary licences and consents, the transfer agreement and the membership agreement) will need to deal with issues such as an indemnity from the LLP to those members giving personal guarantees, the right of outgoing guarantor members to seek release from their guarantees, and the right of the LLP to require the mortgagee or lessor to accept substitute guarantors.

Landlords may also require the original tenant partners to enter into an authorised guarantee agreement in accordance with *section 16* of the *Landlord and Tenant (Covenants) Act 1995*.

Unavailability of consent   5.23

There may however be some instances where the requirement for the consents (see 5.22 above) means that it is not possible for the property to be transferred to the LLP. For example, this could be because an unwilling landlord has the benefit of an unqualified covenant against assignment. Alternatively, if it is known that attempting to transfer will provoke a long and bitter battle with a third party, even if it is thought the battle is winnable, it may simply be felt not worth incurring the cost and anguish of the attempt.

Further, it may be the case that such restrictions in practice prevent the use of the property by the LLP at all, and hence force either abandonment of the idea of forming the LLP, or a move. This would be the case if a mortgagor or lessor was able to refuse consent, and there was a covenant against parting with possession of the property which would be breached by operating the LLP from the premises.

Ascertaining whether any consents will be needed and, if so, whether they are likely to be forthcoming without undue difficulty, should thus be one of the first tasks for the prospective LLP or its advisers to undertake.

Occupation of property by the LLP   5.24

If for any reason it is undesirable, or impossible, for the property to be transferred into the LLP, but it is possible for it to be occupied by the LLP (as, for instance, where partners wish to retain an uncharged property as a personal asset) then thought needs to be given as to the formal recording of the arrangements for that occupation, i.e. by the creation of a lease to the LLP.

This may provide an opportunity for financial planning not previously open to partners, e.g. if the property is owned by all of them, and they had not previously been able to grant a lease to themselves, thus creating a freehold reversionary interest which would be potentially saleable as an investment property at some future date.

Banking matters 5.25

In most cases the bank accounts of the partnership will cease to be operated as at the transfer date, and new ones will be opened in the name of the LLP, with balances simply being transferred from one to the other on that date.

Care should be taken to ensure that arrangements are made sufficiently well in advance with the business's bankers for that to happen, since, for example, it will be an offence for the LLP to continue to use the partnership's cheque books (*CA 1985, s 349(1)* as amended).

In some cases however the transfer may, in respect of all or some of the accounts, be deferred, e.g. because the partnership under the dissolution agreement is to continue to collect pre-transfer book debts. In any event the transfer agreement should make clear what is to happen, and deal with any rights the LLP may require, e.g. to pay into its accounts any cheques made payable to the partnership. The membership agreement should deal in the normal way with such issues as the mandates to be given to the bank, and with issues arising from the possible need for personal guarantees to be given to the bank, e.g. an indemnity, a right to contribution from other guarantors, and arrangements for the provision of guarantors in substitution for outgoing members.

Partners' financial balances 5.26

There will normally be no need for any changes in the accounting structure of the business insofar as the balances attributable to individuals are concerned. All that the transfer agreement will need to record is that the closing balances of the partners' accounts will be the opening balances of the members' accounts. This will be so insofar as capital accounts, current accounts, loan accounts, and deferred tax accounts are concerned. Note, however, the caution in 11.5 *et seq.* below as to the potential importance of transfers between these various accounts.

Only if a change is needed, in order to facilitate compliance with the requirements of the *CA 1985*, with regard to the layout of the information as to members' finances, is any change likely to need to be made. It was suggested by some commentators that, in order to preserve loan relief where partners had borrowed as individuals in order to invest in their capital accounts, it would be necessary for partners to withdraw that capital, repay their lenders, and then borrow afresh to invest in their members' capital account. Fortunately, that cumbersome mechanism seems to have been rendered unnecessary by the Inland Revenue's intention to allow the continuation of relief for the original loan (see *Tax Bulletin No 50* for December 2000, referring to the extension of extra statutory concession ESC A43).

Finance and rental agreements   5.27

Many partnerships will have a range of finance and rental agreements, relating chiefly to such items as cars, computers, etc. The transfer agreement should deal with such issues.

Many of the problems referred to in 5.22 and 5.23 above, in the context of property transfers, will be relevant for this purpose, e.g.:

- the necessity for consents;
- the requirement for guarantees; and
- the possibility of breaches of agreement.

In practice these are less likely to be of sufficient importance to jeopardise the concept of the transfer to an LLP, though it may be necessary in some arrangements for alternative arrangements to be made, e.g. by paying off an agreement from an un–cooperative supplier and refinancing it elsewhere.

Staff matters   5.28

For most partnerships they will themselves be the employers of all staff. There should not be any particular staff issues arising out of the transfer of employment to an LLP, as all staff will be protected by TUPE (the *Transfer of Undertakings (Protection of Employment) Regulations 1981 (SI 1981/ 1794)*, as amended). The transfer agreement need therefore only briefly record that all staff are to be transferred, unless some are to be made redundant at the time of transfer, in which case liability for consequent payments, which by TUPE will normally fall upon the LLP in the first instance, will need to be allocated between the partnership and the LLP.

There are some partnerships which utilise a service company for the purpose of employing their staff, in which case no transfer of service arrangements will apply, though the transfer of ownership of the service company itself will need to be addressed. The transfer agreement may deal with how and when staff are to be told of the change, and what notification of continuity of employment is to be given. (Businesses which are amongst the significant minority which still do not have written contracts of employment may wish to use the opportunity of transfer to put their affairs in order in this regard!)

Value added tax   5.29

The transfer from the partnership to the LLP will normally be of a going concern, and so no VAT consequences in practice will arise. The VAT number will usually continue as before.

One possible exception is if land or buildings are included in the transfer, either because the transferor has elected to waive the available exemption, or because they are new or incomplete buildings which are standard-rated anyway. In those circumstances, for them to be treated on the going concern basis, the transferee LLP will need to waive the exemption.

More care may however be needed if the transfer is in effect a hiving-off of a part only of the partnership's business, where the transferred part needs to be capable of operation in its own right. Similarly, there could be problems if some of the items regarded as indicators of a going-concern transfer are not immediately being passed over, e.g. if the partnership in dissolution is to be the body continuing to render invoices for pre-transfer work so there cannot be said to be a transfer of work in progress. (For a list of these indicators see Tolley's *Value Added Tax 2001–02, para 8.11.*)

Intellectual property   5.30

All partnerships will have some intellectual property matters to consider on transfer, even if only in respect of the use of the partnership's name with the suffix chosen for the LLP. Nearly all will also be not only the owners, but also licensees, of some intellectual property, e.g. the copyright in respect of computer software used by them. Some will also be the owners of intellectual property which is licensed by them to others, e.g. if they themselves are a computer software house, or if as architects they have retained copyright in designs which others are authorised to use.

All of these matters need to be dealt with in the transfer agreement. All intellectual property used by the business, whether as owners or as licensees, is likely to need transfer or assignment to the LLP. The matters noted in 5.13 above with regard to novation of agreements will need to be considered in respect of licences to or by the business. Some licences may not need novating, but simply require notification of transfer to be given to the licensor.

Goodwill   5.31

Many partnerships still have provision for goodwill, either by reason of its having been purchased previously and hence appearing as an asset in the balance sheet, or because the existing partnership agreement provides for an element of goodwill to be paid to future outgoing partners as an entitlement.

The transfer agreement will need to deal with how the balances attributable to the former partnership are to be transferred to the LLP, and the members' agreement will need to cover future entitlements. Accounting treatment will be according to Financial Reporting Standard 10, and this may involve determining a finite period over which the goodwill is to be written off.

Conclusion   5.32

There is no requirement, either in the *LLPA 2000*, or elsewhere in law, for agreement as to any of the matters covered by this chapter to be dealt with in writing (though the subsequent transfer of any freehold or leasehold property would of course have to be written). It would be quite possible for the transfer of the business to be effected without any documentation.

Nonetheless the chapter has drawn attention to a number of the matters which ought to be considered at transfer – and indeed the range of issues covered is by no means exhaustive. If they are not covered, then confusion can arise in future (quite possibly when the people involved are no longer the same as at transfer) and if they are not recorded in an agreement then there will always be scope for disagreement or simply lack of remembrance as to what was agreed. Best practice therefore dictates that an agreement should be drawn up, even if it is simple, and even if in relation to any particular issue it merely records that it had been considered and that no provision was believed to be needed. This chapter should serve as a guide to the topics which ought to be covered, and to cross-refer to other relevant provisions such as the tax consequences of transfer.

6 – Membership Concepts

> This chapter looks at the concept of individuals as members of an LLP. It compares the role of member with that of a partner in an ordinary partnership, and explores the central part played by the concept of agency.
>
> The chapter also considers the special class of 'designated' members, and explores both the obligations which go with that role, and the use which can be made of it in planning the managerial structure of an LLP.

The terminology of membership 6.1

Presumably the term 'member' was chosen by the Parliamentary draftsman to differentiate those individuals concerned with an LLP's business from those concerned with any other form of business vehicle, e.g. partners, directors or shareholders. That aside, there does not seem to be any particular magic in the term, and indeed it may prove difficult for people to get used to using the term as opposed still to describing someone as a 'partner' in an LLP.

The other relevant term, of which more later, is that of 'designated' member. Unhelpfully, this is nowhere defined, and it is left for the members and their professional advisers to spell the role out of the various statutory obligations which are placed on the designated members to the exclusion of their non-designated fellows.

Subscriber members 6.2

The *Limited Liability Partnerships Act 2000* provides simply for two ways of becoming a member.

The first members are those who subscribed their names to the incorporation document (*LLPA 2000, s 4(1)*) with the exception of any such subscribers who have died or (in the case of incorporated members) been dissolved in the interval between signing the incorporation document and the certificate of incorporation being issued. (Draftsmen of agreements to be entered into by subscribers before incorporation, in accordance with *LLPA 2000, s 5(2)*, should bear in mind the possible problems this may create.)

Joining as a member by agreement 6.3

The other permissible route of entry – in addition to being a subscriber member (see 6.2 above) is simply 'by and in accordance with' an agreement with the existing members.

There is no requirement in the *LLPA 2000* itself for such an agreement to be express, let alone in writing. In practice, however, an express agreement is likely to be needed, since the position will be governed either (if there is no partnership agreement covering the point) by the default provision in *regulation 7(5)* of the *Regulations* (see 1.14), which states that a new member may only be introduced with the unanimous consent of all existing members; or under an a provision in a partnership agreement which specifically provides a route to membership, whether in the same terms as *regulation 7(5)* or otherwise.

Eligibility for membership 6.4

Any legal 'person' may be a member of an LLP. Thus individuals, limited companies, or other LLPs may become members. On the other hand ordinary partnerships (or indeed limited partnerships under the *Limited Partnerships Act 1907*) cannot, since they have no legal personality separate from that of their members.

In businesses which have loose 'associations' between different business vehicles, this may well mean it becomes sensible, if they are ever to be formalised, for all to acquire some sort of incorporated status, whether as companies or LLPs, so as to allow for full inter-relationship.

Members are not usually employees 6.5

The *LLPA 2000* makes it clear, in *section 4(4)*, that in normal circumstances, members of an LLP are not employees of that LLP. (This fits with the central plank of the legislation that members are taxed as self-employed, rather than as employees.) It does not, however, prohibit a member also having the dual status of an employee, but merely states that he/she will not unless he/she would be so regarded if the business vehicle were a partnership not an LLP.

In other words, if the members wish to opt for the status of a 'salaried member' as some partnerships choose to have 'salaried partners', i.e. someone held out as a partner/member, they can do so. It has however been indicated by the Inland Revenue, so far only informally, that they will nonetheless (being legally 'members') be taxed under Schedule D.

Members as 'workers' for statutory purposes   6.6

Like partners, however, whilst the lack of 'employee' status (see 6.5 above) means that most of the mainstream employment legislation (unfair dismissal, redundancy, etc.) will not apply to members, since they do not fulfil the test for applicants of being an 'employee'; they may nonetheless be covered by some of the more recent, EU–inspired, secondary employment legislation, particularly that which masquerades as being health and safety legislation.

Examples of the above are the *Working Time Regulations 1998 (SI 1998/1833)* and the *National Minimum Wage Act 1998*, which both use the term 'worker' to define the class of people given rights in accordance with their provisions. Since the definition of 'worker' in each is:

'. . . an individual who has entered into or works under . . .

(a)   a contract of employment; or

(b)   any other contract, whether express or implied and (if it is express) whether oral or in writing, whereby the individual undertakes to do or perform personally any work or services for another party to the contract . . .'

members acting under an agreement (express or implied) between themselves and the LLP will presumably be included. Thought may therefore, for instance, need to be given to whether hard–working members need to sign a contracting–out agreement under *SI 1998/1833, reg 5* or can claim the exemption afforded to those who have the power to determine their own working hours (*SI 1998/1833, reg 20(1)(a)*); and whether tax problems may result from payments assumed by the Inland Revenue to be made to working but actually unremunerated members (e.g. members in a small family business) as to which see *Tax Bulletin* No 50, December 2000 for a statement of Revenue practice.

The basis of membership   6.7

Just as a partner in a partnership is an agent of the partnership (*PA 1890, s 5*) so is a member of an LLP an agent of that LLP (*LLPA 2000, s 6(1)*).

The concept of agency is thus central to the operation of LLPs, and is a constant theme when examining the ways in which they will work in practice. As an agent, a member will owe to the LLP all the duties which any agent owes to his principal, e.g:

- to carry out his principal's instructions;

- to exercise appropriate care and skill;

- to behave honestly and not take inducements or secret profits; and

- to refrain from allowing conflicting interest.

The vital distinction, however, between a partnership and an LLP is that, in the case of the former, each partner is also by virtue of the provision referred to above an agent of each and every one of the other partners; but in the case of an LLP the members are **not** agents of each other. Consequently, they may owe no duties to each other.

No duty of good faith between members   6.8

The word 'may' is used in the last sentence of 6.7 above for two reasons. Firstly, it is quite possible for the members of an LLP to draw up an express duty of good faith as between members, and to insert it in their governing agreement. Secondly, the Government in debate deliberately did not rule out the possibility of such a duty being found by a court to exist by implication.

All they did was to refuse to introduce, and to have to define, a statutory duty of good faith between members. They were not prepared to go further than two specific default provisions requiring members not to compete with the LLP or to benefit from the use of its property name or connection (*regs 7(9), 7(10)*); and to apply *section 459* of the *Companies Act 1985*. Both these provisions are dealt with in more detail elsewhere (see 8.16, 8.17, 12.64 to 12.72). There may well however be instances where courts would be prepared to establish the existence of a duty to act for the common good and not, for example, for some collateral personal advantage.

The problems of providing a duty of good faith   6.9

The difficulties which the draftsman faced, however, and which appear to have been the driving force behind the Government's steadfast refusal, at all stages of debate, to allow a statutory duty of good faith to creep in, are the practical problems of how that duty would be defined and applied.

There is the very real difference that, with a partnership, there is little true distinction between a duty owed to the partnership as a whole, and to the other partners, since the former is merely the aggregate of the latter. With an LLP, however, if duties existed on both levels they would be owed to two entirely separate potential sources of claim, i.e. the LLP as an incorporated entity, and the members as individuals. How could a distinction be drawn as to whose claim was the primary one, or as to which had actually incurred such loss as might be claimable? It is suggested that the Government was correct, and that efforts to adhere to the duty on an individual basis failed to recognise the real consequences of incorporation.

Further, if that is so, it would seem appropriate for any partnership agreement expressly to state that no such duties exist, so as to avoid the insidious risk of any implied duty being argued for. It is of course open to members to take the opposite tack, and expressly to provide for such duties, but if they do they will face considerable difficulties of defining the duty, and providing for its practical application in addition to the duty owed to the LLP.

Limitations on a member's authority 6.10

There may of course, as with any agent, be limitations upon the authority of any particular member. An example would be a member in an accountancy LLP who was, for instance, a corporate finance specialist, and hence was not authorised to carry out audit work and sign an auditor's certificate.

The *LLPA 2000* provides for such limitations in *section 6(2)*, which states that an LLP is not bound by a member's actions if two conditions are fulfilled. (The provisions parallel those in *PA 1890, s 5* applicable to part-ners, though there is no equivalent of *PA 1890, s 8*, specifically stating that the firm will not be bound if there is an agreement between the partners to limit a partner's authority, where a third party expressly cannot rely upon an act outside that limitation if he knows of the agreement.)

Actual lack of authority 6.11

The first condition referred to in 6.10 above is that the member in fact has no authority to act for the LLP in doing the act in question (*LLPA 2000, s 6(2)(a)*). The default position is thus that a member has full authority unless otherwise provided.

It therefore is for an LLP which seeks to limit a member's authority to do so clearly and in a way it could evidence if required. This could be provided for in the partnership agreement; or in a subsequent resolution of the members, duly minuted. If power to introduce such limitations is to be delegated, e.g. to designated members, or to some form of committee, it would be as well for the partnership agreement and/or the resolution granting delegated powers to spell out the rights to restrict an individual's authority.

Third-party lack of knowledge   6.12

The second condition referred to in 6.10 above is that the person with whom the member is dealing must either know that the member has no authority; or alternatively must not either know or believe the individual with whom he is dealing to be a member of the LLP in the first place (*LLPA 2000, s 6(2)(b)*).

In either case the third party cannot rely on the member's actions to bind the LLP.

Requirement for actual knowledge that unauthorised 6.13

The first limb of the test requires actual knowledge on the third party of a lack of authority. In the light of the default position referred to in 6.11 above, it would seem that a third party would be entitled to rely upon a presumption, when dealing with a member of an LLP, that that member did have authority to bind the LLP, unless the lack of authority is brought to his/her attention.

There is no provision for any sort of register of such limitations. Thus the onus will be firmly on the LLP to protect itself, e.g., in the accountancy example in 6.10 above, by including a provision in its standard letter of engagement for new clients of the corporate finance member to the effect that he cannot sign audit certificates. There could be circumstances where clients might find such statements somewhat curious, and it will be a matter of judgment for the members as to how important they regard the promulgation of limitations as being.

Lack of knowledge of the LLP connection   6.14

The other possibility is where the third party neither knows, nor believes, the person to be a member of the LLP at all. Such circumstances would prevail if the third party considered himself to be dealing with the member as an individual, not knowing of his membership status.

The LLP is thus sufficiently fixed with liability if the third party effectively has any reason to believe the person with whom he is dealing is a member (assuming of course that that belief is in fact correct). He therefore does not have to test that belief, e.g. by checking the register at Companies House.

Comparison with directors' authority   6.15

The test as to actual knowledge referred to in 6.13 above does offer a contrast with the provisions of the *Companies Act 1985* in relation to internal limitations on the powers of directors (which can of course be delegated to an individual director).

In *CA 1985, ss 35A* and *35B*, not only are the powers deemed to be free of such limitation in favour of a third party (who is under no obligation to enquire as to limitations) providing that third party is acting in good faith; but also it is specifically provided that mere knowledge of the existence of a limitation does not, of itself, mean that the third party is acting in bad faith. In other words, in the case of a company, knowledge of an act being ultra vires an individual will not necessarily be fatal to a third party's attempt to fix the company with liability, whereas with an LLP it will.

Third parties and former members   6.16

The position becomes more complex when the relationship between third parties and the LLP is considered in the context of the acts of former members. (It should be noted that these provisions only apply if the person in question has completely ceased to be a member, and not merely if his/her abilities are limited by any of the factors in *section 7* – see 6.25 below).

(In those circumstances the starting point is that the person in question is still regarded fully as a member for third party purposes, subject to 6.17 below.)

The effect of cessation of membership   6.17

By virtue of *section 6(3)* of the *LLPA 2000* a third party dealing with an individual who has been but has ceased to be a member of an LLP is (subject presumably to the *LLPA 2000, s 6(2)* limitations referred to above at 6.11 and 6.12) still entitled to fix the LLP with liability **unless** he has had notice that the individual in question has ceased to be a member, or notice of the cessation of the individual's membership has been delivered to the Registrar. In effect, therefore, delivery to the Registrar of notice of cessation of membership becomes immediate implied notice to all the world of cessation.

This could cause practical problems for a third party who, if dealing with a member, might be well-advised to carry out a search at Companies House to see if the person in question is still a member. Further, since there is no concept of a priority period which would apply to ensure that the results of a search held good for a set period, whatever intervening changes might occur, that search would seem to need to be contemporaneous with the transaction in question. Therefore external contracting parties, even though *section 36* of the *Companies Act 1985* provides that an individual may bind an LLP by contract, may wish to have important contracts signed off by more than one member.

The possibility of an individual member's liability   6.18

Notwithstanding the principle of the limitation of the liability of the members of an LLP to their investment in that body, and the existence of that LLP as a separate and incorporated entity, circumstances may still exist where an individual member is personally liable to a third party.

This will principally occur where there is an act or omission of a wrongful (e.g. fraudulent or negligent) nature which is either the direct act or omission of the member in question, or where he is so closely associated with or responsible for it that personal liability will attach to him. Members may well wish to seek to phrase the LLP's terms of engagement so as to limit this risk, by getting clients to agree to the exclusion of members' personal liability. Such exclusion clauses will however be liable to the same limitations as any other exclusion clause, namely that by the *Unfair Contract Terms Act 1977* any exclusion must broadly be 'reasonable' to be valid, and cannot in any event exclude liability for death or personal injury resulting from negligence; and that (if the customer or client is not a body corporate) any 'unfair' terms must be avoided which would transgress the provisions of the *Unfair Terms In Consumer Contracts Regulations 1999* (*SI 1999/2083*).

The scope of personal liability   6.19

The scope of this possibility for personal liability is uncertain (see 6.18 above), and the *LLPA 2000* does nothing to remove or limit that uncertainty.

One view is that an individual would only be liable personally for his own negligent act if he assumed personal liability for the advice, where the third party relied upon that assumption of liability, and where it was reasonable for them to rely upon it. This was applied by the House of Lords to the liability of a company director in *Williams v Natural Life Health Foods [1998] 1 WLR 830; [1998] 2 All ER 577*. It seems however that this would sit uncomfortably with the later decision in *Merrett v Babb [2001] 3 WLR 1*, that a mere employee can be liable for negligence. In that case the Court of Appeal, after an extensive review of case law, including *Williams,* rejected the view that the voluntary assumption of risk was always the appropriate test, and asserted that an alternative was a combination of proximity and foreseeability with it being fair, just and reasonable to impose a duty of care.

The answer may lie in the closeness of the relationship between the negligent individual and the client. The more personally the individual has been involved, even down to the question of whether a personal rather than a business signature appears on documents (one of the features in *Merrett*), and the more the dependence on that individual's advice, the greater the risk.

The co-extensive nature of personal liability   6.20

What the *LLPA 2000* does however provide, in *section 6(4)*, is that where such personal liability does exist, the LLP is liable to the same extent as the individual, provided that the act or omission either was in the course of the LLP's business, or was done with its authority. (It is not that it needs to have authorised the wrongful nature of the act or omission, or that wrongful steps per se can be taken as in the course of an LLP's business: it is merely the general nature of the act or omission itself which needs so to qualify.)

Liability as between members   6.21

An exception to this however is where the individual's liability, for his wrongful act or omission, is to another member of the LLP. Here, the principle of co-extensive liability (see 6.20 above) is excluded by *LLPA 2000, s 6(4)*.

Presumably this was introduced to avoid internal membership disputes resulting in liability falling upon the LLP, e.g. so that if one member does something to the detriment of another in his management or adminis-tration of the LLP, the LLP is not itself liable to make the harm good. The provision does however go further than this, in that it does not require that member A's liability must be to member B in his capacity as a member for the exemption to apply. Thus, if A were to be negligent when acting as a conveyancer for B, his litigation fellow-member in a solicitors'

LLP, in the purchase of a property for the purely private use of B, the exemption would still appear to apply, and the statutory application of co-extensive liability would not come into effect. This would leave B to ordinary principles as to whether he could establish liability against both; and if he did succeed would leave A and the LLP to resolve the extent of their respective liabilities between themselves.

This would seem to be an undesirable, and possibly unintentional, result which might need correcting by future amendment.

Availability of a member's indemnity   6.22

The question therefore arises of whether a member, who is co-extensively liable with the LLP as far as an outsider is concerned, can nonetheless turn to the LLP to indemnify him against the personal liability.

In the case of a 'wipe-out' claim, that indemnity would presumably be worthless, but in the great majority of cases the LLP's assets (and insurance cover – see 6.24 below) will suffice to cover the personal element.

Statutory indemnity   6.23

An agent is generally entitled to an indemnity from his principal, and indeed an indemnity in general terms is provided by *regulation 7(2)* of the *Regulations* (see 1.14). There is however a subtle (and, again, possibly unintentional) difference in wording between the provisions. *Section 6(4)* of the *LLPA 2000*, defining when co-extensive liability will apply, simply refers to a wrongful act or omission 'in the course of the business' of the LLP. *Regulation 7(2)(a)* gives an indemnity for personal liabilities incurred by a member 'in the ordinary and proper conduct of the business' of the LLP.

Can, for instance, a negligent act or omission, be said to be 'ordinary and proper'? In drafting a partnership agreement, it may thus be prudent to deal expressly with the question and to clarify, one way or another, whether such an indemnity is to be granted to cover all liabilities to which *section 6(4)* may apply, or merely some, or none. In addition, provision may be inserted to regulate the right of the LLP to make a contribution claim against the individual as a joint tortfeasor, in accordance with *section 7(3)* of the *Civil Liability (Contributions) Act 1978*. Thus it would be possible for an individual member to be protected (by indemnity) where a third party claimed against him but not the LLP, and (by excluding contribution obligations) where the external claim is pursued only against the LLP and not the individual; and for the position between those two extremes also to be regulated by the agreement.

Availability of insurance for personal liability   6.24

Insurers are only just getting to grips with the principles of LLPs. Early indications are that they will not regard the change from partnership to LLP status as being of particular importance to them, since the risk they are insuring will not alter. Further, it seems to be the case that they will regard the possible co-extensive liability of an individual as included within that risk, so that one policy will provide cover for both the LLP and the member.

However, it is a point which individuals will be keen to ensure is covered when making their insurance arrangements and when drafting the partnership agreement. Also, they will need to consider this in detail when leaving the LLP and examining what run-off cover is to be provided for personal liabilities which may not emerge for many years, especially in the light of recent developments in case law which suggest that liability for negligence may in practice be almost unlimited in time. The case of *Cave v Robinson Jarvis & Rolf [2001] EGCS 28*, following *Brocklesby v Armitage & Guest [2001] 1 All ER 172*, seems to make an allegation of deliberate concealment under *section 32* of the *Limitation Act 1980*, such as to make the limitation period effectively inapplicable, ludicrously easy to establish. This has been the subject of much comment in both the legal and insurance industry and press, but unless *Cave* is taken to the House of Lords (which appears unlikely) and successfully appealed, this would appear to be with us to stay. The Law Society for one is to press for reform in this area.

Restrictions on management or administration   6.25

The *LLPA 2000* provides that in certain circumstances members may not 'interfere' in the management or administration of the business of the LLP. This applies, by *section 7(1)*, if a member has:

- ceased to be a member;
- died (though it is difficult to see how a member could die without ceasing to be a member!);
- become bankrupt or been wound up;
- granted a trust deed for the benefit of his creditors; or
- assigned all or part of his share in the LLP (whether absolutely or by way of charge or security).

No restriction due to voluntary arrangements etc. 6.26

One notable omission from the list in 6.25 above is where a member (whether individual or corporate) enters into a voluntary arrangement under the *Insolvency Act 1986*. Such a member thus retains full capacity to act in the running of the LLP's business.

In practice, this would often be essential if such an arrangement was to succeed, particularly as individual arrangements for members will often need to be combined with such an arrangement for the LLP itself. Other omissions are for corporate members, where some form of insolvency-related provisions apply which stop short of a winding up, e.g. receivership, administration or administrative receivership. Again, full capacity to act as a member is retained.

Application of the prohibition 6.27

The prohibition in 6.25 above applies not only to the member or former member himself, but to his appropriate representatives. Thus it applies to the personal representatives of a deceased member; to the trustee or liquidator of a bankrupt or wound up member; to the trustee under a trust deed; or to a member's assignee.

The last example appears wholly illogical in circumstances where the assignment is absolute (rather than by way of security) and consented to in such manner as the constitution of the LLP may require (unanimity being the default requirement under *regulation 7(5)* of the *Regulations*). In such circumstances it becomes necessary to write into the provision, for it to have a practical effect, a limitation that the prohibition upon an assignee ceases upon his/her becoming a member in his own right.

Practical extent of the prohibition 6.28

The extent of the prohibition (see 6.25 above) is also unclear. Although it says that such a member or representative may not 'interfere' in the 'management or administration' of the business of the LLP, sadly, neither of those terms is defined anywhere in the *LLPA 2000* or the *Regulations*. Nor is any guidance offered by comparison with the *Company Directors Disqualification Act 1986* which (by *section 1*) forbids a disqualified person to 'be concerned or take part in the promotion, formation or management' of a company – clearly importing a number of different concepts.

It is easy to imagine sets of circumstances where there could be dispute as to whether the section was being breached – e.g. where a bankrupt member acting as site manager for a construction LLP continues so to act, in a role which is part of the external business of the LLP but must involve some administration for it.

Sanctions for breach of the prohibition   6.29

The likelihood that the uncertainty considered in the previous paragraphs would normally be expected to lead to possible litigation, to allow the courts to settle the limitations of the statute's wording, is however reduced by the fact that the section appears to be fairly toothless anyway.

Breach does not give rise to any criminal sanction. Nor does a breach give rise specifically to the right for the authorities to seek an order under the *Company Directors Disqualification Act 1986*, save possibly in the limited circumstances where the LLP is being wound up and the act can be alleged to have been a 'breach [by the member] of his duty as such member' (*CDDA 1986, s 4(1)(b)*). It would seem therefore to be a section usable only by the fellow-members of the member under the disability to restrain his or his representatives' activities. Thus it appears to be no more than another default governance provision, even if one which, at least ostensibly, is not capable of being excluded by agreement. Since, however, its enforcement would only arise if the other members wished positively to take action, it seems likely to amount to much the same thing in practice.

The right to continued payments   6.30

A final part of the prohibition provision (see 6.25 above), and a further weakening of any effect it may have, is that, by *section 7(3)* of the *LLPA 2000*, the section does not in any event limit the right of any member to whom the section applies to receive any monies from the LLP as a result of the ban imposed.

Thus, for instance, a member who becomes bankrupt, but whose membership is not automatically terminated under the terms of the partnership agreement, and who therefore continues to work for the LLP but without the ability to interfere in its management or administration, will still be entitled to the same remuneration as he was before. If such management was a key part of his work, the other members might wish to restrict his/her remuneration to reflect the change in his duties. Unless the partnership agreement gives them such a right, they will not however be able to, and will face the choice of paying up or declining to implement the prohibitions imposed by the section.

Registration of members' details   6.31

The name and address of each subscribing member needs to be stated in the incorporation document, by virtue of *section 2(2)(e)* of the *LLPA 2000*. In the case of an individual member, 'address' means normal residential address. In the case of an incorporated member it means the registered office. *Section 18* so specifies.

Concern has been expressed at the need to give residential addresses for some who may fear that to do so would put them at risk. This has been highlighted by the attacks on directors of companies targeted by protest groups, such as Huntingdon Life Sciences Ltd. The concern also applies however to professionals working in areas where emotions run high, such as solicitors doing family work. The Government has legislated for the possibility of company directors seeking 'Confidentiality Orders' under the terms of the *Criminal Justice and Police Act 2001*. A consultation paper as to how these should be provided for in detail was published by the DTI in October 2001. One of the specific questions posed in that paper was whether LLP members should be afforded the same protection as directors, the DTI's view being that they should. Since a very short period of time (one month) has been provided for this consultation process it may be assumed that there is serious Governmental momentum to implement such provisions sooner rather than later.

7 – Designated Members

The *Limited Liability Partnerships Act 2000* contains a completely new concept of 'designated members', as an optional sub-set of members.

This chapter examines the logic behind this concept, the way in which designated members are to be appointed and notified, the powers and duties applicable to designated members, and the ways in which a partnership agreement can be framed to accommodate the different options which designated members can offer for structuring the governance of an LLP.

Reasons for the creation of 'designated members' 7.1

In the explanatory notes to (what was then) the Limited Liability Partnerships Bill, the Government gave, as one of five reasons for introducing the legislation, its concern that the existing partnership law did not give a suitable base for the structural requirements of a business with very large numbers of partners.

With one exception, however, the legislation does not appear to address this problem at all. The limited default provisions it contains for the management structure of an LLP are based very closely on partnership law. Its main administrative requirements come from the *Companies Act 1985* but, though there is much about accounting requirements, disclosure etc., there is nothing to equate the management structure of an LLP to that of a company, e.g. by a shareholder/director style divide. The sole exception is the concept of designated members, which is totally optional in the sense that there is no need for an LLP to differentiate between ordinary and designated members, and indeed the default position is that there is no such difference.

What are designated members for? 7.2

The answer to this seemingly straightforward question (see 7.1) is that it is almost entirely up to the LLP, if it opts to have designated members at all, to decide what they should be and should do. All that the *LLPA 2000* does is to impose certain administrative duties (and therefore penalties for breach of those duties) upon them.

Further, even those limited duties were considerably weakened during the last stages of progress of the legislation through Parliament. For instance, in earlier stages, it was to have been the duty of the designated members alone to prepare, pass and file the LLP's accounts. By the time of the final version of the legislation, the duty to prepare and pass accounts had reverted to the generality of the membership, and it merely remains the duty of the designated members to sign the accounts thus passed and file them at Companies House.

What is a designated member?   7.3

There is no useful definition within the *LLPA 2000* of what a designated member is. They can be individual or corporate members.

LLPA 2000, s 8 deals with how members are appointed as being designated, how that designation can be removed, what particulars of designation require filing at Companies House, etc; but says nothing at all about what designation means. The definition section, *LLPA 2000, s 18*, states merely that 'designated member' shall be construed in accordance with *section 8* – as neatly circular a definition as you are likely to find anywhere!

Duties of designated members   7.4

The answer to the question of what is a 'designated member' therefore seems to be that a designated member is defined, not by what he is, but by what he must do. Those obligations may be created in one of two ways. Firstly, there are those which are imposed by the statute or the *Regulations* (see 1.14 above). A table of the main requirements is set out as Table A below. The second possibility is that they can be created by the partnership agreement.

Table A

Statutory requirements of designated members

Statutory provision	Refer to paragraph	Nature of obligation
LLPA 2000, s 8(5)	7.9	Sign and deliver Form LLP8 as notice to registrar that either all members are to be designated; or that only certain individuals are.

Statutory provision	Refer to paragraph	Nature of obligation
LLPA 2000, s 9(3)	4.5; 4.6	Sign and deliver Form LLP288a, LLP288b or LLP288c as appropriate, as notice to registrar of certain changes in membership details.
LLPA 2000, Sch, para 4	3.12	Ensure compliance with any direction of the Secretary of State to change the LLP's name.
LLPA 2000, Sch, para 5	4.1	Sign and deliver Form LLP3 as notice to the registrar of a change of the LLP's name.
LLPA 2000, Sch, para 9	3.13	Sign and deliver Form LLP287a as notice to the registrar that the LLP's registered office is situated in Wales.
LLPA 2000, Sch, para 10	3.13	Sign and deliver Form LLP 287 as notice to the registrar that the LLP's registered office has changed.
CA 1985, s 233	10.16	Sign accounts once approved by membership.
CA 1985, ss 242–244	10.25	Deliver signed accounts and ancillary documents to the registrar.
CA 1985, ss 363, 713	4.9	Sign and deliver annual return in Form LLP 363 to the registrar.
CA 1985, ss 385–388A	10.57	Appoint auditors.
CA 1985, s 390A	10.64	Fix auditors' remuneration.
CA 1985, ss 391, 391A	10.68	Remove auditors from office.
CA 1985, s 392	10.70	File with registrar notice of auditors' resignation.
CA 1985, s 392A	10.71	If required by resigning auditors, convene members' meeting to consider resignation and circulate auditors' statement.
CA 1985, s 403	12.31	File in Form LLP403a or LLP403b memorandum of satisfaction of charge on the LLP's property.
CA 1985, s 652A et seq	17.40, 17.41	Apply in Form LLP652a for the LLP to be struck off the register or, in Form LLP 652c, for such an application to be withdrawn.
IA 1986, s 2(3)	13.7	Prepare terms of proposed voluntary arrangement and supporting statement of affairs.
IA 1986, s 2(4)	13.20	Apply to court for replacement of nominee of arrangement.

Statutory provision	Refer to paragraph	Nature of obligation
IA 1986, s 84	15.2	Deliver to registrar copy of determination for voluntary winding up.
IA 1986, s 89	15.5	Make statutory declaration of solvency in support of proposed members' voluntary winding up.
IA 1986, s 99	15.11	Make sworn statement of affairs in connection with proposed creditors' voluntary winding up, and appoint one of them to attend at and preside over creditors' meeting.
Criminal Justice Act 1967, s 9	7.17	Accept service of statements of evidence in criminal proceedings.

Creation of designated powers by agreement   7.5

It can be seen from the above (see 7.4) that statute does not really vest any management powers in the designated members, but merely requires them to perform certain largely administrative and regulatory duties, with the consequential penalties for breach of those duties. In that respect, designation would seem to be an unenviable status, and something of a poisoned chalice.

If LLPs wish to make no more of the status than that, it would seem that they may well choose to treat the burden equally, and to have all members as designated members. (It is not possible to have a limited number of designated members, and to offer them an indemnity from other members against any personal financial penalties suffered by them, since such penalties will be in the nature of fines in criminal proceedings, and such an indemnity would therefore be void as being against public policy.)

Using the opportunity of designation   7.6

What the Government has done, however, is at least to offer the option of a differentiation in the status of different groups of members, which can be positively built upon by a partnership agreement, in order to create a more corporate style of management structure.

Thus there would be nothing to prevent an LLP, in its partnership agreement, from approximating the status of designated members to that of directors, and delegating a large range of management powers to them, subject to such controls by the general membership as they might wish to retain. The likelihood, therefore, is that it is the larger LLPs which will seek to take advantage of these provisions, and make something of the status of designation.

Designation of all members   7.7

There are two possibilities, at the stage of incorporation, as to how the issue of designation can be approached.

The incorporation document, Form LLP2, in accordance with *section 8(3)* of the *Limited Liability Partnerships Act 2000*, asks whether all the members for the time being are to be designated members. If the relevant box is ticked, then not only will all the originally subscribing members become designated members, but so will all subsequently joining members. (Each member, whether as subscriber or when later joining, has to indicate by Form LLP2, or Form LLP288a, as the case may be, whether he consents to become a designated member. Presumably, if all are supposed to be designated, but the relevant box is not ticked in respect of any particular member, then the paperwork will be rejected by Companies House.)

Designation of particular members   7.8

If, however, Form LLP2 (see 7.7 above) indicates that not all are to be so treated, then only those particular members whose details show that they are to be designated will be so. There must be at least two of them, or the incorporation document will be rejected by Companies House.

Those members so specified remain designated until their status is changed, either by positive action being taken, or by reason of their ceasing to be a member at all. Others may join their ranks, by means either of an existing member becoming designated, or a new member joining and being designated from the start.

Changing the approach   7.9

The LLP is able, at any time, to change its general approach, by *LLPA 2000, s 8(4)*.

Thus, if it has initially said that all members are to be designated, it can subsequently change to specify only certain members as being designated. Alternatively, if it has initially named particular members, it can determine henceforth to treat all members for the time being as designated. Notice to either of the above effects must be delivered to the Registrar in Form LLP8. If the change affects the status of any particular member, then Form LLP288c will also need to be filed in respect of that member.

Changes where certain individuals are designated members   7.10

Where the provisions at any time in force require certain named members only to be designated members, then the choice of those named can still be changed at any time. Any member may become or cease to be a designated member by agreement with the other members. Form LLP288c needs to be filed.

It is notable however that, unlike cessation of actual membership where, by virtue of *LLPA 2000, s 4(3)*, the default position is that a member may resign his membership upon reasonable notice, there is no equivalent right in the absence of agreement to resign the status of designation whilst retaining membership. If the ability for a member to do this is desired, it must therefore be expressly included in the partnership agreement.

Reduction in numbers of designated members   7.11

There is no requirement that the number of designated members must in any way be proportionate to the overall number of members. Thus, if there are 50 members, there is still no obligation to have more than two designated members.

It is however provided by *LLPA 2000, s 8(2)* that, if the number of designated members falls to one or none, then automatically all members become designated members. This could happen because of e.g. death or resignation. There is no period of grace during which members can appoint to fill the vacancy, without the automatic provision coming into effect. It will therefore always be prudent, for all except the smallest of LLPs (where probably all members will be designated anyway) to have three or four designated members at least, to avoid this possibility.

Automatic cessation of designation   7.12

A member automatically ceases to be a designated member, if he ceases to be a member at all (*LLPA 2000, s 8(6)*). In other words the designation cannot exist independently of membership, so there is no equivalent of a non-executive director having no shares or other stake in the business.

Note however that the prohibitions in *LLPA 2000, s 7* (as to e.g. bankrupt members – see 6.25 above), though they prohibit a member 'interfering' with the management or administration of the business, and hence would prevent a designated member exercising many if not all of the functions attaching to designation, do not actually affect his continued status as a designated member. Thus if, in a ten–member LLP, there were only two designated members, and one of those two became bankrupt, even though that one could no longer function as a designated member, the number of designated members would not be deemed to drop so as to invoke the automatic changes provided for in *LLPA 2000, s 8(2)* – see 7.11 above.

Notice of appointment etc. of designated member 7.13

Amongst the changes in membership details which need to be notified to the Registrar under *section 9(1)* of the *Limited Liability Partnerships Act 2000*, is the situation where a member either becomes a designated member, or ceases to be so designated. Form LLP288c then needs to be filed.

The exception is where all members for the time being are designated, when, by virtue of *LLPA 2000, s 9(2)*, the ordinary notice of accession to or cessation of membership will suffice without a separate notice dealing with designated status.

Stated obligations of designated members 7.14

There is no statement of principle, in either the *LLPA 2000* or the *Regulations* (see 1.14 above), as to what duties may be owed by designated members to the LLP, or to their fellow members, over and above the obligations of an ordinary member.

It seems as if the only instance of extra responsibility is to the regulatory authorities, and hence the public, enforceable by means of the various criminal sanctions to which designated members are exposed, which their undesignated brethren are free of.

Contrast with proposals for directors' responsibilities 7.15

Contrast the situation described in the previous paragraphs with the approach of the Company Law Review Steering Group which in *Modern Company Law for a Competitive Economy: Final Report*, published in July 2001, proposes to build upon existing common law obligations of directors by establishing a legislative statement of directors' duties covering:

- obedience to the company's constitution and to prior binding decisions;

- acting in good faith to promote the company's interests;

- maintaining independence of judgement;

- exercising care skill and diligence;

- avoiding conflicts of interest;

- not using company property or information for personal interest or benefit;

- not gaining personal collateral benefit from exercising directors' powers; and

- considering creditors' interests if insolvency threatens.

Underlying obligations   7.16

Some of the duties in 7.15 above are likely to apply to all members anyway, in the LLP context, e.g. the limited provisions as to duties of good faith in *SI 2001/1090, regs 7(9)* and *(10)*. Some may be considered inappropriate where there is not the degree of separation of interests and powers that can occur in a company's shareholder/director structure.

If however the status of designation is to be used to create a class analogous to directors (and, if not, it is difficult to see how LLPs can in structural terms satisfy the Government's concern referred to in 7.1 above) then, in the absence of either legislative provision or any specific common law guidance as to designated members' particular obligations to other members, and to other stakeholders in the LLP (staff, creditors etc.), it is left for either the courts in application of general common law principles, or the draftsman of the partnership agreement, to fill the gap. An instance of the former might be for a court to rule that designated members have a duty to exercise reasonable care and skill. In the latter case, provision could be made either way, e.g. by imposing duties upon the designated members in the partnership agreement, or by specifically excluding the application of potential duties.

Criminal Justice Act statements   7.17

One miscellaneous duty of the designated members is that, if there are court proceedings involving the LLP where, under *section 9* of the *Criminal Justice Act 1967*, there are witness statements to be served on the LLP, it is the task of the designated members to receive them.

8 – Governance of the LLP

This chapter starts by examining the overall question of whether a partnership agreement is needed for an LLP. It puts the default provisions provided by the *Regulations* (see 1.11 above) into context, looks at them in detail, and compares them with their predecessors under the *Partnership Act 1890*.

The chapter suggests ways in which properly drafted terms can replace or improve upon the default provisions. Lastly, it draws attention to areas which are not touched upon at all, but which nonetheless should be provided for in a partnership agreement for the LLP.

General

Introduction 8.1

The philosophy of the *Limited Liability Partnerships Act 2000* is that it is for the members of an LLP to arrange their own affairs as they think fit. In many instances, during the passage of the legislation through Parliament, the Government refused to adopt a prescriptive stance on matters where the only consequences were of an internal nature.

Partly in order to achieve this, and to avoid attempts to import partnership concepts and case law into the LLP arena, partnership law in any shape or form was expressly excluded from applying to LLPs unless specifically applied by the *LLPA 2000* or any other statutory provision (*LLPA 2000, s 1(5)*). Eventually, they did include a minimal level of default provisions, in *SI 2001/1090, regs* 7 and 8 (see 1.11 above).

Part of the theory seems to have been that, unlike an ordinary partnership which can be created without any formality (or even without knowing that the effect of the steps being taken is to create the relationship of partnership), the creation of an LLP requires the conscious taking of a number of decisions and public steps, so that it is reasonable to expect members to go through the process of deciding how they wish to regulate matters between themselves. Experience of those professionals who have had much to do with either partnership or company disputes suggests this may be optimistic!

The concept of a partnership agreement   8.2

Unless therefore an LLP and its members are content to rely on the default provisions, they will wish to have their affairs regulated by agreement(s). Such an agreement is referred to by *SI 2001/1090, reg 7* (somewhat inconsistently, in the light of the use of the term 'member' as opposed to 'partner') as a 'limited liability partnership agreement'.

Notably, there is no requirement for any such agreement to be express, let alone in writing. Thus, any agreement, even an implied or verbal one, may be sufficient to displace the majority of the default provisions, i.e. those in *SI 2001/1090, reg 7*. The only exception is the provision of *SI 2001/1090, reg 8* that an ability to expel a member can only be imported by express (but again not necessarily written) agreement. The possibilities for evidential arguments about the existence or otherwise of implied or verbal agreements can only be imagined, and this situation should be avoided wherever possible.

The parties to appropriate agreement(s)   8.3

The statute clearly contemplates two classes of agreement:

● an agreement between the members; and

● an agreement between the LLP itself on the one hand and its members on the other,

since in *section 5(1)(a)* of the *Limited Liability Partnerships Act 2000* there is reference to the existence of the one sort of agreement 'or' the other.

In practice, however, it is likely that one document will suffice for both purposes. It does, however, need a change of mindset, on the part of the draftsman of such a document, from the usual drafting of a partnership agreement, as he has constantly to bear in mind whether the obligation or right he is creating is in fact that of individual members, or of the LLP as a corporate entity, acting through its members.

Pre-incorporation agreements   8.4

It is specifically provided that it is possible to formulate an agreement to govern the operation of an LLP before its formal existence commences.

LLPA 2000, s 5(2) provides that an agreement made before incorporation, if made between the subscribers to the incorporation document, can impose obligations upon the intended LLP, so as to take effect 'at any time' after its actual incorporation.

It is seemingly possible therefore to make such an agreement effective immediately after incorporation. It may however be prudent, as the moment of incorporation will not be known until after the event, to make the commencement of the agreement relate either to the receipt of the certificate of incorporation, or the transfer of a business to the LLP, or a specific date set sufficiently far in advance to allow for the comfortable completion of the incorporation process. (One provision which should normally thus be included is an indemnity for pre-incorporation liabilities incurred by subscribing members on behalf of the future LLP, as the default indemnity conferred by *SI 2001/1090, reg 7(2)* only covers things done in the ordinary and proper course of the LLP's business, or to preserve its business or property, neither of which would seem capable of application to pre-incorporation events.)

The default provisions

The default provisions generally   8.5

Many of the default provisions will appear familiar to any draftsman, having been largely lifted from the *Partnership Act 1890*. However, it should not be assumed that the default provisions are appropriate for an LLP setting, and they should not be automatically incorporated either by leaving any reference to their subject matter out of an agreement, and hence impliedly accepting them; or by repeating them in an agreement.

Further, it is worth remembering that partnership law has been expressly excluded by *LLPA 2000, s 1(5)*, so the interpretation of familiar principles in partnership case law may or may not be applied by courts in future to these provisions, depending on whether the judiciary take the opportunity to consider the actual words used in an unfettered manner.

The default provisions therefore need consideration on an individual basis, as set out at 8.6 to 8.16 below. In what follows, the default provision itself is set out in bold type, and the *PA 1890* counterpart then follows in italics, with the relevant regulation and section numbers given.

Equal division of capital and profits   8.6

'All the members of a limited liability partnership are entitled to share equally in the capital and profits of the limited liability partnership.' (*SI 2001/1090, reg 7(1)*.)

> 'All the partners are entitled to share equally in the capital and profits
> of the business, and must contribute equally towards the losses whether
> of capital or otherwise sustained by the firm.' (PA 1890, s 24(1).)

This first default provision seems simple, but is far from being so. It provides that all members of an LLP are entitled to share equally in its capital and profits. The first limb of that statement requires careful consideration. It implicitly assumes that the initial capital, whatever that may be, has been contributed equally. That may well be the case in a start-up situation, but is considerably less likely to be so if the scenario is that of the transfer of an existing partnership business into an LLP. If the transferred capital is unequal, then it should be noted that this provision is not merely talking about the distribution of future capital profits (or indeed losses) but about the ownership of existing capital as well, since it talks about capital 'and' profits. Thus if, in a partnership, A owns £100,000 of capital, and B owns £50,000, and they decide to transfer the business into an LLP without any express agreement, this regulation on the face of it provides that they are entitled to share equally in the capital, i.e. £75,000 each. Member A may well argue that there is some form of implication to be inserted by reason of the prior differential, but it places the onus upon him to prove that in order to restore the status quo.

Further, it begs the question as to what constitutes 'capital'. If the definition of capital is taken to be the aggregate of the sums which, on winding up of the LLP, would be payable to the members after realisation of all the assets and payment of all the debts (including debts due to members), then that effectively includes not only original or specifically introduced capital sums, but also retained and unallocated profits. Even if shares of profit entitlement are equal, the reality is that retained profit levels are extremely unlikely to be equal, unless all drawings and payments to be treated as drawings are also exactly equal. If (as will be the case for many businesses) prudence dictates that funds are retained within the LLP to pay individual members' (almost certainly differing) tax bills, notwithstanding that the actual legal liability is a purely personal one, that of itself will result in a differential between the amounts charged to each member's account with the LLP. Even if, therefore, equal division of 'capital', in the sense of specifically introduced capital, is required, then a careful definition of it is needed. (This may also be relevant for the purpose of calculating available loss relief for trading (i.e. other than professional) LLPs.)

The second limb of the provision refers to profits. Since it does not differentiate, this must be assumed to include profits of a capital nature. If there is specific provision for unequal ownership of capital, it may well therefore make sense for there to be a provision for correlative division of capital profits. Thus if, in the above example, the status of A and B has been preserved by a statement that the capital of the LLP at the outset belongs two-thirds to A and one-third to B, and a capital asset such as a building transferred from the partnership's beneficial ownership into the LLP's name is sold at a profit, A will presumably want two-thirds of that profit, not just a half, even if the operating profits of the LLP are being split equally as per the default provision.

In many cases, of course, equal division of profits will not, for operational reasons, be the desired split, and specific provision will need to be made.

Another point to make in regard to this provision is that (unlike its counterpart in the *PA 1890*) it does not refer anywhere to apportionment of losses. 'Profit' is not defined anywhere so as to include losses. Although of course any loss will show as that in the accounts of the LLP, as a separate entity, nonetheless it will in practice impact upon the members' several interests in the LLP, and thus its effect needs to be apportioned in just the same way as profits. Again, consideration needs also to be given to whether there should be any differentiation between the ways in which operating losses and capital losses are to be borne. To extend the above example, if A is to take two-thirds of any profit on the sale of the building, he should equally expect to bear two thirds of the burden of any losses on it, even if he is only suffering one half of the general operating losses.

As an overlay to all this, the accounting treatment of LLPs (as shown by the consultation draft of the Statement of Recommended Practice) indicates (see 11.7) that it is not until the moment that profits and losses are actually allocated or divided (whatever sharing agreements have previously been reached) that they cease to be treated as reflecting on the level of 'other reserves' of the LLP and come to affect the level of debts owed to individual members, which are therefore provable in a winding up.

In short, it is extremely difficult to think of any scenario where this default provision is safe to cover the reality of the members' positions in regard to the absolutely central concepts of capital and profits, and it should always be the case that a properly worded express provision should apply. There is no particular surprise in this, since the similar provision in the *PA 1890* has in practice almost always been displaced by express provision in any partnership agreement.

Indemnity to members   8.7

> **'The limited liability partnership must indemnify each member in respect of payments made and personal liabilities incurred by him–**
>
> **(a) in the ordinary and proper conduct of the business of the limited liability partnership; or**
>
> **(b) in or about anything necessarily done for the preservation of the business or property of the limited liability partnership.'** (*SI 2001/1090, reg 7(2)*.)

> 'The firm must indemnify every partner in respect of payments made and personal liabilities incurred by him—
>
> (a)   In the ordinary and proper conduct of the business of the firm; or
>
> (b)   In or about anything necessarily done for the preservation of the business or property of the firm.' (PA 1890, s 24(2).)

This provision is less problematical, though it may require some refinement. It provides an indemnity to an individual member, from the LLP, in two circumstances. It is worth bearing in mind one fundamental difference between the indemnity thus granted to a member, and that granted to a partner in a partnership by the PA 1890. In the latter case, the indemnity is a liability of all partners, and can be called upon to the extent of their personal assets. In this instance, however, the indemnity will only bind the available assets of the LLP itself, which may be far less extensive. This is accordingly one area where the principle of limitation of liability may work against the interests of a particular member (though, of course, in favour of all others) and members should accordingly be careful of allowing themselves to get into a position where they are dependent on such an indemnity to any extent which is significant when viewed against the asset base of the LLP.

One case where the matter may well be out of their hands is that of negligence, where there is sufficient evidence of a direct link between the act or omission giving rise to the negligence claim and the individual member to render him personally liable. There, in addition to the question of whether the default wording of the indemnity is wide enough to cover the situation, the risk of an indemnity claim being beyond the asset base of the LLP (perhaps in the situation where the claim exceeds the business's cover level, or where insurers either disallow a claim or are themselves insolvent) may be a relevant concern.

Reference has been made elsewhere to the potential for exclusion in the partnership agreement of the reverse of this indemnity (see 6.23 above, and the surrounding paragraphs), i.e. the right for the LLP to recover a contribution from an individual member in circumstances where a third party chooses to sue only the LLP for, e.g. negligence, even though that third party could have established co-extensive liability against the particular member if it had chosen to do so, because of his assumption of responsibility for the negligent act or omission. Should the LLP have the right to seek a contribution against the member as a joint tortfeasor under the *Civil Liability (Contributions) Act 1978*, or should that right be excluded, as allowed by *section 7* of that legislation (see 6.23 above)? If the philosophy of the agreement is that the LLP should bear all claims, and an indemnity is therefore granted to members for occasions when action may be taken against them by third parties, clearly it makes no sense to allow the situation where, merely because there is no direct claim, the LLP can recover from the member.

Further, the right to seek a contribution could well give rise to great internal strife, with the other members effectively trying to establish a contribution claim against their fellow member when this has not even been contended for by the third-party claimant. It is suggested that the course of action most consonant with the idea of seeking limited liability protection in the first place is to grant members an indemnity against negligence, and to bar contribution claims against them, relying on the remedy of expulsion if needed for future protection. The alternative, to say that the indemnity to members did not extend to third-party tortious claims against them, and that contributions could be sought from them, seems contrary to the corporate concept of an LLP.

As mentioned, the indemnity itself has two limbs, which can be shortly considered. The first is where the member has made any payment, or incurred any liability, in the 'ordinary and proper course' of the LLP's business. The second is where such a payment or liability arises from anything 'necessarily done for the preservation of the business or property' of the LLP. Any agreement is likely to contain such an indemnity, but there are still areas of concern. For one thing, from the LLP's viewpoint, there is no provision that, in return for the indemnity, the member has promptly and fully to provide vouchers and evidence to support his claim.

Secondly, from the member's stance, there may be times when he acts, with the full knowledge and consent of other members, outside what could normally be considered the scope of the 'ordinary' course of the business, or takes steps which are considered desirable but may not be strictly 'necessary' for the preservation of the LLP's business. He would reasonably wish and expect the indemnity to extend to cover such circumstances, if they are nonetheless genuinely for the LLP's benefit, but it would not extend that far on the statutory wording. One option when drafting a partnership agreement would be to provide for such extended circumstances to apply to the indemnity if the act in question was either approved in advance, or subsequently ratified, in such circumstances as the agreement provided, e.g. by the designated members, or a management board etc.

Participation in management   8.8

'Every member may take part in the management of the limited liability partnership.' (*SI 2001/1090, reg 7(3)*.)

'Every member may take part in the management of the partnership business.' (PA 1890, s 24(5).)

This short provision says simply that every member may take part in the management of the LLP. All members thus start from an equal theoretical standing in this respect. In all but the smallest of LLPs, this is unlikely to be the case in practice. Even if all members have an equal say in major management issues (accepting new partners, opening new offices etc.) they are likely either to have their own management roles, or to play no active part in routine management, rather than everyone participating in every management decision.

The partnership agreement may provide for this differentiation, or it may be left to more informal and more flexible decision-taking. Bear in mind also that the member's rights under this provision, and any express counterpart in an agreement, are subject to the provisions of *section 7* of the *LLPA 2000*, preventing e.g. a bankrupt member from interfering in the management or administration of the LLP. (As a sidelight, this provision is an illustration of the fact that the functions of the designated members, as laid down in the statutory provisions, are not considered to be managerial functions. During the consultation process which accompanied the drafting of the legislation, it was considered whether it should in fact be only designated members who managed, but this was eventually rejected, and this default provision was substituted.)

No entitlement to members' remuneration 8.9

'No member shall be entitled to remuneration for acting in the business or management of the limited liability partnership.' (*SI 2001/1090, reg 7(4).*)

'No partner shall be entitled to remuneration for acting in the partnership business.' (PA 1890, s 24(6).)

In this provision 'remuneration' presumably equates in common parlance to salary, since of course it does not mean that members shall not receive any return for their membership, but merely that it shall come through the medium of a profit share. It applies to two potential aspects of a member's activities. Firstly, it states that he will not be entitled to remuneration for 'acting in the business' of the LLP. Since there is now a distinction between the 'business' and the 'management', the former presumably means providing the goods or services which the LLP exists to sell, and is more likely to be applicable to a member of an LLP in the professional services field than a retail or manufacturing LLP, since in the former case the member himself is likely to be responsible for the direct delivery of client services.

Secondly, it provides similarly for anything done in the management of the LLP. If, therefore, a professional services partnership wishes to reward a member for taking on a managerial role in addition to his client service role, it will need specifically to do so. In drafting terms, this really fits with the requirements referred to in the consideration of the default provision on profits in 8.5 above, so that any special arrangements for prior profit shares, etc. should be taken care of in an express agreement.

If it is envisaged that there may at any stage be salaried members, this possibility, and the need for remuneration to be paid to them, will need to be spelled out (though figures may be left to less formal documentation). The reason for this is that salaried members will be full members (unlike their salaried partner equivalents who are merely held out as partners and need not be party to the partnership agreement) in the sense that they will have completed just the same Companies House paperwork as their profit-sharing brethren, and be regarded as having equal rights and obligations. Any sense in which this is not the case thus needs specifying.

Unanimity for new members and assignments   **8.10**

'**No person may be introduced as a member or voluntarily assign an interest in a limited liability partnership without the consent of all existing members.' (SI 2001/1090, reg 7(5).)**

'No person may be introduced as a partner without the consent of all existing partners.' (PA 1890, s 24(7).)

Two separate aspects are rolled into one in this provision. The first is that unanimous consent is required for the introduction of a new member. This may well still be desired in all but the largest LLPs, since this has often been regarded even in large partnerships as one of the fundamentals which do indeed require unanimity, so personal is the relationship between individuals practising as partners. This does however seem an anachronism in the corporate setting of an LLP, especially in the larger ones, and particularly in the light of the fact that members are not agents of each other and may well not owe each other fiduciary duties.

In any event, the provision as written is potentially undesirably restrictive, in that actual and active consent of all members is needed. Thus any move to introduce a new member could effectively be defeated, even by a member who was not prepared openly to vote against the admission, by his absenting himself from any meeting where the matter was to be considered. The requirement is not that all members present and voting at a duly convened meeting must be in favour, but that all must. Similarly, if a member is prevented from participating in a decision by absence or illness, that would debar admission. Even if, therefore, unanimity is desired, thought should be given to whether that should in practice mean a vote by all those present and voting at a properly convened and quorate meeting of members, rather than relying on the default provision.

The second limb, to which all the same considerations apply as are mentioned in the last paragraph, is that unanimous consent is required for the assignment of any member's share in the LLP. Such assignments may perhaps be thought to be likely to be more frequent than assignments of partnership shares, as LLPs are after all corporate bodies, and the equivalent of a share sale in a limited company is more applicable. The default provision still leaves the situation however where, in theory, consent could be given under this provision but, if the arrangements did not go so far as admitting the assignee as a member in his own right, the assignee could not participate in the LLP's management or administration, as provided by *section 7(2)* of the *LLPA 2000*. (This broadly follows the idea in *section 31* of the *PA 1890* that an assignee's only right is to receive the appropriate share of profits, and not in any way to participate in the firm.) Draftsmen will therefore need to consider firstly whether unanimity is appropriate for assignment, or an unfair restriction on a member's right to realise their investment in the LLP; and whether consent to an assignment should also be automatically classed as consent to the assignee's admission as a member.

Majority decisions 8.11

'Any difference arising as to ordinary matters connected with the business of the limited liability partnership may be decided by a majority of the members, but no change may be made in the nature of the business of the limited liability partnership without the consent of all the members.' (*SI 2001/1090, reg 7(6)*.)

'Any difference arising as to ordinary matters connected with the partnership business may be decided by a majority of the partners, but no change may be made in the nature of the partnership business without the consent of all existing partners.' (PA 1890, s 24(8).)

Having provided that admission and assignment both require unanimity, *SI 2001/1090* (see 1.14 above) goes on to provide that with one exception, i.e. a change in the nature of the LLP's business, all other decisions can be reached by a simple majority of members. A curious term is however used in the regulation, following the *PA 1890*, namely that all decisions as to 'ordinary' matters connected with the LLP's business can be so decided by simple majority (other than as excepted). What then of decisions as to extraordinary matters, if the reason they are extraordinary is nothing to do with the specific exception? Must the provision be read so as to imply that all matters, other than the specific exceptions of admissions, assignments or changes in the nature of business, are *ipso facto* ordinary – or is there an unspecified class of matters for which the *LLPA 2000* does not specify what majority is appropriate? The only decided case on the parallel provision in the *PA 1890*, *Highley v Walker (1910) 26 TLR 685*, held that the admission of a partner's son to the business was 'ordinary'. Once again, a clearer express provision would be desirable.

For the exception, of the change in a business's nature, the same provisions apply as in 8.10 above in regard to the requirement for consent of all members, not just those attending a properly convened and quorate meeting. The other difficulty with this provision is that there is no definition of what constitutes a change in the 'nature of the business' of the LLP. Must it be such a change as involves the abandonment of the former nature of business, or is an enhancement such as to call the exception into play? In other words, if an accountancy firm wishes to start a professional recruitment agency, it would undoubtedly be a change in the nature of the business if accountancy were to be abandoned in favour of recruitment; but what if what is started is merely a small off-shoot providing a new service to existing clients, not intended or likely to provide more than a small percentage of the overall operation's turnover? It is no doubt a 'change' in the nature of business, since there was previously no business of the nature of recruitment, but is it such an extraordinary change as logically to require a different decision-taking structure from, for instance, moving the firm's office, for which no exception is made?

Access to books and records   8.12

> **'The books and records of the limited liability partnership are to be made available for inspection at the registered office of the limited liability partnership or at such other place as the members think fit and every member of the limited liability partnership may when he thinks fit have access to and inspect and copy any of them.' (*SI 2001/1090, reg 7(7)*.)**

> *'The partnership books are to be kept at the place of business of the partnership (or the principal place, if there is more than one), and every partner may, when he thinks fit, have access to and inspect and copy any of them.' (PA 1890, s 24(9).)*

Part of the debate which arose, during the passage of the legislation through Parliament, concerning the respective rights of ordinary members and designated members, related to the ability of the former to have access to the books and records of the LLP. In the end, the compromise position was not to enshrine such a right in statutory terms, but to put it in the default provisions where it is of course capable of being excluded by agreement. (This is different from the right of all members to receive a copy of the accounts, which is enshrined in *section 238(1)* of the *Companies Act* 1985 (as modified).)

The requirement is twofold. Firstly, it requires that the books and records (which presumably, these days, must be interpreted as including computer records) must be kept either at the LLP's office, or at such other place (singular) as the members think fit. (There is no requirement for the Registrar to be notified of the chosen place.) Secondly, it gives any member the unfettered right, when he thinks fit, to have access to, and to copy, any of the books and records.

The provision refers to the 'books and records' of the LLP, without in any way defining that term. There is no qualifying word such as 'financial' or 'accounting', and it must seemingly go beyond the financial records, since *section 222* of the *Companies Act 1985* (as modified) gives a similar right to members in respect of the LLP's 'accounting records', and if that were all that *SI 2001/1090, reg 7(7)* was supposed to apply to, it would largely be redundant (save for the express right to copy as well as inspect). It seems logical to consider the provision as including source documents for the preparation of accounts.

Further, if a purposive approach to construction is used, i.e. that the idea underlying the provision is to enable all members, in order to protect themselves and to discharge their managerial responsibilities, to form an independent view as to the position of the LLP, then it presumably would need to include documents relevant to that, such as:

- deeds;
- leases;
- finance agreements etc.

It may well go so far as to include records such as personnel files, etc. It will thus need adapting for a multi-site LLP, since the regulation applies only to one 'place', and it would otherwise be impossible to devolve functions and record-keeping to different sites. This provision is likely to need modifying therefore in many cases, and may also need some limits put upon it for larger LLPs, where the management may prefer to avoid the administrative burden of permitting such access.

Obligation to disclose information 8.13

'Each member shall render true accounts and full information of all things affecting the limited liability partnership to any member or his legal representatives.' (*SI 2001/1090, reg 7(8)*.)

'Partners are bound to render true accounts and full information of all things affecting the partnership to any partner or his legal representatives.' (PA 1890, s 28.)

This is one provision which sits uncomfortably with all the others. It requires all members to render true accounts and give full information of all things affecting the LLP. That in itself is not an unreasonable requirement of an agent, when defining its obligations to his principal. The requirement however is not that the member should give such disclosure to the LLP, which is the principal, but that he should give it 'to any member or his legal representatives'. Seemingly therefore other members, and only they – to the exclusion of the LLP – have the right to call for such disclosure or to take action if it is not forthcoming.

This cuts across the whole idea that there is no duty of good faith in an LLP between members directly, as distinct from such a duty being owed to the LLP itself. Since the Government refused time after time to create such a direct duty, and set its face against derivative actions (with the sole exception of allowing for actions under *section 459* of the *CA 1985* and even they can under *section 459(1A)* be excluded for LLPs by agreement) it seems strange that they have allowed this exception. It is also unhelpful that, following the *PA 1890*, 'legal representatives' is nowhere defined. Is it restricted in its effect to those who have the legal power to represent a member, e.g. a trustee in bankruptcy or a donee of a power of attorney; or would it be apt, in accordance with common parlance, to include a member's duly appointed solicitors? There is not even any case law in respect of the *PA 1890* provision – even if that were to be regarded as persuasive – to offer guidance. It is suggested that a draftsman of a partnership agreement should seek to retain a consistent regime by excluding this provision as it stands, and replacing it by a similar duty owed by members to the LLP itself.

Profits from competing business   8.14

> **'If a member, without the consent of the limited liability partnership, carries on any business of the same nature as and competing with the limited liability partnership, he must account for and pay over to the limited liability partnership all profits made by him in that business.' (*SI 2001/1090, reg 7(9)*.)**

> *'If a partner, without the consent of the other partners, carries on any business of the same nature as and competing with that of the firm, he must account for and pay over to the firm all profits made by him in that business.' (PA 1890, s 30.)*

There are two provisions which limit the ability of a member to profit from other activities at the expense of the LLP. Together they are the closest that the *LLPA 2000* gets to expressing a duty of good faith as being owed by a member. The duty is however owed to the LLP itself, and not to other members as individuals. This first limb has three elements, i.e. that in order for a member to be obliged to account for and pay over to the LLP all 'profits' made by him in a business other than the LLP:

- the business must be of the same nature as the LLP;

- the business must be competing with the LLP; and

- the LLP must not have consented to his carrying on the business.

The provision is therefore fairly limited in its scope. It certainly does not extend as far as the limitation found in many partnership agreements, banning partners from carrying on any other business at all without consent. It is not even enough for the business to be of the same nature as that of the LLP but it must also be competing with the LLP. If therefore the business is of the same nature, but is targeting a completely different customer or client group, it is presumably not caught by the provision.

Drawing lines of interpretation as to whether a business is of the 'same nature' as, or is 'competing with' the LLP is an exercise which may be difficult. Calling for an account to be taken by the court, in order to determine the extent of the 'profit' which is to be repaid by the offending member to the LLP if the offence is proved, will also be a complex and potentially costly process. Again, therefore, any help which can be offered by the draftsman of a partnership agreement to clarify the circumstances in which, and the extent to which, any such restriction will apply, will be useful.

Use of the LLP's name or connection etc. 8.15

'Every member must account to the limited liability partnership for any benefit derived by him without the consent of the limited liability partnership from any transaction concerning the limited liability partnership, or from any use by him of the property of the limited liability partnership, name or business connection.' (SI 2001/1090, reg 7(10).)

'Every partner must account to the firm for any benefit derived by him without the consent of the other partners from any transaction concerning the partnership, or from any use by him of the partnership property name or business connexion.' (PA 1890, s 29(1).)

The provision which is associated with that last mentioned is one which forbids unauthorised transactions concerning the LLP, or the improper use of the LLP's property, name or connection. Again, it is the LLP which is the party having the benefit of the right, and hence the ability to enforce it, rather than any particular member. The provision is wider in its scope than that in 8.14 above, since it refers to 'benefit' rather than 'profits' and is thus apt to cover benefits in kind etc. The activities which may trigger a claim are also very broadly stated, and so may appeal to draftsmen of partnership agreements. (The wording of the final part of the provision is less clear than its 1890 predecessor, and it needs the words 'or its' to be read into it, before 'name or business connection' to make sense.)

A number of cases noted to *section 29(1)* of the *PA 1890* in *Halsbury's Statutes, Vol 32 (4ᵗʰ edition, 2001 reissue)* may (bearing in mind the caution against using *PA 1890* cases at all) be illustrative of the scope of this provision. Two instances where the offending partner was held to account were where there was a secret commission (*Fawcett v Whitehouse (1829) 1 Russ & M 132, 8 LJOS Ch 50*), and where a partner was selling his own goods to the firm (*Bentley v Craven (1853) 18 Beav 75*). The provision was not however breached where one partner bought the interest of another (*Cassels v Stewart (1881) 6 App Cas 64, 29 WR 636, HL*); where a partner formed an independent company (*Fuller v Duncan (1891) 7 TLR 305*); where a partner bought a reversionary share in a building from which both the partnership and his sole businesses were conducted (*Bevan v Webb [1905] 1 Ch 620, 74 LJ Ch 300*); and where two partners bought a property independent of the partnership (*Trimble v Goldberg [1906] AC 494, 75 LJPC 92, PC*).

The right to expel members   8.16

'No majority of the members can expel any member unless a power to do so has been conferred by express agreement between the members.' (*SI 2001/1090, reg 8*.)

'No majority of the partners can expel any partner unless a power to do so has been conferred by express agreement between the partners.' (PA 1890, s 25.)

The final default provision is of a slightly different nature from the others. Instead of being a provision to be included unless specifically excluded, it is one which forbids the inclusion of one term by implied agreement alone. It prohibits the expulsion of any member by any form of majority vote, unless the power to do so has been conferred by express agreement. It does not prescribe what majority should be needed, and it would accordingly be open to an LLP to opt for a simple majority. It does not require that the express agreement shall be written or even recorded in writing (e.g. membership meeting minutes).

Many LLPs may think that they would not wish to include a power of expulsion, since that would run contrary to the partnership ethos they wish to retain, but in fact many will do so without realising it, e.g. with regard to the ability to require a member who suffers long-term illness to retire. In cases under the similar provision under the *PA 1890* (or earlier provisions) it has been held that a power to expel, if conferred, must in any event be exercised with the utmost good faith (*Carmichael v Evans [1904] 1 Ch 486; 73 LJ Ch 329*); and for the benefit of the partnership as a whole (*Blisset v Daniel (1853) 10 Hare 493 at 522, 1 Eq Rep 484*). Draftsmen should therefore ensure that the circumstances in which expulsion is possible, and the decision taking processes which are necessary for it, are defined carefully.

Additional provisions

The need for additional provisions 8.17

In effect, any LLP partnership agreement will have three overlapping elements. One is simply those provisions which will be familiar from any partnership agreement – governing administrative matters such as banking, holidays etc. These are not examined here. The second is those matters which are covered in the default provisions above, and which may either be adopted as they are or, preferably, improved upon by the draftsman.

The third is those provisions which are not appropriate to partnership agreements, and not covered in the default provisions, but which it would be prudent to include in any well-drafted agreement, since they refer to matters which may arise in the running of the LLP for which there is no other provision made. This part of this chapter suggests some such provisions.

Ratification of pre-incorporation contracts 8.18

One aspect of the consideration of pre-incorporation contracts has already been considered in 8.4 above, namely the need for the indemnity to members to be extended to include cover for acts properly done on the LLPs behalf in the run-up to incorporation.

The correlative provision which it would be prudent to include in any partnership agreement – especially if does itself precede incorporation – is that the LLP should subsequently adopt and ratify any such pre-incorporation contracts.

Liability under personal guarantees 8.19

Personal guarantees are likely to be needed in a number of circumstances, for many LLPs. It may be that they will be required from all members, e.g. if the LLP trades on a substantial overdraft, when the bankers may require such guarantees.

On the other hand, it may well be that only some are called upon. For instance, if a ten-partner firm converts to an LLP, and wishes to transfer the lease of the premises from which it trades, from the names of the four most senior partners, in whom it has for years been vested, into the name of the LLP itself, then it would not be unusual for the landlord to require those four individuals personally to guarantee the obligations in the lease.

In either instance there are two aspects to be considered. Firstly, it should be checked that the indemnity given to individual members by the LLP is apt to cover liability incurred under the guarantee. Secondly, the position needs to be considered where that indemnity may be insufficient to cover the liability, so that there is resultant personal liability on one or more particular members. In most cases, it would be inappropriate for that liability to remain solely with those giving the guarantee, but rather it should be shared amongst the members. The agreement should therefore provide for how that sharing should take effect.

Meetings and voting 8.20

There are many instances in the *LLPA 2000* where reference is made to decisions being taken by either the members or the designated members. There are also a number of instances where reference is made to meetings being held e.g. *section 392A* of the *Companies Act 1985* as modified (meetings to consider auditors' resignation) and *section 89* of the *Insolvency Act 1986* as modified (meetings to give declarations of solvency on voluntary winding up), which again may concern either all or merely the designated members. There is even provision in some cases where the right is given to apply to the court to determine the procedures to be adopted for calling meetings, e.g. *section 92(3)* of the *IA 1986* as modified, dealing with provisions for filling a vacancy in the office of liquidator.

What does not appear, however, and what should therefore be provided for in the agreement, is what the mechanics for meetings should be. The questions which need resolving (and the answers to which may differ between meetings of the general membership and the designated members, who may thus require different provisions) will include:

● who has the right to call meetings;

● what notice of them must be given;

- can notice be abridged;

- who is to chair meetings;

- what is an appropriate quorum;

- what majority or majorities can determine what matters;

- is proxy voting allowed; and

- when and how can written resolutions take the place of meetings?

Designated members' roles   8.21

Part of the consideration which will be relevant to meetings will concern the division of roles between members and designated members (unless all members are to be designated) (see Chapter 7).

There are certain roles which statute reserves to the designated members, e.g. the appointment of auditors, but there may well be other matters which members wish to delegate, and which will need to be provided for.

Duty of good faith   8.22

As has been mentioned in various places above, the Government on many occasions refused to spell out a duty of good faith between members, as opposed to one between each member and the LLP. It accepted however, that there might well be circumstances in which such a fiduciary duty might be implied, but said that they would leave it to the courts to find and define any such duties.

Clearly such uncertainty is undesirable. The opportunity should therefore be taken to remove that doubt by either stating explicitly that no such duties are to be implied; or that they are – in which case the extent of those duties should be spelled out. It is suggested that the former is the more desirable way of proceeding, as otherwise if there is any breach of duty the fundamental question arises as to who – LLP or individual member – has the right to seek remedies for that breach.

Termination of membership   8.23

Some aspects of termination of membership are touched upon either in the default provisions (the right to withdraw on reasonable notice) or in normal partnership provisions (the right to expel for default etc.). The purpose of mentioning the topic here is to draw attention to the fact that neither of those sources provides the comprehensive code to govern termination which any well organised LLP will need, especially bearing in mind that members may not just be individuals, but corporations (whether companies or other LLPs) which will have their own circumstances for termination, e.g. dissolution rather than death.

The provisions will need to cover carefully the circumstances in which termination will take place, and what the consequences are to be. Most important under this latter heading is the requirement for comprehensive provisions defining the amounts and methods of withdrawal applicable to members' interests in the LLP after termination. Here there are no default provisions at all (save for the undesirable – and excludable – remedy of action on the ground of unfair prejudice under *section 459* of the *Companies Act 1985*).

Insolvency provisions – voluntary arrangements   8.24

Insolvency for LLPs is covered at length elsewhere (see Chapters 13 to 18) but there are three aspects of it which are relevant to the drafting of a partnership agreement.

The first relates to voluntary arrangements ('VAs'). If the LLP proposes a VA under *section 1* of the *Insolvency Act 1986* (as modified), it may be that modifications are proposed to it by a creditor. The chairman of the creditors' meeting must then seek the approval of the LLP to those modifications, under *section 4(5A)*. In the absence of agreement before the close of that meeting the LLP is deemed not to have agreed, and hence the VA cannot proceed. To avoid the need for potentially damaging adjournment of the meeting, there thus needs to be someone present at the meeting who is authorised to give consent on behalf of the LLP. For all but the smallest LLPs it will not be practical for all members to be present, so the agreement should deal with who that should be.

Insolvency provisions – determination to wind up   8.25

The *Insolvency Act 1986* refers in many instances to a 'determination' by the LLP to wind itself up, but nowhere does it provide what constitutes a determination, or how such a determination is to be reached.

To take an extreme example, would it be a 'determination' for the only two members of a small LLP, drowning their sorrows over a pint together, to decide that they cannot continue, and have to call it a day? The question is facetious, but the point is serious, since much flows from the timing of the 'determination', as it is this which constitutes the commencement of the winding up and many matters flow from that. The agreement should therefore provide carefully for the manner and timing of the making of any such determination.

Insolvency provisions – members' voluntary contributions   **8.26**

Perhaps the most curious provision in the whole of the LLP legislation is that found in *section 74* of the *Insolvency Act 1986* (as modified), which states that, in a liquidation, a member will only be liable personally to contribute if he has agreed to make such a contribution.

Since that would appear to negate the whole purpose of seeking the limited liability protection of an LLP, it would seem unlikely that this would frequently be the case, so that it would be wise to include a provision confirming that no member has agreed to make any such contribution.

There may however be practical reasons for such an agreement to be entered into (see 17.4 to 17.7 below). Either way, the draftsman of the original partnership agreement should make the position very clear.

9 – Taxation of LLPs

This chapter looks at the various taxes which may affect an LLP, and members' interests in it, namely income tax, capital gains tax, inheritance tax, stamp duty, national insurance and value added tax.

It starts from the general theme that the intention is for tax transparency, i.e. that it is the members of the LLP who are the taxable parties, rather than the LLP; and examines the exceptions to that rule, and various tax avoidance provisions. Steps which need to be taken in mitigation of potential tax liabilities, especially for stamp duty, are indicated.

General

Introduction 9.1

The avowed intent of the Government in legislating for the tax consequences of LLP formation has been to achieve transparency, i.e. to arrange matters so that the authorities look through the entity of the LLP to the underlying members' interests in it, so that the LLP itself is not a taxpaying party.

In broad terms, when considering the tax positions of various business vehicles, the above means that an LLP equates to a partnership rather than a company, and has the consequent advantages and disadvantages. Thus, like a partnership, tax is payable on profits earned, whether or not they are distributed to members or retained within the LLP for working capital; whereas with a company tax is payable at a lower rate when earned, but a second taxable event occurs when profits are distributed (whether by way of salary, directors' remuneration, or dividends). The allocation of profits to members of an LLP (as distinct from the sharing arrangements) will not constitute such an event (see 11.7 below).

Effect of conversion to LLP status 9.2

As a result of what is said at 9.1 above, in effect, when a partnership converts its business to that of an LLP its members will not notice any real change in the tax provisions which apply to them. With the one exception of stamp duty, where active steps need to be taken within a year of incorporation if duty is to be avoided on any transfers of assets from the partnership (or its nominees) to the LLP, the change should be seamless and automatic.

This follows on from the introduction of the self-assessment regime in the late 1990s, under the *Finance Act 1994* and later legislation, at which time the partnership as a whole ceased to be liable for the payment of the tax liabilities of the constituent partners. It also follows the pattern which has been adopted in respect of the LLP regime in the US, which will have the effect of making it easier for those LLPs with interests on both sides of the Atlantic to harmonise the tax regimes under which they work.

Exceptions 9.3

That is not to say that the Inland Revenue has given in without a fight! It has been concerned to preserve the overall amount of the tax take, and therefore has been and still is considering what loopholes it needs to stop up, in order to prevent the use of the vehicle of the LLP simply for tax saving purposes.

In this respect, the Revenue's approach differs from that of other jurisdictions, particularly with regard to investment and property LLPs, and the suggestion has been made that other countries may benefit from having businesses choose their regimes as offering a better home than the UK model.

Finding the provisions 9.4

Much of the relevant law is to be found in the *Limited Liability Partnerships Act 2000* itself, although it mostly operates through inserting provisions in other statutes. In addition, however, much of the anti-avoidance legislation appeared as last-minute amendments to a raft of measures in the *Finance Act 2001*, passed just before the dissolution of Parliament prior to the General Election of that year.

Further, the Revenue's interpretation of the legislation, which will be important to any attempt to understand its likely interpretation, is to be found in the December 2000 edition (Issue No 50) of its publication 'Tax Bulletin', which can be found on the Revenue's website www.inlandrevenue.gov.uk/bulletins. Also helpful on the VAT front is Business Briefing No 3 of 2001 (February 2001) from HM Customs and Excise, which can be found on www.coi.gov.uk/coi/coipress.nsf.

Income tax

The main provisions 9.5

The provisions of the *LLPA 2000* referring to income tax are to be found in *section 10(1), (2)*. Sadly, they work exclusively, and clumsily, by inserting four extra sections, and one phrase, into the *Income and Corporation Taxes Act 1988* (*ICTA 1988*).

General treatment of LLPs 9.6

The first, and easiest to comprehend (and, for the majority of partnerships seeking to convert to LLPs, the only one they are really likely to be interested in) is a new *section 118ZA, ICTA 1988*.

This new provision deals with the general treatment of LLPs, and provides that a trade, profession or business carried on by an LLP, with a view to profit, shall be treated as carried on in partnership by its members, and not by the LLP as such. For any LLP passing that test, there will therefore be no difference between the tax treatment before and after conversion from a partnership, i.e. it will be the members who will be taxed according to the regime appropriate to them (be it income tax under *ICTA 1988, s 111* for a member who or which is an individual or an LLP; or corporation tax under *ICTA 1988, s 114* for a member which is a limited company). Thus for instance the existing rules for the 'catch-up charge', relating to changes in work-in-progress provisions, will continue.

Similarly, it is provided that the LLP's property shall be treated as partnership property, so that for instance there is no balancing event for capital allowance purposes, thus preserving those allowances. The transfer of business from a partnership to an LLP part way through the tax year will not mean that two sets of returns need to be filed by partners/ members (even if the accounting year changes). Such returns will need to be signed by a nominated member, and default penalties may fall on him if returns are not in on time, according to the normal rules (for which he may well want an indemnity from his fellow members.)

One peculiarity is that (though the position is not yet clear or certain) the Revenue is believed to have indicated that even 'salaried' members will be treated as taxable under Schedule D – since they are 'members' within the statutory definition – even if in a partnership context they would have been taxed under Schedule E.

Non-trading etc. LLPs 9.7

The Inland Revenue however takes the view that this – to its mind, favourable – treatment (see 9.6 above) only applies to LLPs actively engaged in a trade, profession or business. It does not class the holding of investments, or of property for investments, as falling within these categories. It has therefore indicated an intention to legislate to provide that:

- Income derived from a property investment LLP, by a member which normally enjoys tax exemption on its income by reason of being a pension fund, the pension business of a life insurer, or the tax exempt arm of a friendly society, will nonetheless be taxable.

- Relief on interest payable by a member on a loan for capital introduced into an LLP will not be available if that LLP is an investment LLP.

Non-profit-making LLPs 9.8

It is also possible for an organisation to be engaged in a trade, business or profession, but not to seek to make a profit. Classically, this would apply to charitable or philanthropic organisations. Such an organisation should probably not be an LLP at all, since *section 2(1)(a)* of the *Limited Liability Partnerships Act 2000* requires that the business to be incorporated as an LLP should have been formed 'with a view to profit', but to make doubly sure, this phrase is repeated in the newly created *ICTA 1988, s 118ZA* (see 9.6 above).

Should a charity or philanthropic organisation therefore somehow succeed in getting registered as an LLP, it would nonetheless not have the advantages of transparency.

Continuation of availability of reliefs 9.9

A number of reliefs will continue to apply with no break. The most significant are as follows:

- Relief on interest payable on a loan for monies to be invested into the partnership business will continue once those monies are passed to the LLP.

- Overlap relief (i.e. the relief available to a partner leaving a partnership as compensation for the double taxation element applicable to him under the commencement rules when he joined the partnership) will continue to be available when he leaves the

LLP, provided that the LLP takes over all of the partnership's business, or at least sufficient part for the change not to be considered a 'demerger' of the partnership.

● Higher rate relief for continuing annuity payments continues to be available (and will also be available for incoming LLP members who accept future liability in respect of such annuities). Even if such annuity liability is not transferred to the LLP, the former partners who keep up the payments will continue to obtain such relief until they leave the LLP, or the business carried on by the LLP ceases, whichever is the earlier.

● The provisions for the 'catching-up charge', payable when partnerships moved from e.g. the cash basis to the 'true and fair' basis for their accounts, will continue to be phased as if there had been no change.

Loss relief 9.10

A distinction is drawn, when looking at loss relief available to members of an LLP, between those LLPs whose business involves the carrying on of a profession, and others (referred to in this paragraph as 'trading LLPs'). The difference arises not when looking at what losses can be claimed against future profits of the LLP itself, but in respect of the 'sideways loss' provisions, i.e. the ability of a member to set a loss in the LLP against other income he has.

Essentially, there are no restrictions for professional LLPs, but for trading LLPs the member can only set off such of his originally subscribed capital as has not been withdrawn, or already used in respect of previous years' losses. For this purpose the member's share of retained profit does not, unless the partnership agreement expressly provides otherwise, count as capital. (The logic behind this is that such undrawn profits once allocated count as a debt from the LLP to the member, and thus rank with the unsecured creditors in a winding up. The danger therefore of an agreement providing that undrawn profits shall be counted as capital is that the member would then lose the chance of getting part of his undrawn profits by way of dividend in a winding up, unless all creditors were paid in full.)

The detailed examination of losses is beyond the scope of this work. A useful example of how these rules could work is in the Tax Bulletin referred to in 9.4 above. If that is not sufficient reference should be made to a specialist tax work.

Capital gains tax

General position 9.11

The position in respect of capital gains tax (CGT) for LLPs is straightforward unless and until the LLP ceases to trade. By *LLPA 2000, s 10(3)*, a new *section 59A* is inserted into the *Taxation of Chargeable Gains Act 1992 (TCGA 1992)*.

This new provision applies to the position where an LLP carries on a 'trade or business with a view to profit'. (Note that, in distinction to the new *section 118ZA, ICTA 1988*, this does not refer to an LLP carrying on a 'profession' with a view to profit. This however merely reflects the difference in terminology used elsewhere in *ICTA 1988* and *TCGA 1992*, and does not imply that transparency in respect of CGT does not apply to professions.)

Treatment as a partnership 9.12

By virtue of the new *section 59A(1)* of the *TCGA 1992* (see 9.11 above), in three respects, the position of an LLP is treated as if it were that of a partnership. Thus:

- assets held by the LLP are treated as if they were held by the members, as partners;

- dealings by the LLP are treated as if they were dealings by the members acting in partnership (and not by the LLP as such);

- CGT chargeable to the members of the LLP on the disposal of its assets is assessed and charged on the members separately.

Therefore, a transfer of assets into the LLP's name has no adverse effect on such matters as indexation, retirement relief or taper relief. Further, the Revenue has indicated that if annuity rights and obligations are transferred, on substantially the same terms as before, neither the business nor any annuitant will be regarded as making a chargeable disposal.

Cessation of transparency 9.13

It is however possible that the right of the members of the LLP to take advantage of this favourable regime may cease, e.g. if they cease to carry on their trade or business, or if it should be held that it is not being carried on for profit. In those circumstances, by virtue of *TCGA 1992, s 59A(2)*, the picture changes completely.

In such an event, the LLP becomes liable for the tax on the disposal of any of its assets, as if it were a company; and the members as individuals become liable for CGT on any disposal by them of their interests in the LLP itself.

Movement between the two regimes   9.14

It is quite feasible for an LLP to move between the two possible CGT regimes as detailed above, e.g. by stopping, and then restarting, its trade.

There is no logical reason why any such change would necessarily involve an actual disposal of assets. Lest there be any doubt, *TCGA 1992, s 59A(3)* provides that any such move, in or out of the realms of transparency, does not of itself constitute any deemed disposal of assets. It looks therefore as if it is simply a case, with any actual disposal, of asking whether, at the time of disposal, the LLP satisfies the *section 59A(1)* test – if it does, the tax will fall on the members, but if it does not it will fall on the LLP.

The Revenue has however indicated that if there is merely a temporary cessation, e.g. a disposal of assets from one trade in order to raise funds to start another business, then it will still regard the assets as being disposed of by the members, not the LLP.

Cessation of trade   9.15

The actual position is however less simple than that, for *LLPA 2000, s 10(4)* goes on to insert another new provision, *section 156A*, into the *TCGA 1992*, which deals with the consequences of a 'cessation of trade'.

That phrase is defined (by *TCGA 1992, s 156A(3)*) as meaning the time when *section 59A(1)* ceases to apply to an LLP. That does not, as has been seen, necessarily mean a permanent cessation of trade. There may well therefore be arguments in individual borderline cases as to whether a pause in trade in sufficiently marked to constitute a cessation.

The effect of cessation on deferred gains   9.16

The problem is that, if there is a cessation, a charge to tax upon a member arises, without the need for any actual disposal, at the time of cessation, if he himself had acquired the asset for a consideration reduced under *section 152* or *153* of the *TCGA 1992*, i.e. if there had been any 'rolled over' element of gain held in respect of the asset.

Imagine, for instance, a sole trader who sold his shop in order to go into partnership; invested the proceeds with his new partners in the joint purchase of a new, larger, building; claimed roll-over relief in respect of his sale; transferred the building to a new LLP as successor to the partnership; and then ceased to operate the trade of the LLP which goes into liquidation. He as an individual would, under *TCGA 1992, s 156A* be liable for tax on cessation on the rolled over element of gain. To make matters worse, the Revenue has also indicated that taper relief will not be available to any member thus liable for gains. The liquidator will then be liable for any gain made during the liquidation period itself.

Revenue concession 9.17

There is however some light to throw over this otherwise gloomy position. The Revenue has indicated that it will only seek to implement this provision (see 9.16 above) in the case of insolvent liquidation, or if the LLP, having ceased its business, is not acting in a timely manner to brings its affairs to a close.

So long as the reason for the termination of business is not tax avoidance, and that the period of informal winding up is not over-protracted, then transparency can continue until completion of the process, or until a liquidator is formally appointed. In other words, it is only if it feels that it will lose out by allowing transparency to continue that the Revenue will stand on their rights under this section.

The provision is however such that, if partnerships have large amounts of gains rolled up into their assets, they may be put off forming LLPs, since the idea of a tax bill in advance of an actual disposal of property, at a time when almost by definition finding the funds to meet the bill is likely to be difficult, will be highly unattractive.

Inheritance tax

General position 9.18

The position on inheritance tax is refreshingly straightforward. By *section 11* of the *LLPA 2000*, a new *section 267A* of the *Inheritance Tax Act 1984* is added. This gives four instances in which, for the purposes of that and any related statutes, LLPs are to be treated as partnerships. Thus:

- property which an LLP owns, uses or occupies, is treated as if used, owned or occupied by the members, as partners;

- any business carried on by the LLP is treated as if carried on by the members, in partnership;

- any incorporation, change in membership or dissolution of an LLP is to be treated as if it were the formation, alteration or dissolution of a partnership;

- any transfer of value made by or to an LLP is treated as if made by or to its members in partnership, not by or to the LLP as such.

The effect therefore is that all reliefs etc. which are available to partners will continue to be available to them as members of the LLP which takes over from the partnership. The Revenue has confirmed that there will be no adverse effect even if the LLP might otherwise be regarded as a close company.

Stamp duty

General position   9.19

The general idea with stamp duty is that no *ad valorem* duty will be payable on the transfer of assets held by a partnership, or by trustees or nominees on its behalf, into the ownership of the LLP itself.

The idea of such a transfer is attractive in many cases, as it will avoid the fictions often necessary for partnerships, where freehold or leasehold properties are held by up to four partners as trustees for the generality of the partnership, and will facilitate the transfer of beneficial ownership on changes in the constituent members of the firm.

Further, for leasehold properties, a transfer of the lease into the LLP's name will be necessary for the protection of the rights enjoyed under Part II of the *Landlord and Tenant Act 1954* by those tenants who occupy premises for the purpose of their business (since if it is the LLP which runs the business, but it is not officially the tenant, it will not have the standing to seek a new tenancy etc.).

Such a desirable transfer of assets is however potentially the most hazardous part of the tax arrangements which will be applicable to an ordinary partnership on the change to an LLP. There are both time traps, and technical qualifications to be cleared, if the benefit of the exemption is to be obtained.

Time limit   9.20

The first problem is timing. By *section 12(1)* of the *LLPA 2000*, no duty is chargeable upon an instrument by which property is transferred or conveyed by anyone to an LLP, in connection with the incorporation thereof, provided that two conditions are met (see 9.21 and 9.22 below) and provided that the date of the instrument is within the period of one year beginning with the date of incorporation.

The catch is that it is the date of incorporation, not the date of the transfer of the business to the LLP, which is relevant. Shortly after the *LLPA 2000* came into effect on 6 April 2001, it became apparent that some firms had registered LLPs at a time when they had not taken the decision to transfer their businesses to those LLPs, simply to secure their first choice of name. Not only had they possibly committed an offence under *section 2* by inaccurately stating on the incorporation document that they had 'associated for carrying on a lawful business', but they had inadvertently started the clock running as to the time within which, if they did decide to go ahead with their new LLPs as trading vehicles, they had to get their property transfers complete if they wished to avoid stamp duty. This is a strict statutory time limit, and it does not appear that the Revenue would have any discretion (let alone incentive) to extend the period.

Identity of the transferor   9.21

Assuming the time limit (see 9.20 above) can be complied with, the first condition, under *LLPA 2000, s 12(2)*, is as to the identity of the transferor of the property. Two categories of transferor fulfil the condition.

The first category is a person who is himself a partner in a partnership, where the partnership is comprised of all the persons who are, or are to be, members of the LLP, and no one else. In other words, it will not suffice if there are partners in the partnership of the transferring partner who are not going to be members of the LLP, e.g. because they are retiring. Similarly, the condition will not be met if there are members of the LLP who were not partners in the partnership.

A further category of acceptable transferor, if the property is held on behalf of such a partnership as is referred to above, is someone conveying as nominee or bare trustee for one or more of the partners in that partnership. Such a person will, by *section 12(4)*, qualify as a 'bare trustee' for a partner if that partner has the sole right to direct how the property shall be dealt with. (Any apparent restriction on that right arising from any charge, lien or other right of the trustee to resort to the property for the payment of duty, taxes, costs or other outgoings is ignored for the purposes of this test.)

Beneficial interests in the property   9.22

The second condition (see 9.20 above), in *LLPA 2000, s 12(3)*, concerns the beneficial interests in the property transferred or conveyed. With one exception, the proportions of the property to which the members in the LLP are entitled, after the transfer, must be exactly the same as they were entitled to at 'the relevant time' (see 9.23 below).

The idea is that if ten partners were beneficially entitled in equal shares before the transfer, then ten members must be so entitled, in the same shares, afterwards. There is one logical flaw in this requirement, which is that, after transfer, no person has any share in the beneficial ownership of the property itself – it belongs to the LLP as a corporate entity and all that any individual has is an interest in the LLP. The Revenue has however said that it proposes to ignore this, and look at the underlying interests in the LLP, when ascertaining what beneficial shares it considers members to have. The exception referred to, found in *section 12(3)(b)*, is that changes in the underlying beneficial interests will be allowed, provided they do not result from any scheme or arrangement wholly or partly designed for the avoidance of liability to any duty or tax. Thus, for instance, any change due to the death of a partner will not upset the relief.

The 'relevant time'   9.23

Both conditions (see 9.20 to 9.22 above) need to be fulfilled at 'the relevant time'. Thus the identity of the transferor has to be satisfactorily established at the relevant time; and the beneficial interests after conveyance or transfer have to be the same as they previously were at the relevant time.

This is defined by *LLPA 2000, s 12(5)*. Normally, the relevant time will be immediately before incorporation. If however the property transferred was not acquired by the transferor until after incorporation (as where a partner acquires a property after incorporation of the LLP but in anticipation of the transfer of the partnership business to it) then the relevant time will be immediately after acquisition.

Revenue concession on changes   9.24

Taking these conditions and the definition of the relevant time together (9.21 to 9.23 above), it would appear that the relief would be lost if there were any change at all in the constituent partners/members. It would thus be impossible at the time of incorporation itself for outgoing partners to retire, or new blood to be brought in as members, even though in operational terms that might be just the most desirable moment.

Fortunately, the Revenue has indicated that it will be generous in its interpretation, and allow changes of partners/members the instant before or after incorporation, though they will in such circumstances wish to see all associated documentation, and may call for further supporting information. It seems therefore that if circumstances permit, it might still be prudent for outgoing partners to retire well in advance of incorporation, and for no new members to be appointed until the property transfer process is complete, to avoid having to argue the finer points of timing with the Revenue.

An illustration of difficulties 9.25

There are great dangers in all these conditions, to those LLPs incorporated rapidly after 6 April 2001, without any definite intent to transfer the partnership business to them. It can be seen that not only was the clock running against them from the moment of their incorporation, but also the chances of their failing to fulfil the conditions as to the common identity of the partners/members, and the common beneficial interests before and after transfer, will increase as time, and the chance of changes in the partnership, go on.

It is believed that some such partnerships, believing they could effectively form an LLP on a nominee basis, elected to do so with only two nominee partners as members. If they should decide to go ahead and transfer their business to an LLP, they would appear to have no chance of fulfilling the conditions and if, as seems likely, they have property to transfer, they would have to form a second LLP which did comply, and then swap names simultaneously if the Registrar permits, leaving the first-formed LLP to be later struck off as dormant, and transferring the property to the second.

Stamping of exempt instruments 9.26

By *LLPA 2000, s 12(6)(a)*, an instrument of transfer or conveyance which, by reason of the above exemption (see 9.19 above), does not have to have duty actually paid upon it, nonetheless has to be produced in accordance with *section 12* of the *Stamp Act 1891*, to be stamped so as to show that it is not chargeable or is duly stamped.

If the instrument is not so produced and stamped then, by *section 12(6)(b)*, full duty is payable upon it as if the exemption did not apply.

National insurance 9.27

By *section 13* of the *LLPA 2000*, a new *section 15(3A)* is introduced into the *Social Security Contributions and Benefits Act 1992*.

The provision states shortly that, where income tax is or would be payable by a member of an LLP, in respect of profits or gains arising from the trade or business carried on by the LLP, then Class 4 contributions are payable as if the trade were being carried on by the members of the LLP in partnership. In other words, members who are individuals are potentially liable to pay such contributions; but corporate members (companies or LLPs) are not. The Revenue has also pointed out that Class 2 and Class 3 contributions may also be payable, just as with a partnership.

Value added tax

General position   **9.28**

The *LLPA 2000* itself is silent on VAT. HM Customs and Excise Business Briefing, as referred to in 9.4 above, is however helpful as to the position of LLPs in relation to VAT.

There are no surprises. The LLP itself becomes a potentially registrable entity. If there is a transfer of a partnership's business to the LLP, the normal rules applying to the transfers of going concerns will apply and, if the partnership ceases to exist, it may be possible for the LLP to take over the partnership's VAT registration number. (One practical problem which may arise is if not all of the partnership's business is transferred to the LLP, in which case the going concern rules, which are beyond the scope of this work, will need examining carefully to see if a sufficiently major part of the business is being transferred for the rules to apply.)

The members are not regarded for VAT purposes as supplying services to the LLP, so do not themselves have to register. LLPs will, as bodies corporate, be able to join VAT groups if they fulfil the normal conditions requiring common control of the constituent bodies within a group.

10 – Accounts and Auditing

This chapter looks at the requirements of legislation and standards as regards the accounting and auditing aspects of LLPs.

The chapter is in seven parts. It starts by setting the legislative scene for accounts, etc., and looking at the structure of the legislation and how it can best be read and understood. The duties as to record-keeping and the preparation of accounts, which fall upon members, are then considered; before moving on to the designated members' responsibilities for the approval of accounts, and the reports which go with them. Then the requirements for the delivery and distribution of accounts, to the registrar on the one hand, and to members and debenture holders on the other, are reviewed. Provisions for voluntary, or compulsory, correction of defective accounts are discussed. The important topic of exemptions from the full stringency of these requirements, as made available to small and medium-sized LLPs, is fully covered. Lastly, the respective rights and duties of LLPs and their auditors are reviewed.

Introduction

The overall accounting picture 10.1

Much of what has gone before has indicated the similarities of LLPs to the partnerships from which they have derived. This has especially been so in the field of the taxation treatment of LLPs.

It may seem paradoxical, therefore, that at the point where one turns to look at the accounting treatment of LLPs, which might logically seem the opposite side of the coin from taxation, one moves completely across to the area where the legislation equates LLPs to companies, and not to partnerships. If you think of an LLP, for all accounting purposes, as fundamentally a sub-species of company, you will not go far wrong.

The structure of the legislation 10.2

The *Limited Liability Partnerships Act 2000* itself, in its 19 sections, is completely silent as to accounting and auditing requirements. Rather, it works through the medium of incorporating, by means of the *Regulations* (see 1.14 above), large chunks of the *Companies Act 1985*. *SI 2001/1090, reg 3* states that the provisions of *Part VII* of the *CA 1985*, which deal with accounts and audit matters, shall apply to LLPs. It makes, for ease of interpretation, some specific changes in those provisions, as far as nomenclature is concerned. Thus, it says that references to a company include references to an LLP, and that references to a director, or an officer, of a company, include references to an LLP. It has a 'sweeper-up' of a modification, by saying that such further modifications as are needed by the context to give effect to the *CA 1985* provisions are to be deemed incorporated.

So far, so good. Where the ease of reading comes to a grinding halt, however, is in *SI 2001/1090, reg 3(2)(d)*, which states that the provisions of *Part VII* of the *CA 1985* apply subject to the modifications set out in *Schedule 1* to *SI 2001/1090*.

The extent of Schedule 1   10.3

It should be noted that, in the case of *Schedule 1*, **all** provisions of *Part VII* of the *CA 1985* are incorporated. Thus if a section in that *Part* is not referred to in the *Schedule*, the result is not that it does not apply to LLPs at all, but rather that it applies in its original form, no amendment being necessary.

(That is not the case when it comes to *SI 2001/1090, Sch 2*, where **only** those provisions listed from the more general parts of the *CA 1985* will apply to LLPs.)

Reading Schedule 1   10.4

SI 2001/1090, Sch 1 is in two columns. In the left-hand column is set out the number, and a brief description, of the *CA 1985* provision to which reference is being made. In the right-hand column is the particular modification, whether that be to omit, alter or add to the original provision.

The problem is that, to make sense of *Schedule 1*, a reader therefore needs °to have before him not only that *Schedule*, but also a copy of the *CA 1985*, onto which he must mentally superimpose the amendments from the schedule. When the *LLPA 2000* was going through Parliament, much was made of the difficulty which this treatment caused to readers. The Government's answer was firstly that that was unavoidable in the light of the desire to avoid having to amend primary legislation to mirror any subsequent changes in the *CA 1985* (particularly as those were envisaged in the wake of the Company Law Steering Group's Review and the likelihood of consequent legislative change); and secondly that the private sector would fill the gap. In that latter regard they were correct, and any prospective reader of the legislation is commended to *Tolley's Limited Liability Partnerships – the New Legislation*, by Douglas Armour, in which, in addition to the original text of the LLP legislation, the relevant provisions of the other main legislation affected by and incorporated by the *LLPA 2000*, i.e. the *Companies Act 1985* and the *Insolvency Act 1986*, are set out in their full, modified, form.

Future legislative change 10.5

Mention was made above (at 10.4) of the Company Law Steering Group's Review. The Steering Group's final report, published in July 2001, proposes many substantive changes to the regime governing the accounting and auditing requirements of companies, and hence, from now onwards, for LLPs subject to the same regime.

It remains to be seen however which of the Group's recommendations become law, but in the light of the fact that the Review was DTI-inspired, incorporated very extensive consultations and has had the co-operation of the Parliamentary Draftsman's Office in preparing its recommendations, it would seem surprising if its views did not for the most part get an airing in the life of the current Parliament. Reference is made throughout this chapter, therefore, to the Steering Group's recommendations, as they may well be considered relevant to any decision as to whether, and if so when, to convert to an LLP.

Statement of Recommended Practice 10.6

One of the Steering Group's recommendations is that even more force and status than at present should be given to non-legislative standards, created by bodies given statutory backing for the purpose, but then left to make, and to develop, their own codes.

One such standard is the Statement of Recommended Practice (SORP for short) in respect of LLPs, which hopefully will be published, after consultation, in 2002. At the time of going to print, a consultation draft of the SORP, issued by the Consultative Committee of Accountancy Bodies, has been circulated and reference will be made to this where appropriate.

Preparation of accounts

General record-keeping requirements 10.7

The accounts to be prepared by an LLP have a number of different stakeholders whose interests they must serve. Firstly, there are the regulatory and taxation authorities. Secondly, there are those who are to conduct business with the LLP. Thirdly, there are the members themselves.

Part VII of the *CA 1985* thus starts off, in *section 221* as modified (which imposes record-keeping duties) by stating that those records must be such as to disclose the LLP's financial position with reasonable accuracy at any time, and to enable members to ensure that the balance sheet and the profit and loss account of the LLP satisfy statutory requirements. A parent LLP has the responsibility for ensuring that any subsidiaries, which may not themselves need to fulfil these requirements, nonetheless keep such records as will enable the parent so to comply. A failure to comply is an offence on the part of all members of the LLP, unless an individual member can persuade a court that he acted honestly and that his default was, in all circumstances, excusable.

Records which need keeping   **10.8**

Section 221 as modified (see 10.7 above) indicates with some particularity the nature of the records which must be kept. These include:

- day-to-day entries for all sums received and paid by the LLP;
- similar entries for the items to which those sums refer;
- a record of all assets and liabilities;
- for trading LLPs:
  - year-end stock statements;
  - stocktaking statements from which the above derive;
  - statements of all goods sold and bought (otherwise than by way of normal trade).

It is worth noting that the use of the phrase 'at any time' connotes more than just that the LLP must be able to produce 'true and fair' accounts at the end of the year. The members must have such records as will enable them to produce a snapshot of the LLP's full financial position at any mid-term stage. Some form of computerised management accounting system will therefore, for all but the very smallest of LLPs, be essential to enable the members to fulfil their obligations under this section. By *DTC (CTC) Limited v Gary Sargeant [1996] 1 WLR 797*, an accountant to whom records have been passed for the purposes of accounts production, cannot exercise a lien over them for unpaid fees if the effect of that would be to place the LLP in breach of its statutory obligations under this section.

Location of records 10.9

The above records may, by *section 222* of the *CA 1985* (as modified), be kept either at the registered office of the LLP, or at any other place the members decide. Wherever they are, however, they must be open to inspection at all times by all members.

The suggestion, at earlier stages of the legislation, that only designated members should have full access to the records, was not followed. Nor, since this is an unequivocal statutory requirement rather than a default provision for the LLP's governance in *regulation 7* of the *Regulations* (see 1.14 above), is this something which can be altered by the LLP's partnership agreement. Members are therefore in a more fortunate position than company shareholders, since it is only company officers who have this right in a company context.

There are specific provisions for what records have to be sent to Great Britain, if the place the members decide to keep the records generally is outside the jurisdiction. Again, unlike in the early draft legislation, all members, not just designated ones, are potentially liable for any breach of these requirements, although the same defence as in *section 221* is available to any individual member if his conduct was honest and excusable.

Duration of record keeping 10.10

Records must be kept for at least three years, under *section 222(5)* of the *CA 1985* (as modified).

Other statutory requirements which may affect many of the same documents may however require a longer period of keeping, e.g. the six years for which all tax records must be kept, or even the 20 years for which the Revenue can go back in the case of alleged fraud or negligence under *section 36* of the *Taxes Management Act 1970* (as amended). Any member who has failed to take all reasonable steps to ensure compliance with the above, or who intentionally causes any default in meeting this obligation, is guilty of an offence.

Accounting reference dates 10.11

LLPs are to have accounting reference dates in the same way as companies, by *section 224* of the *CA 1985* (as modified). The first such date will normally be the last day of the month in which the anniversary of its incorporation falls.

It may however, by *section 225* (as modified), alter that date, and may even make such a change retrospective for one year. Notice in form LLP225, which any member may sign, needs to be filed. The effect of the change may be to shorten or lengthen the accounting period, i.e. from incorporation or the last accounting reference date, as the case may be, up to the newly chosen date. The period thus created, however, cannot be more than 18 months nor, in the case of the first accounting period, less than six. Any notice to lengthen an accounting reference period cannot normally be given within five years of a previous extension by like means.

Financial years, by *section 223* (as modified), basically follow accounting reference dates, though seven days leeway is allowed. If an LLP has a subsidiary undertaking to which these concepts do not apply, it has to ensure that its financial year follows that of the parent LLP, unless there are good reasons to the contrary.

The duty to prepare accounts   10.12

The accounts which an LLP is obliged to produce, under *section 226* of the *CA 1985* (as modified), as what are referred to as its individual accounts, are a balance sheet and a profit and loss account for each financial year. These must be on the basis that they offer a 'true and fair' view of the LLP's affairs.

The responsibility for the production of these accounts is that of all members, not merely, as had been previously proposed, that of the designated members. Where the LLP is a parent LLP, then under *section 227* (as modified) it must, in addition to its individual accounts, prepare consolidated accounts for itself and all subsidiary undertakings, unless it is itself a subsidiary of another undertaking, and that undertaking is itself under an obligation to prepare consolidated accounts, and the conditions set out in *section 228* (as modified) are complied with. (The detailed requirements as to consolidated accounts set out in *sections 228 to 231* inclusive (as modified) are considered beyond the scope of this work, and specific reference to them should be made by any affected LLP or their advisers.)

The format of accounts   10.13

As already stated (in 10.12 above), and whether individual accounts or consolidated ones, all accounts must be on a 'true and fair' basis. In order to achieve this, they must follow the requisite format as provided by the appropriate schedule to the *CA 1985*, i.e. *Schedule 4* for individual accounts, or *Schedule 4A* for consolidated accounts (both as modified).

If those schedules are not of themselves enough to include all information necessary to give a true and fair view, then that additional information must be given in the accounts or a note to them. Equally, if observance of the requirements of those schedules would prevent a true and fair view being given, they may be varied, but a note of the reasons for and effects of the departure from the norm must be given in a note to the accounts. The detail of those provisions is such as to be beyond the scope of this work.

Disclosure of members' interests etc.   **10.14**

In Chapter 11 below, there are detailed provisions as to what disclosure of members' financial positions is required by the legislation. At this point, however, it is worth noting in passing that *section 232* of the *CA 1985*, and thus *Schedule 6*, which is imported by it, does not generally apply. That schedule contains many requirements relating to benefits which directors may gain from a company, e.g. not just straight emoluments, but also pensions, compensation for loss of office, loans, quasi-loans etc. Most of these do not apply, by virtue of this section, to members, who are only subject to the particular requirements examined in Chapter 11, albeit that some particular provisions of *Schedule 6* are, as set out in that chapter, applied by *paragraph 56A* of *Schedule 4*. (Note also the provisions as to members' annuities etc. as referred to in 5.10 above.)

Approval of accounts and report

Approval of accounts   **10.15**

The members as a body have, as above (see 10.12), the responsibility for producing the accounts. Similarly, they have the responsibility for approving them, under *section 233(1)* of the *CA 1985* (as modified).

No process is however offered for how that approval is to be given for, as already noted, there is no provision for an annual general meeting, or indeed any other form of meeting, for their approval, unless one is to be put into place by the LLP's partnership agreement. When considering whether to place such a requirement into an agreement, it may be worth bearing in mind the suggestion of the Steering Group report that, for all new private companies, there should be no requirement to hold an AGM unless a suitable majority votes to opt into a scheme of having such a meeting. Perhaps therefore the LLP legislation may be anticipating a trend against meetings which will become more widespread. If not a meeting however, by what means are the members of an LLP to signify the approval of the accounts which is needed of them since, as will be seen, such approval is not to be shown by their signing the accounts themselves?

The agreement should provide for some form of process which is demonstrable and acceptable, and affords some protection to members against any suggestion that they have approved accounts which they have not, since by *section 233(5)* if the accounts do not comply with the statutory requirements, all members may be responsible if they either knew or were reckless as to compliance. That liability will apply to any individual member if he was 'party to' the approval of the accounts, and he will be considered as being so if he cannot show that he took all reasonable steps to prevent the accounts being approved.

Signing of accounts   10.16

It is however left for a designated member, under *section 233(1)* of the *CA 1985* (as modified), to take the step of signing them off, albeit that that is on behalf of the total membership. It is the balance sheet which has to be signed, and the name of the signatory must be stated on all copies of the balance sheet. The copy of the accounts delivered to the Registrar must be so signed.

If these requirements are not complied with, then the LLP as an entity, and any member (i.e. not just any designated member) who is in default commits an offence. There is no guidance as to what would place an individual in default, i.e. would it only be if he actually distributed an unsigned copy, or would it be enough for him to have known or suspected of the proposed distribution? Clearly, it is in the interests of all members to ensure that all copies are properly signed.

Directors' report   10.17

There is no equivalent, for LLPs, of the requirements for a directors' report, as in by *sections 234* and *234A* of the *CA 1985*. Such a report normally requires two things, namely a fair review of the company's development during the course of the year, and its position at the end of it; and the directors' recommendations as to dividends. Clearly the latter would be inappropriate for LLPs, but it seems surprising that the former is omitted.

The directors' report also needs to include the information contained in *Schedule 7* to the *CA 1985*, covering such items as:

● changes in asset values not revealed in the accounts;

- political and charitable donations;
- employment and training of the disabled;
- involvement of employees in the business; and
- policy and practice on payments to creditors.

This omission indicates the Government's view that such information is not of interest to any outsiders, e.g. financers, customers or suppliers of the LLP, which seems a surprising conclusion. This is particularly so in the light of the fact that the trend seems to be for more disclosure, rather than less, as evidenced by the fact that the Steering Group's report recommends (admittedly only for public and large private companies) the new concept of an Operating and Financial Review ('OFR') giving a review of the business, its performance, plans and prospects, as well as information as to relationships with employees, suppliers and customers; environmental and community impact; and risk management. It may be that some of the more go-ahead LLPs may seek to pass this sort of information onto the public, whether compelled to or not.

Submission of accounts to auditors   10.18

The next step in the progress of the normal LLP's accounts, in theory, is that they are to be submitted to the LLP's auditors, in accordance with *section 235* of the *CA 1985* (as modified). (The question of whether a particular LLP will be large enough to require the appointment of auditors is dealt with at 10.54 below.)

In practice, of course, the accounts will have been prepared by the auditors anyway. The auditors must state whether the accounts have been properly prepared in accordance with statute, and in particular whether they present the required true and fair view of the LLP's position. The auditors' report must confirm their identity, and it and every copy of the accounts delivered and filed must be signed by them. If those statements and signatures are omitted, it is the LLP, and any member of it in default, which are in breach and commit an offence, not the auditors themselves. As before, all members thus have an interest in ensuring proper processes are in place to ensure compliance.

Duties of auditors   10.19

In preparing their report, the auditors have to observe duties imposed on them by *section 237* of the *CA 1985* (as modified). They have to take into account whether:

- proper accounting records have been kept;

- adequate returns have been made by branches they have not visited; and

- the individual accounts agree with original accounting records

If not satisfied, or if they do not get sufficient information or explanation, they must state that in their report. The requirement for such an audit is going to be new for those LLPs which are subject to it, as even those professional businesses which, like solicitors, are used to an element of audit, i.e. in respect of their client accounts, will not have had to suffer it in respect of their own office accounts.

There is concern as to the associated costs and resource commitments, and this may be a major possible disincentive to conversion to LLP status. Not only the LLPs themselves will be affected. Increasingly, for self-defensive reasons, auditors have been seeking to obtain external confirmation of companies' positions, and this has led to some controversy, e.g. by requesting companies' solicitors to confirm, in extremely broad terms, the legal health and freedom from threat of the company, which has led to Law Society advice that such questions should go unanswered. Such attempts will no doubt be made in respect of LLPs which are subject to audit.

Delivery and distribution of accounts

Distribution to members 10.20

Once signed, the accounts must be distributed within a month, according to *section 238* of the *CA 1985* (as modified). A copy of the accounts, with the auditors' report, must be sent to each member, and to every holder of a debenture from the LLP.

It is worth remembering that for this purpose 'member' will include a salaried member, and it will not therefore be possible (as still happens with some salaried partners in partnerships) for accounts to be withheld from such members. This distribution must be within ten months of the end of the relevant accounting reference period. If copies are sent out over a period, they are only deemed to have been sent on the last day of that period. In the event of default, the LLP itself, and every member in default, is guilty of an offence.

Electronic publication 10.21

There is however a new twist to the requirement for distribution, namely that it can now be done by electronic means.

The *Companies Act 1985 (Electronic Communication) Order 2000 (SI 2000/3373)* introduced some new sub-sections into *section 238* of the *CA 1985*, and of those *sections 238(4A)* and *238(4B)* (as modified) are relevant for LLPs. These provide that copies of the accounts can be sent electronically to members or debenture holders, if the prospective recipient has notified a suitable electronic address to the LLP for that purpose. Further, the publication of the accounts etc. on a website may be regarded as sufficient for delivery, if the LLP and the member or debenture holder have specifically agreed this, and if the LLP notifies him, in an agreed manner, of the fact of that publication and the necessary address and access arrangements for that site. In other words, if the parties agree, it would be possible for the LLP to put its accounts on a website, and e-mail the recipient to say that they are available and, if the site is a secure one, what password etc. they will need to access the documents.

This pattern is likely to be developed further in future, as for instance the Steering Group's report recommends shortening the ten-month period for distribution of accounts, on the basis that modern methods of production and distribution should allow members earlier and easier access.

Demands for additional copies $\qquad$ 10.22

In addition to the distribution obligations above (in 10.20 and 10.21), the LLP is obliged to provide a member or debenture holder with an extra copy of the accounts and auditors' report on demand, under *section 239* of the *CA 1985* (as modified). Again, this may be done electronically if the prospective recipient agrees and gives an e-mail address.

The additional copy must be sent within seven days of the demand. The LLP, and any member in default, will be guilty of an offence if this is not done. If, in such proceedings, the defence is raised that the demanding member has already been sent an additional copy, the burden of proof that that is so rests on the defendant.

Ancillary publication requirements $\qquad$ 10.23

There are, in *section 240* of the *CA 1985* (as modified), a number of ancillary requirements with regard to the publication of accounts by LLPs.

First, there are two restrictions with regard to the statutory accounts, each being designed to ensure that any reader of the accounts gets the full picture. On the one hand, therefore, the accounts cannot be published without the auditors' report (if applicable). On the other, if the LLP is part of a group, the individual LLP's accounts cannot be published without the accompanying statutory group accounts.

Beyond that, an LLP may wish to publish accounts (i.e. a profit and loss account and/or a balance sheet) which go beyond, or are differently presented from, the statutory accounts. If so, those non-statutory accounts must state that they are not the statutory accounts, and whether the relevant year's statutory accounts have been filed with the registrar. They must also exclude the auditors' report, but state whether such a report was prepared for the relevant year and, if so, whether it contained any qualification, or statement as to inadequate records etc.

'Publication', for the purpose of invoking the requirements of this section, is widely defined to include any form of publishing, issuing or circulating the document in such a way as to make it available to the public in such a way as to invite the public (or a class of the public) to read it. Although in this case there is no specific reference to electronic publishing, this would presumably be broad enough to include publication on a website. LLPs should therefore be careful, if publishing any form of accounting data on their websites, e.g. a summary profit and loss account to show how well they are doing, or the equivalent of a company's preliminary announcement or interim report, to observe the provisions of this section. Any LLP contravening the section, and any member in default, is guilty of an offence.

Going public with the accounts   10.24

A key difference between partnerships and LLPs is the obligation to go public with the enterprise's accounts, by delivery of a copy of the accounts and, if appropriate, the auditors' report, to the Registrar, under *section 242* of the *CA 1985* (as modified).

There are two main areas of concern. One is the disclosure of the members' own positions, which is looked at in Chapter 11 below, dealing with specific disclosure requirements. The other is the mere fact of how the business is doing, where the fears are of the reactions of those associated with the business, e.g. as customers or staff.

The argument runs like this. If the business is seen to be doing well, and making large profits, will customers claim they are being overcharged, and staff claim they should share in the profit by increased salaries? On the other hand, if the business is doing badly, will customers feel they would be safer to take their business elsewhere, and staff be searching for posts elsewhere? Many professional partnerships in particular have a great attachment to the secrecy that partnership status affords them, even though some seem to use it in a curious manner. For instance, the managing partner of one major accountancy firm, commenting adversely upon the established practice of Ernst & Young (now the first UK LLP) of freely publishing its accounts in its annual report, boasted of the fact that his firm's profit per partner was higher than Ernst & Young's anyway – thus removing one of the main points in favour of the secrecy he was advocating!

It will of course be for each business to decide for itself whether the publication of accounts is too high a price to pay for the advantages of LLP status, but it is suggested that it would be naïve to base that decision on the view that, for instance, staff cannot tell how well a business is doing from signs other than published accounts, e.g. annually renewed expensive partners' cars on the one hand, or suddenly arranged meetings with the bank manager on the other!

The process of delivery of accounts   10.25

The obligation to deliver to the Registrar the LLP's signed accounts, and auditors' report if appropriate, is that of the designated members only. Accounts delivered in a language other than English must be properly translated.

(There is provision in *section 710B* of the *CA 1985* (as modified) for rules to be made to allow for certain specified documents, in relation to LLPs whose registered office is in Wales, to be delivered in Welsh, with the obligation for the production of a translation being then upon the Registrar rather than the LLP.)

The consequences of default for designated members   10.26

Potentially, all designated members (not the LLP itself) are guilty of an offence if the accounts etc. are not delivered within the specified period, currently ten months from the close of the financial year in most cases (*CA 1985, s 244(1)*) (as modified) – though note that the Steering Group report recommends that this be reduced to seven months.

In that event, not only are designated members liable to a fine, but they also face a daily default fine for continued contravention. Further, it is possible for any member, any creditor, or the Registrar, to serve notice upon designated members in default requiring compliance, and, if that notice is not complied with, to apply to the court for an order that the designated members, or such of them as the court specifies, shall comply within such period as the court specifies. The court has, in these circumstances, power to award costs against the designated members.

There are two specific provisions as to potential defences to prosecutions for offences under this section. It is a defence for the accused to show that he took all reasonable steps for ensuring timely compliance. However, it is unsurprisingly not a defence to show that the requisite documents had not been prepared in the first place.

The consequences of default for the LLP 10.27

As mentioned (in 10.26 above), there is no criminal sanction against the LLP itself for failure to deliver its accounts in time. There is however a civil sanction under *section 242A* of the *CA 1985* (as modified), which is in addition to, not in substitution for, any liability of the designated members. This penalty is claimed by the Registrar. Again, it is no defence to say that the documents had not been prepared.

The penalty is calculated on a time basis, by reference to the gap between the time when the accounts should have been delivered, and the day when they actually are. The potential penalties are as follows:

Length of period of delay	Amount of penalty
Not more than three months	£100
More than three months but not more than six months	£250
More than six months but not more than twelve months	£500
More than twelve months	£1,000

Accounts in ECUs 10.28

It is possible for accounts to be delivered and published which show the LLP's results in ECUs (otherwise known as Euros). This can be done in one of two ways. In each case the treatment in ECUs must be in addition to, not as a replacement for, showing the figures in sterling.

Either they can be shown alongside the sterling equivalent on the same document, or an additional copy showing the amounts in ECUs only can be supplied. In either case the rate of conversion must be as at the balance sheet date, and that rate must be shown in notes to the accounts. Such accounts count as statutory accounts, i.e. the provisions applying to the publication of non-statutory accounts referred to in 10.23 above do not apply to them.

Appending the accounts of subsidiary undertakings
10.29

An LLP may be the parent of an undertaking which is not required to form part of a group's consolidated accounts by reason of the subsidiary business's activities being so fundamentally different from those of the parent, and others in its group, that to include them would prevent the giving of a true and fair view of the group's activities (*CA 1985, s 229(4)* (as modified)).

Such a subsidiary may be either an incorporated subsidiary, registered abroad and having no place of business in Great Britain; or an unincorporated undertaking (e.g. if an LLP is a partner in a partnership of which it has control). In that event, in order to ensure that a complete picture of the group's activities is available, *section 243* of the *CA 1985* (as modified) requires that the LLP shall, when delivering its own accounts, also deliver a copy of the subsidiary undertaking's individual accounts (or group accounts if the subsidiary undertaking is itself a parent of others) and any required auditors' report. The accounts in question must be for a period ending not more than a year before the end of the parent LLP's own accounts. If not in English, a translation must be supplied (subject to the same point regarding accounts supplied in Welsh as in 10.25 above). Penalties for breach of these requirements are the same as for failure to deliver the main accounts.

Exceptions to the requirement to append
10.30

There are however exceptions to these requirements, under *section 243(5)* of the *CA 1985* (as modified).

A subsidiary undertaking need not produce accounts specially for the purpose of this section – i.e. if the subsidiary is not itself obliged by law to produce accounts it need not do so. Similarly, a document need not be appended if it would not be required to be published anywhere else in the world, though in that case the LLP's accounts shall refer to it and state why it is not appended.

Lastly, where the subsidiary is itself a parent, and it and all its subsidiaries are of such a nature that they are excluded from consolidation in the LLPs accounts by reason of having businesses of a different nature as above, but the subsidiary itself produces consolidated group accounts, then the LLP does not need to append such of the ultimate subsidiary accounts as are included in those consolidated group accounts. Thus, if 'Joe Bloggs LLP' has an overseas subsidiary 'Fred Bloggs Inc', which in turn has subsidiaries A, B, and C, and if Fred Bloggs Inc produces consolidated group accounts for itself, A and B, then what Joe Bloggs LLP needs to append to its accounts are the consolidated group accounts for Fred Bloggs Inc, and the individual accounts for C.

Time for delivery of accounts   **10.31**

As mentioned already (see 10.26 above), the normal period within which the accounts need to be delivered to the Registrar is ten months from the end of the relevant accounting reference period, under *section 244* of the *CA 1985* (as modified). (If the Steering Group's recommendations are followed, this may in future be reduced to seven months.)

If however the accounting reference period in question is the LLP's first, and is itself longer than a year, then the last date for delivery is the later of:

- ten months from the first anniversary of the LLP's incorporation; or
- three months from the end of the accounting reference period.

Variations of time for delivery   **10.32**

There are three possible variations on the above theme (in 10.26 and 10.31) permissible under *section 244* of the *CA 1985*.

First, there is provision for a three-month extension to the normal period, as of right, if the LLP has interests outside Great Britain (i.e. the UK, the Channel Islands, and the Isle of Man) and notice in form LLP244 is filed. (Curiously, the *Regulations* say that such a notice must be given by a designated member, but the Companies House form provides for the possibility of signature by either a designated member or a member.) Secondly, if the LLP has served notice in Form LLP225 to shorten the accounting reference period, then the period for delivery of the accounts is the later of:

- the normal period from the end of that shortened period; or
- the date of the Form LLP225.

Lastly, there is provision that application may be made to the Secretary of State for an extension to the period for delivery. He may grant or refuse at his discretion, and, if he grants the request, shall notify the LLP of the period for such extension. There are no guidelines offered in relation to the circumstances in which such discretion is likely to be exercised in the LLP's favour.

Correction of defective accounts

Voluntary corrections 10.33

With the best will in the world, it is possible for accounts to be defective, and the legislation recognises this by allowing a number of ways for the correction of defects.

The first, in *section 245* of the *CA 1985* (as modified), is an opportunity for voluntary correction, if the members (not just, it should be noted, the designated members) believe that the delivered accounts did not comply with the statutory requirements. They may then prepare and deliver revised accounts, provided that the revisions shall be confined to correcting the non-compliances and making any necessary consequential alterations.

The legislation then provides for regulations to be made for how such revised accounts are to be dealt with, and the *Companies (Revision of Defective Accounts and Report) Regulations 1990 (SI 1990/2570)* apply, as modified. These provide for the details of how the revised accounts are to be dealt with, either by way of substitution of complete accounts, or a supplemental note to the original versions. They also provide for the same penalties in respect of default as apply to the original delivery obligations.

Requirement of explanation by the Secretary of State 10.34

It may be that the Secretary of State is not satisfied that an LLP's delivered accounts (whether revised or not) comply with the statutory requirements. If so, he can, under *section 245A* of the *CA 1985* (as modified), serve notice upon the members (not the LLP itself, as the accounts are the members' responsibility) indicating the areas of his concern, and requiring an explanation within a specified period, of not less than a month.

The Secretary of State can extend that period later if he thinks fit. If by the end of the period he is not satisfied with the explanation given (or indeed if none has been given) and if there has been no voluntary revision of the accounts, then he may make application to the court.

Application to court regarding defective accounts 10.35

An application, under *section 245B* of the *CA 1985* (as modified), may be made by the Secretary of State himself, or by someone authorised by him. This application is twofold. Firstly, it is for a declaration that the accounts do not comply with statutory requirements. Secondly, it is for an order requiring the members to prepare revised accounts.

A notice of the application, with a background statement, must be given by the applicant to the Registrar. If the court orders the preparation of revised accounts, it may give directions with regard to:

- the auditing of the accounts as revised;
- how members shall bring the revisions to the attention of third parties who may have relied upon the originals;
- such other matters as it thinks fit.

The court may also order that the costs of the application, and the extra costs incurred by the LLP itself in putting matters right, shall be borne by such of the members as were party to the original approval of the defective accounts, i.e. every member other than any who took all reasonable steps to prevent approval. Its discretion in making such an order for costs and expenses is wide, and it may differentiate even amongst those members who were party to the approval. It must consider whether particular members knew, or should have known, that the accounts were defective. It may order different members to pay different amounts, and may exclude particular members from such obligations entirely, even if they were technically party to the original approval. Once proceedings are concluded, the applicant must notify the registrar of the outcome.

Authorisation of applicants 10.36

The Secretary of State may, by statutory instrument, under *section 245C* of the *CA 1985* (as modified), authorise various people to make applications to the court as described above, either generally, or for specific classes of case. Anyone who is to be thus authorised must:

- have an interest in securing compliance by LLPs with the statutory accounting requirements;
- have satisfactory procedures for securing such compliance;
- have such procedures for receiving and investigating complaints about LLPs' accounts;
- be a fit and proper person to be authorised.

Currently, the body so authorised is the Financial Reporting Review Panel Limited, under the *Companies (Defective Accounts) (Authorised Person) Order 1991 (SI 1991/13)*. If anyone seeks such authorisation, it may be refused on the grounds that someone else is already authorised and so a further appointment is unnecessary. Authorisation may be revoked (again by order) in which case provision shall be made for what is to happen to any pending proceedings. Authorised persons, and those connected with them (staff or members of governing bodies thereof) are protected from action against them in respect of anything relating to investigating whether there are grounds for application, determining whether to make such an application, or publication of its reasons for any such decision. The protection does not apply, however, to anyone acting in bad faith.

Exemptions for small and medium-sized LLPs etc.

General 10.37

There are a number of exemptions from the full requirements of the *CA 1985*, in relation to accounting and auditing, which benefit 'small' and 'medium-sized' LLPs.

Broadly, these affect the requirement for audit to occur at all, the format of the LLP's accounts and the extent of disclosure of members' finances. Since the latter is one of the most contentious issues surrounding LLPs, these provisions are important to understand, as the determination of precisely which set of provisions is likely to apply if a partnership converts to an LLP could be a major factor in deciding whether to convert or not. The criteria which determine whether any particular LLP comes within these exemptions relate to turnover, the balance sheet total, and the number of employees.

Qualifying conditions 10.38

The qualifying conditions for any financial year will, under *section 247* of the *CA 1985* (as modified), be met by an LLP if, in that year, it fulfils at least two of the three relevant criteria, as follows:

Small LLP	
Turnover	Not more than £2.8 million
Balance sheet total	Not more than £1.4 million
No. of employees	Not more than 50

Medium-sized LLP	
Turnover	Not more than £11.2 million
Balance sheet total	Not more than £5.6 million
No. of employees	Not more than 250

If the accounting period is not one of twelve months, the maximum turnover figures are proportionately adjusted. The balance sheet total refers to total assets, not net assets. The staff numbers refer to the average number of staff employed during the year, calculated on a monthly basis (remembering that, by virtue of *section 4(4)* of the *LLPA 2000*, the members will not be regarded as employees for this purpose: see 6.5 above).

When qualifying conditions need to be met   10.39

Normally, under *section 247* of the *CA 1985* (as modified), an LLP will, in order to qualify as a small or medium-sized LLP, need to meet the above criteria not only in respect of the year for which it seeks the exemption, but also the immediately preceding year. This does not apply in the LLP's first accounting year, however, i.e. there is no attempt to look at what the accounting position of any predecessor partnership may have been.

Further, there is provision for a gap of a year in which the criteria are not met, when the exemption will not be lost. Thus, if an LLP meets the criteria for a small LLP in years 1, 2 and 4 of its existence, but not year 3, it will nonetheless be treated as a small LLP for all four years.

Exemptions for small LLPs   10.40

Generally speaking, the accounts of LLPs need to be drawn up in accordance with the very detailed provisions of *Schedule 4* to the *CA 1985* (as modified). For small LLPs, however, the less stringent requirements of *Schedule 8* to the *CA 1985* (as modified) will apply, and the accounts delivered to members and debenture holders need only comply with that schedule. Further, if the members so determine, the copy accounts delivered to the Registrar need not include a profit and loss account at all, and need only give an abbreviated balance sheet in accordance with the provisions of *Schedule 8A* to the *CA 1985* (as modified).

Thus the amount of information as to the LLP's affairs disclosable to the public will be very limited, though members will get more. Usual signing requirements and time limits apply to the shortened accounts, and they must also contain a statement that they have been prepared under the small LLPs exemption provisions.

Exemptions for medium-sized LLPs   10.41

As might be expected, the extent of the exemptions for medium-sized LLPs are less generous.

Such an LLP's accounts, firstly, need to be produced under the general requirements of *Schedule 4* to the *CA 1985* (as modified), but do not need to give a statement as to whether they have been prepared in accordance with applicable accounting standards, or whether there have been any material departures from such standards. That applies to the accounts whether sent to members etc, or delivered to the Registrar. In relation to the latter there are also other relaxations, namely that most sources of income can be presented as one item, rather than being particularised. Any accounts which take advantage of this exemption must bear a statement to that effect.

Authorised persons under the Financial Services Act 1986   10.42

Despite the exemptions in the previous paragraphs, there are however certain types of business where it is judged to be against the public interest to allow anything less than full public disclosure of the LLP's financial position. The ambit of the above exemptions is accordingly limited by *section 247A* of the *CA 1985* (as modified).

The first, and potentially most important of those restrictions, under *section 247A(1)* is where the LLP was, at any time during the year in question, an 'authorised person' under the *Financial Services Act 1986*. At one fell swoop that removes the benefit of the small and medium-sized exemptions from the vast majority of solicitors' and accountants' LLPs since, as they will almost certainly need to be holders of a certificate from their respective 'recognised professional bodies' (i.e. the Law Society or the Institute of Chartered Accountants in England and Wales) under *section 15* of that Act (even if they do not carry on discrete investment business) they will be 'authorised persons'.

This seems entirely illogical. If it is necessary for public protection to have the accounts of authorised persons fully made public, it should make no difference what the nature of the business vehicle chosen by the authorised person is, i.e. partnership, LLP or company. What *section 247A* achieves, however, is to say that whilst a partnership need make no disclosure of its accounts whatever, an authorised LLP must make full disclosure, whatever its size. To use a phrase favoured by the Government in recent times, this does not seem to be 'joined-up thinking'!

The authorisation regime is to change as from 1 December 2001 with the bringing into force of the relevant sections of the *Financial Services and Markets Act 2000*. One of the matters which businesses which have converted to LLPs, or are considering converting, will have to take into account is whether the benefits of authorisation under that Act outweigh the possible benefits of the small or medium-sized LLP accounting exemptions. Further, happily, many fewer firms will need to be authorised anyway, since this will (broadly) cease to be a requirement for those whose investment business is purely ancillary to their normal work, and who do not do discrete investment business.

Other businesses which cannot take advantage of above exemptions   10.43

The other relevant restrictive provisions are *sections 247A(2)(3) of the CA 1985* (as modified). *Section 247A(2)* provides that a group is ineligible for the exemptions if any of its members is:

● a public company;

● a body corporate able to offer shares or debentures to the public;

● an authorised institution under the *Banking Act 1987*;

● an insurance company to which *Part II* of the *Insurance Companies Act 1982* applies;

● an authorised person under the *Financial Services Act 1986*.

Section 247A(3) states that a parent LLP will not qualify unless the whole of its group complies as a small or medium-sized group, as set out below (see 10.44 below).

Small and medium-sized groups   10.44

Section 247A(3) of the *CA 1985* (see 10.43 above) introduces the concept that not only may an individual LLP be considered as small or medium-sized, but so may a group.

Here, the requirements for qualification are set out in *section 249* (as modified). The principles and amounts are similar to those for individual LLPs, but the idea is introduced of being able to consider either gross or net figures. 'Net' in this context means after making the set-offs and other adjustments provided for in the modified *Schedule 4A* to the *CA 1985*. The LLP can use whichever of the gross or net figures is more favourable to it. Figures are aggregated across the whole group. The qualifying conditions are thus:

Small group	
Aggregate turnover	Not more than £2.8 million net, or £3.36 million gross.
Aggregate balance sheet total	Not more than £1.4 million net, or £1.68 million gross
Aggregate number of employees	Not more than 50

Medium-sized group	
Aggregate turnover	Not more than £11.2 million net, or £13.44 million gross
Aggregate balance sheet total	Not more than £5.6 million net, or £6.72 million gross
Aggregate number of employees	Not more than 250

The provisions for the years in which the group needs to qualify are the same as for individual LLPs, save that the reference to the first financial year is to that of the parent LLP. The accounts for the subsidiaries, which fall to be aggregated, are those for the financial years being either coincident with the parent's financial year, or ending last before the end of the parent's financial year, save that if those figures cannot be obtained without disproportionate expense or undue delay, the last available figures shall be taken.

Exemptions for small and medium-sized groups
10.45

Under *section 248* of the *CA 1985* (as modified), an LLP which is the parent of a small or medium-sized group need not prepare group accounts, unless any member of the group comes within one of the same list of ineligible types of business as is referred to in 10.44 above.

Further, by *section 248A* of the *CA 1985* (as modified), if an LLP has taken advantage of its own qualification as a small LLP to prepare individual accounts in accordance with *Schedule 8* rather than *Schedule 4*, but is nonetheless preparing group accounts (e.g. because the group is ineligible for the *section 248* exemption) then those group accounts can also be prepared under *Schedule 8*, subject to minor variations as to the balance sheet set out in section *248A(3)*.

Exemptions from audit requirements
10.46

Sitting by the side of the above exemptions from certain requirements as to the contents of the accounts are some exemptions as to the requirements for the auditing of those accounts.

These exemptions use, but build upon, the above definition of a small LLP for their applicability. Thus, in respect of any financial year, an LLP will be deemed, under *section 249A* of the *CA 1985* (as modified), to be totally exempt from the requirement for any form of audit if, using the same principles of calculation as are referred to in 10.38 above, it not only qualifies as a small LLP, but also has a turnover of not more than £1 million, and a balance sheet total of not more than £1.4 million.

If exempt under these provisions (or the provisions referred to in 10.49 below) the accounts themselves need (under *section 249E* of the *CA 1985*, as modified) not refer to an auditors' report in the copies for members and debenture holders, or include such a report in the copy delivered to the Registrar.

Cases where section 249A audit exemption does not apply   10.47

There are a number of types of LLP to which the above exemption (see 10.46) cannot, however, apply. These, by *section 249B* of the *CA 1985* (as modified), are:

- an insurance broker listed by the Insurance Brokers Registration Council under *section 4* of the *Insurance Brokers (Registration) Act 1977*;

- an authorised person, or an appointed representative, under the *Financial Services Act 1986*;

- a special register body as defined in *section 117(1)* of the *Trade Union and Labour Relations (Consolidation) Act 1992*;

- an employers' association as defined in *section 122* of that latter Act;

- a parent LLP or a subsidiary undertaking.

Further provisions relating to parent or subsidiary LLPs   10.48

Section 249B of the *CA 1985* is however qualified in two sets of circumstances. Thus an LLP which is a subsidiary undertaking will not lose its audit exemption for a year if it was dormant during that year.

Further, an LLP which is either a parent LLP or a subsidiary undertaking will not lose its audit exemption if it was a member of a group meeting certain additional qualifications. Those qualifications are:

- that the group qualifies as a small group (see 10.44 above);

- that it is not an ineligible group (see 10.43 above);

- that its aggregate turnover in the year is not more than £1 million net or £1.2 million gross;

- that its aggregate balance sheet total is not more than £1.4 million net or £1.68 million gross.

In short, therefore, for an LLP which is a member of a group to qualify for the audit exemption, the whole group must qualify.

Exemptions for dormant LLPs   10.49

Section 249AA of the *CA 1985* (as modified) introduces the concept of a dormant LLP, and includes the possibility of an LLP which has been dormant since its foundation.

This latter concept in particular seems not to sit well with the requirements of *section 2(1)* of the *LLPA 2000* that the incorporation document must contain a declaration that two or more members have 'associated for carrying on a lawful business with a view to profit'. Nonetheless, this provision in the *CA 1985* allows an exemption from the audit requirements of that Act if the LLP has thus been dormant since birth, or has been dormant since the end of the previous year, provided that it both qualifies as a small LLP (see 10.38 above) and does not have to prepare group accounts for the year in question. This exemption does not however apply to an LLP which is an authorised person under the *Financial Services Act 1986*.

For an LLP to be considered 'dormant' it must not during the year in question have had any 'significant' accounting transaction, i.e. one which needs recording under the general accounting duties under *CA 1985, s 221* (see 10.8 above) other than payment of fees to the Registrar for a change of name or for the filing of an annual return, or a penalty for late delivery of accounts.

One final provision applying to dormant LLPs is that, by *section 249E(1A)* of the *CA 1985* (as modified), if the LLP has used the dormant exemption, then its accounts may be prepared as if it were a small LLP even if it is a member of an ineligible group (see 10.43 above).

Statements by LLPs exempt from audit requirements   10.50

If an LLP is entitled to take advantage of any of the above audit exemptions, then by *section 249B(4) and (5)* of the *CA 1985*, the balance sheet prepared must contain a statement by the members as to the exemption which is being taken advantage of, and confirming that the members acknowledge their responsibility for proper keeping of accounting records, and preparing accounts in accordance with the statute which give a true and fair view of the LLP's position.

This statement must appear in the balance sheet above the signature to the accounts (see 10.16 above).

Future possible variations in small and medium-sized exemptions   10.51

The Steering Group report has considered in some details the future development of the various exemptions referred to above, and they recommend a number of changes.

The authors of the report support continuing the use of the three reference criteria of turnover, balance sheet total, and staff numbers. They suggest that the definition of a small company, and hence small LLP, should be extended to the maxima currently permitted under European Union law (which maxima have apparently already been adopted by most other member states). These changes would double the turnover and balance sheet limits, from £2.8 million and £1.4 million to £4.8 million and £2.4 million respectively. The maximum staff number of 50 would however remain unchanged. They also recommend abolishing the status of a medium-sized undertaking or group altogether, as the differences from normal requirements are so slight.

Future possible variations in small company accounts   10.52

The next step by the authors of the Steering Group report was to consider what accounts a small LLP, according to their new definition, should prepare.

They suggest that for all accounts, including those for small bodies, the format for accounts should be moved away from statute to a non-statutory Standards Board. They have prepared a draft of such standards which are suggested for small enterprises. One currently available exemption which, however, they recommend abolishing, is the ability for small companies to deliver merely abbreviated balance sheets to the Registrar. They regard those as next to useless, and suggest that the accounts which small LLPs should deliver to the registrar should be the same as those they are obliged to give to members and debenture holders. Delivery, they suggest, should be within seven months of year end, not ten.

Future possible variations in audit exemptions **10.53**

The authors of the Steering Group report have also considered the audit exemptions. In particular, they have looked at those enterprises which, though qualifying as small, do not gain the audit exemption because their turnover or balance sheet totals are above £1 million or £1.4 million respectively.

They suggest two options. The first is that that intermediate banding should disappear altogether, so that all small bodies (subject no doubt to the ineligibility of certain types of business) meeting their suggested criteria (see 10.51 above) should be exempt from audit. The second is that, if it can be made to work, companies or LLPs in that intermediate band should be required to have, not an audit, but an independent professional review, or 'IPR' for short. This would be a lesser, and less costly, investigation by an outside professional, possibly an IPR practitioner not having an auditor's full qualifications. A pilot scheme for IPRs is being conducted.

Auditors

Introduction **10.54**

The provisions of the *CA 1985* applying to auditors are not found in *Part VII* of that Act, and so their incorporation into the LLP legislation comes not via *Schedule 1* to the *Regulations* (see 1.14 above), but via *Schedule 2*, which covers general provisions in that Act.

Unlike *Schedule 1*, which operates by including all of *Part VII* unless expressly excluded, *Schedule 2* works on the opposite basis, i.e. only those provisions which are specifically included (as modified) will apply to LLPs. Amongst those so included are *sections 384* to *394A*, which deal with the role of auditors in the LLP context. Much is written in all the standard texts on company law as to the position, rights and especially obligations and duties of auditors (see, for example, the 'Auditors' chapter (A9001 onwards) in *Tolley's Company Law*). That is considered beyond the scope of this work, as an auditor's duty to an LLP client will not differ from his duty to a company.

Duty to appoint auditors   **10.55**

By *section 384* of the *CA 1985* (as modified), each LLP which is not exempt must appoint an auditor or auditors.

Those which are exempt are those which are either small or dormant, using the tests examined in the last part of this chapter (see 10.37 onwards), as confirmed by *section 388A* of the *CA 1985*.

Eligibility for appointment   **10.56**

Those eligible for appointment are, by virtue of *section 384(4)* of the *CA 1985*, simply those who would be eligible for appointment as auditors to a limited company. That qualification in turn is to be found in *Part II* of the *Companies Act 1989*, and so that batch of statutory provisions is incorporated into the LLP legislation by *section 384(5)* of the *CA 1985*.

It is beyond the scope of this work to go into detail as to auditors' qualifications, but suffice it to say that any auditor registered under *section 35* of the *CA 1989* will be able to audit an LLP's accounts. This qualification may well pose a practical problem for many partnerships considering conversion, particularly for those who are at the smaller end of the market but do not actually rate as 'small' within the statutory provision, and for their advisers. Such firms may well, for many years, have been very satisfied with the services provided by their accountants, who may not themselves be registered auditors. It would be natural for them to turn to those advisers for input as to the merits or otherwise of conversion. This must create a conflict of interest for such advisers since, if they recommend conversion, they are in practice likely to lose the client. This conflict may be unavoidable, but is something of which both sides should be aware.

Appointment of auditors by designated members   **10.57**

The appointment of auditors is reserved by *section 385* of the *CA 1985* (as modified) to the designated members, and is one of the most significant of their tasks.

For the first financial year of the LLP for which such an appointment is needed (not necessarily, of course, the first year of the LLP's existence if exemptions are initially available to it) the appointment must be made before the end of that financial year. Thereafter, the appointment must be made, in respect of any financial year, not later than two months after the approval of the accounts for the preceding financial year. The expiry of that two-month period also marks the latest possible date for the termination of the period of office of the auditor appointed for that preceding year, the concept thus being that there should always be a validly appointed auditor.

Appointment by members if designated members default 10.58

The situation could however arise where the designated members fail to comply with their statutory duty. Such failure does not of itself render the designated members liable to prosecution. The problem however comes with regard to the procedure if there is such default.

At first sight, *section 385(4)* of the *CA 1985* appears to offer a solution, in that it provides that the members generally may, if the designated members do not exercise their powers of appointment, step in and take over, with power to make an appointment at a meeting convened for that purpose. There are however two difficulties associated with that. Firstly, there is no mechanism in any of the legislation for the calling of such a meeting, and so this is one of the areas where the draftsman of the partnership agreement should have filled the gap. Secondly, there is no period of grace. Presumably, it cannot be said that the designated members have failed to exercise their powers until the very last day upon which it would be legitimate for them to do so. Can the membership generally start the procedure for calling a meeting earlier than that date, in anticipation of default, or must they wait until there is actual default, and then suffer a period of, say, two or three weeks whilst the notice calling the meeting has its currency?

Appointment by Secretary of State if designated members default 10.59

The difficulty mentioned in 10.58 above is compounded by the fact that the members are not the only ones who can act to fill the gap. So can the Secretary of State, under *section 387* of the *CA 1985* (as modified). Further, it is incumbent on the LLP, if appointment has not been made by the due date, to serve notice of that fact upon the Secretary of State within seven days of the last day for appointment, and failure to give such notice renders the LLP itself, and every designated member who is in default, liable to prosecution and, in addition to normal remedies, to a daily default fine.

If, therefore, the members of an LLP have given the designated members until the last day for appointment and then, on the designated members' default, have served a notice convening a meeting 21 days later, and have served the statutorily required notice upon the Secretary of State, it would appear at least theoretically possible for the members and the Secretary of State each to make a valid appointment of auditors. This may all sound far-fetched, but it does reinforce the need for the membership generally to ensure that they have the right, under the partnership agreement, to know what is happening in this regard, and the ability to act promptly to remedy any default on the part of the designated members.

Filling casual vacancies 10.60

If a casual vacancy occurs in the office of auditor, this may be filled by the designated members. If there was initially a joint appointment, any surviving or continuing auditor may continue to act, which may be a point commending joint appointments where possible.

The relevant provision here is *section 388* of the *CA 1985* (as modified).

Appointment where exemptions expire 10.61

If it becomes apparent that an LLP, which was previously exempt as 'small' or 'dormant' from the requirement to appoint auditors, has ceased to be exempt, then *section 388A* of the *CA 1985* (as modified) provides for the appointment of auditors by the designated members, such appointment to be of effect until two months after the approval of the accounts for the year in question.

There is however no stipulation (quite naturally, since the exemption could be lost at any time) of when such an appointment must be made. That in turn makes it difficult to operate the provisions of *section 388A(5)*, which gives the membership generally the power, to be exercised at a meeting called for the purpose, to appoint in the event of default by the designated members. Apart from the previously referred to problem of there being no statutory provision for such meetings, there is the difficulty of being able to point to any particular moment when default occurs.

Auditors' rights to information 10.62

Once appointed, auditors acquire wide-ranging powers of enquiry under *section 389A* of the *CA 1985* (as modified). They have a right of access, at all times, to all the LLP's financial documentation, and are entitled to require all members to supply such information and explanation of any matter as they think fit. Any member who, knowingly or recklessly, gives any such information or explanation which is misleading, false, or deceptive, commits an offence.

Similarly, any subsidiary company or LLP and its auditor may be required to give information or explanation and, if it fails to do so, it and every officer in default is guilty of an offence, as is any auditor of it who fails to comply without reasonable excuse. In respect of an unincorporated subsidiary, the parent LLP is obliged to take all steps reasonably open to it to obtain the information required by the auditors and, if it fails to do so, it and every member in default is guilty of an offence.

Auditors' rights to attend meetings 10.63

An LLP's auditors are entitled (but not obligated), under *section 390* of the *CA 1985* (as modified), to attend meetings of the LLP in certain circumstances.

That sounds unexceptionable, but the difficulty once again is that the Act and the legislation incorporated into it make virtually no provision for meetings of the LLP. The rights apply to any meetings where any part of the business to be conducted concerns the auditors in their statutory functions. They are entitled to receive notices of and communications concerning the meeting as if a member, and to attend and be heard at the meeting in respect of the relevant part(s) of it. If the chosen auditor is itself a body corporate or a partnership, it needs to nominate, in writing, an individual to attend such a meeting on its behalf.

Remuneration for audit work 10.64

The remuneration of the auditors for their work in their capacity as auditors shall normally be fixed by the LLP, as provided by *section 390A* of the *CA 1985* (as modified).

The statute provides that the decision shall be taken by the designated members, or in such manner as the members of the LLP may determine. It would thus be open to the LLP, in its partnership agreement, to leave the decision to the designated members or, at opposite ends of the spectrum, to delegate the decision to a particular member (e.g. the equivalent of a finance director) or to reserve it to the membership generally.

If the auditor is appointed by the Secretary of State (see 10.59 above) he determines the remuneration. The LLP's accounts must state the amount paid to the auditors, for their audit work, as remuneration, which for these purposes includes expenses and any benefits in kind (which must be stated and valued).

Non-audit work undertaken by auditors   **10.65**

There is growing concern, amongst those whose responsibility are the principles of ensuring public protection through corporate governance, about the apparent conflict of interest where a firm acts not only as auditors of a body corporate, but also as its advisers in much more general work. This is reflected not just in this country, but also in the US and internationally.

There is no doubt that in many cases the audit work is priced low by firms, in order to gain entry to the more general and more lucrative advisor's role. There have been suggestions that there should actually be a statutory bar to a firm acting in both capacities. That has not yet been implemented, but there are controls designed to make the amounts paid for such non-audit work as transparent as possible.

Remuneration for non-audit work   **10.66**

The controls referred to in 10.65 above are to be found in *section 390B* of the *CA 1985* (as modified), and in regulations made under *section 390B(1)* thereof, namely *the Companies Act 1985 (Disclosure of Remuneration for Non-Audit Work) Regulations 1991 (SI 1991/ 2128)* as amended.

Those provisions between them require that information as to the remuneration (which for this purpose includes benefits in kind, which must be detailed and valued, but does not include expenses) paid for such work must be given for not only the year of the accounts in question, but also the previous year. To ensure that the provisions are effective, there are detailed definitions of who is an 'associate', both for the business being audited, and for the auditors themselves, and the remuneration which must be disclosed relates to the aggregate of all services provided to the LLP in question or its associates, where the auditors or their associates are also the auditors.

The auditors are obliged to supply sufficient information for the LLP to identify any associates of the auditors for this purpose. None of the disclosure provisions, however, apply to any LLP which qualifies as either 'small' or 'medium-sized' (see 10.33 above).

Auditors' lien   **10.67**

In order to ensure payment of their fees, auditors are regarded as having a lien over all books, records and other papers in their possession, whether these relate strictly to their work as auditors, or to other professional work undertaken for the LLP being audited – *Woodworth v Conroy [1976] QB 884.*

This may however be weakened, as mentioned in 10.80 above, if the exercise of this lien might interfere with the LLP's obligations as to record keeping – *DTC (CTC) Limited v Gary Sargeant [1996] 1 WLR 797.*

Removal of auditors 10.68

There could be many, perfectly proper, reasons for getting rid of a particular firm of auditors. The problem is that there could also be one very improper reason, namely that they are doing too good a job, and asking questions which those being audited are neither willing to have asked, nor to answer.

For the protection of others associated with the business, and its creditors, there need accordingly to be special safeguards built into the process of removal of auditors. Whilst, therefore, *section 391* of the *CA 1985* (as modified) gives the designated members the right at any time to remove an auditor from office (subject, of course, to any contractual consequences which may flow from that removal), they are also required to give notice of that removal to the Registrar within 14 days, failing which the LLP and every designated member of it who is in default will be guilty of an offence.

Rights of removed auditors 10.69

The designated members who seek to remove an auditor from office, either during his term of office or simply by failing to re-appoint him at the expiry of that term, are obliged by *section 391A* of the *CA 1985* (as modified) to give that auditor not less than seven days' prior notice in writing of their intention.

The auditor in question still has, under *section 391(4)* of the *CA 1985*, the theoretical right to attend any meeting of the LLP at which his term of office would otherwise have expired, or at which his replacement is to be proposed – but that right is likely to be illusory in the LLP context, in the light of the fact that there is no statutory requirement for such a meeting to be called in the first place, as the designated members can simply deal with everything themselves.

More useful is that the auditor being so removed, or not being re-appointed, may make representations of reasonable length to the LLP, and request that they be distributed to all members. That request must be complied with within 21 days, or else the LLP and any designated member in default will be guilty of an offence. There is however a protective ability for the LLP, or any other aggrieved person (not even necessarily a member) to apply to the court for relief against the obligation thus to circulate the auditors' representations, on the grounds that the auditors' rights are being abused to secure 'needless publicity for defamatory matter'. On considering such an application, the court has discretion to award the LLP's costs (whether or not it is actually a party to the application) wholly or partly against the auditor.

Resignation of auditors 10.70

Similarly, whilst an auditor's resignation may be for any one of a number of perfectly normal reasons, it might be because of his concern at wrongdoing within the LLP, and therefore again protection needs to be built in. By *sections 392* and *394* of the *CA 1985* (both as modified), an auditor can resign at any time by depositing at the LLP's registered office:

- notice of resignation; and

- a statement of any circumstances, connected with his resignation, which he considers should be brought to the attention of the LLPs members or creditors (or, if all is well, that there are no such circumstances).

The notice of resignation is not effective unless accompanied by the statement. An effective notice may take effect either on the date it is deposited, or on such later date as it specifies. The LLP must then send a copy to the registrar within 14 days, or it, and every designated member in default, will be guilty of an offence.

Rights of resigning auditors 10.71

If, in the statement referred to above (in 10.70), a resigning auditor has indicated that he believes there are circumstances which should be brought to the attention of the LLP's members or creditors, then he may at the same time, under *section 392A* of the *CA 1985* (as modified), deposit with the LLP a notice requiring the designated members to convene a meeting of all members.

The purpose of the meeting is for him to give such explanation of the circumstances surrounding his resignation as he thinks fit. The designated members must act to call the meeting within 21 days of the notice from the auditor requiring them so to do, and the meeting must be not later than 28 days from the date of the notice calling it. If this does not happen every designated member who did not take all reasonable steps to ensure that a properly convened meeting was called will be guilty of an offence.

Auditors' statement to members 10.72

The auditor may also, then or later, request the LLP to circulate to all members a statement of reasonable length of the circumstances applicable, in advance of the meeting. If this is not delivered too late for circulation to be practical, the LLP must then state in any notice of the meeting that such a statement has been made, and circulate copies.

If it is not so circulated, either because the designated members fail to comply with their obligations, or because it was delivered too late, the auditor may read it at the meeting. He is in any event entitled to attend the meeting. Similar rights to those referred to in 10.69 above, for the LLP or any aggrieved person to apply to the court in respect of an allegedly defamatory statement, apply.

Deposit of statement of circumstances 10.73

Reference has been made in 10.70 above to the deposit of a statement by a resigning auditor. That obligation not only applies, however, to the act of resignation, but also to a decision by the auditor simply not to seek re-appointment, or to removal by the designated members or their failure to reappoint.

If the auditor does not seek re-appointment, the statement must be deposited not less than 14 days before the designated members' time for appointing his successor runs out; and if there is any other cause, it must be deposited not later than 14 days after his term of office expires. If an outgoing auditor fails to comply with this obligation, he is guilty of an offence, unless he can show that he took all reasonable steps and exercised all reasonable diligence (*CA 1985, s 394A* (as modified)).

Distribution of statement 10.74

If the statement is to the effect that there are circumstances which the auditor believes should be brought to the attention of members or creditors, then the LLP has 14 days from the date of the statement's deposit to make a choice. It can either distribute the statement to all members, and all holders of debentures from the LLP; or it may apply to the court, and notify the auditor of that application (*CA 1985, s 394(3),(4)*, as modified)). If it fails to do either then it, and every member in default, will be guilty of an offence (*CA 1985, s 394A(4)*, as modified).

To complete the loop, the auditor must, unless within 21 days of deposit of the statement he is notified by the LLP of an application to the court, then send a copy of his statement to the registrar within a further seven days (*CA 1985, s 394(5)*, as modified).

The court's powers on application   10.75

The court's powers on an application under the modified *CA 1985, s 394(3)* (see 10.74 above) are similar to those referred to in 10.69 and 10.72 above. There are basically two possible outcomes, depending on whether the court is satisfied that the auditor is using the statement to secure needless publicity for defamatory matter.

If it is so satisfied, it shall direct that copies of the statement shall not be sent out; and it may order the auditor (even though not a party to the application) to pay the LLP's costs in whole or in part. In that event the LLP must, within 14 days of the court's order, send to all members and debenture holders a statement setting out its effect. If however the court does not believe the allegation of a defamatory reason, the LLP must within 14 days of the court's decision to that effect send copies of the auditor's statement to all members and debenture holders, and notify the auditor of the court's decision. Again, in those circumstances, it is for the auditor to complete the loop by sending the notification of the court's decision to the registrar within seven days of receipt.

Power of court to grant relief from auditor's liability   10.76

The final provision of the legislation relating to auditors is found in *section 727* of the *CA 1985* (as modified). It deals with the situation where an auditor seeks relief from what would otherwise be a finding of fault against him.

The section can apply to any proceedings against the auditor (whoever the claimant may be) for negligence, default, breach of duty or breach of trust. If the court holds the view that the auditor is, or may be, liable for such an act or omission, it may nonetheless relieve him, either wholly or partly, from that liability, either absolutely, or on such conditions as it thinks fit. To do so, it must be satisfied that the auditor has acted honestly and reasonably, and that, in all the circumstances, he ought so to be excused.

There is also a power for the auditor, if he is fearful that such proceedings may be brought against him, to apply in advance for such relief, and the court has the same powers in respect of such a pre-emptive application as it would have on a substantive one.

Supplementary matters

Accounting standards 10.77

Statutory force is given to the concept of the establishment of accounting standards, set by various accountancy bodies, by *CA 1985, s 256*, as modified. The section gives power for regulations to specify those bodies which may set such standards. Such bodies may be funded by the Secretary of State. In an LLP's case, the standards will be such as are relevant to its particular circumstances and accounts. In practice, the LLP will be governed by a range of Financial Reporting Standards and, importantly, by the Statement of Recommended Practice which, as mentioned elsewhere in this work, will be published by the Consultative Committee of Accountancy Bodies after the conclusion of the current consultative process.

Such standards may be expected to play an even greater role in future, as the Company Law Steering Group, in its report, recommends that they should increasingly supplement formal Parliamentary regulation, since they are considered more flexible and more reflective of best professional practice.

Parent and subsidiary undertakings 10.78

Sections 258 and *259* of the *CA 1985*, as modified deal with the relevant definitions in respect of those LLPs which are linked to each other, or to other organisations, as a 'parent' or an 'undertaking', as referred to in various places, such as accounting groups.

The basic concept is that of an 'undertaking' which can be either:

- a body corporate, whether:
    - ○ a limited company, or
    - ○ an LLP,
- an unincorporated association carrying on a trade or business, whether for profit or not.

In other words it will encompass just about every sort of business other than a sole trader or practitioner.

An undertaking, A, is the parent of a subsidiary undertaking, B, if:

- A holds a majority of the voting rights in B; or

- A is a member of B and has the right to appoint or remove a majority of its board of directors;

- A has the right to exercise a dominant influence over B, either:

  ○ by virtue of provisions in B's memorandum or articles, or

  ○ by virtue of a contract giving it such control,

- A has a participating interest in B and either:

  ○ actually exercises a dominant influence over B, or

  ○ A and B are managed on a unified basis.

For these purposes, there is no specific indication that a majority of the members of an LLP would be regarded as equivalent to the board of directors of a company, but on the other hand there is the general provision in *Regulation 5(2)(b)* of the *Regulations* that references to directors include references to members of an LLP, so this would seem to bring LLPs within this limb of the definition. Similarly, *Regulation 5(2)(e)* equates an LLP's partnership agreement to a company's Memorandum and Articles. An undertaking can be regarded as a member of another even if its membership is indirect, i.e. through the medium either of another subsidiary undertaking, or by a nominee holding shares in the ultimate subsidiary.

Reference to the holding of shares, in the case of an LLP, i.e. an undertaking which does not have share capital, but does have capital, will be to rights to share in the capital of the LLP.

Participating interests 10.79

The other expression used in a number of instances which is given a definition section is that of a 'participating interest', as in *section 260* of the *CA 1985*, as modified. Using the same definition of 'undertaking' as in 10.78 above, it indicates that A will have a participating interest in B if it holds that interest 'on a long term basis for the purpose of securing a contribution to its activities by the exercise of control or influence arising from or related to that interest'. Such an interest will be rebuttably presumed if A holds 20% or more of the shares in B. Such interests can be held through the medium of subsidiaries, or nominees.

11 – Disclosure of Members' Interests

> This chapter looks in detail at one of the most controversial aspects of the LLP legislation, namely the requirements for public disclosure of members' personal financial interests in the LLP.
>
> The impact of this disclosure varies considerably according to the size of the LLP, and those variances are considered fully. Overall, the examination in the chapter suggests that the burden is not as heavy as many may fear, and should not in many cases prove a disincentive to the conversion of existing businesses into LLP format.

Introduction   11.1

In many ways, it would have been logical for the contents of this chapter to have been considered in Chapter 10, along with the rest of the requirements for the format of an LLP's accounts.

However, frequently, businessmen and professionals considering conversion to LLP status have been concerned above all with the question of the extent of their obligation publicly to disclose their personal financial positions in relation to the LLP, and so it was decided to give the topic particular prominence by allotting a chapter to it.

The underlying principles   11.2

From the outset, having determined to take the LLP legislation down the route of a body corporate, rather than a sub-species of partnership remaining an unincorporated undertaking, the Government was clear that the price to be paid for the protection which limited liability status would afford members of an LLP was to be the obligation to make some disclosure.

The Government's intention in doing so was not that those examining the accounts should know everything about the members' finances; but rather that they should be able, by examining the accounts, to consider the overall financial health of the LLP, and how that was matched by the members' own willingness to invest their funds in it. In other words, this is intended to give reassurance to those dealing with the LLP that, notwithstanding its limitation of liability, their chances of having their contracts honoured are reasonable.

The degree of disclosure   11.3

In light of the Government's intention with the legislation (see 11.2 above), the legislation is not particularly concerned with information as to the position regarding any individual member, but rather with the aggregate members' position.

After all, the situation with an LLP, where the two constituencies are the members and outside contracting parties, is markedly different from that relating to a company, where there are three interested groups, i.e. the directors, the shareholders, and outside parties. In that scenario, it is the need for protection of the shareholders from exploitation by the directors for their own benefit that gives rise to many of the detailed disclosure requirements (though how effective those are in the real world is a matter of some debate).

Comparison with other jurisdictions   11.4

Mention is made elsewhere of the development of the LLP idea from the model of the US version of the concept, both initially by individual states, and later, by means of the application of the revised Uniform Partnership Act. In those states which have brought in the principle the LLP is not, unlike the UK, a newly created and separately incorporated body. It is simply a development of the existing partnership which determines to avail itself of limited liability protection. As such, it is not necessary for it to make any public declarations of its finances, any more than it is for a partnership (save that some states have minimum capital requirements, though these are largely directed at possible malpractice liabilities, and can often be covered by insurance).

Therefore there were some pleas to the effect that, if UK LLPs' members had to make personal disclosures which their overseas rivals did not, that would put them at a commercial disadvantage. Such pleas fell on deaf Governmental ears.

Requirements for non-exempt LLPs – the balance sheet   11.5

As mentioned above, the requirements of LLPs vary according to the business's size. To start with, therefore, the position is that applying where there are no exemptions available to the LLP. That being so, its accounts will fall to be prepared under *Schedule 4* to the *Companies Act 1985* (as modified).

In the *CA 1985*, two options are offered for the format to be adopted for the layout of the balance sheet (though, once chosen, a format has to be adhered to). For these purposes, it makes no difference which is chosen. In each format, two main headings relevant to the disclosure of members' interests are given, namely 'Loans and other debts due to members', and 'Members' other interests'. Each of those headings is then split, either by note (12) in the first main heading, or in the balance sheet itself in the second main heading, into three sub-headings which have to be shown separately, as follows:

- Loans and other debts due to members:
  - ○ the aggregate amount of money advanced to the LLP by the members by way of loan;
  - ○ the aggregate amount of money owed to members by the LLP in respect of profits;
  - ○ any other amounts.
- Members' other interests:
  - ○ members' capital;
  - ○ revaluation reserve;
  - ○ other reserves.

Loans etc. 11.6

The provisions clearly draw a distinction between capital on the one hand, and other amounts owed to members on the other. The first grouping is of the amount which the members would be entitled, on the face of it, to require to be repaid to them. There is no requirement to state whether there are any provisions restricting their right to take these monies out, e.g. by limiting the circumstances in which loans can be repaid, or requiring members to leave undrawn profits in the business. The presumption in the outsider's mind must therefore be that these monies would rank equally with any debt owed to him by the LLP (since, unlike in a partnership scenario, the LLP and the members will be separate legal entities, and the members will have the same rights as any other creditor, depending on whether or not they have taken any security, as they would be entitled to do (subject to the usual requirements as to registration of charges etc.)).

The amounts which have to be disclosed under the first two headings are clearly aggregates, with no need for individual amounts to be stated, but the position is less clear with regard to the last item, 'any other amounts'. It is arguable that this is still an aggregate requirement, in keeping with what has gone before, but it would have been easy for the provision to spell that out, and there might be some suggestion that more detail needed to be given of such (by definition unusual) amounts, so that a cautious accountant might, by way perhaps of a note to the accounts, wish to spell this out.

Members' other interests   11.7

The heading 'Members' other interests' (see 11.5 above), and the three items in it, seem oriented more to what may be considered long-term investment in the business, and, by means of the inclusion of reserves, of the true, rather than nominal values of that investment.

One aspect to be aware of is that, according to the draft SORP, profits earned by the LLP but not yet allocated or divided, will be regarded as included in 'other reserves' and thus an equivalent to capital. In some ways, in terms of third-party protection, the distinction is artificial, since capital can be withdrawn just as loans can (but either would be subject to the special provisions requiring repayment of withdrawals found in *section 214A* of the *Insolvency Act 1986*, discussed at length in Chapter 17). It is perhaps true that there would be a reasonable expectation that capital would remain in the business on a long-term basis.

Profit and loss accounts   11.8

In *Schedule 4* to the *CA 1985* (as modified), there are again two possible formats for profit and loss accounts which are available for LLPs, but again there is no difference between them in this respect.

'Profit' in this context effectively ignores members, and therefore the profit figure is calculated without heed to any profit share distributable to, or any other form of remuneration payable to, members. Further, any statement as to interest payable by the LLP must exclude interest paid to members.

Notes to the balance sheet — paragraph 37A information   11.9

The notes to the balance sheet have to give various supplemental information by virtue of *Schedule 4* to the *CA 1985*. In the case of LLPs, there is a new *paragraph 37A*, which requires a note to give information under six headings. In each case it is again the aggregate amounts which are required, with no individual breakdowns.

The aggregate amounts required are in respect of:

● loans and other debts due to members at the start of the year;

● contributions by members during the year;

● transfers to or from the profit and loss account during the year;

● monies withdrawn by members or applied on their behalf during the year;

● loans and other debts due to members at the balance sheet date;

● loans and other debts due to members that fall due after one year.

Once again, the intention is simply that the overall pattern of the movement of funds between the LLP and its members shall be visible, so that a third party can see whether the overall flow of funds is into or out of the business, or whether it is in equilibrium.

Notes to the profit and loss account — paragraph 56A information

Average number of members 11.10

The third and final batch of information which needs to be given, and perhaps the most contentious, takes the form of a note to the profit and loss account, under *paragraph 56A* of *Schedule 4* to the *CA 1985* (as modified).

This deals with members' remuneration etc, and, for the first time, makes some individual details available. It starts by requiring the note to give the average number of members for the year in question, with the average being worked out on a monthly basis to allow for variations over the year. Once that figure is given, it will not require any reader of the accounts to be Einstein to work out the average profit per member. That is hardly going to be radical news, however, once the overall profit is public, for it would not be difficult for anyone to find out from other means, e.g. an LLP's letterhead, or the statement of ownership to be kept at its registered office, or simply a search of the Companies House records, what the number of members at any given point in time happens to be. This requirement of itself therefore adds little to the burden of disclosure.

Highest earning member 11.11

There is however a second layer of information which needs to be given under *paragraph 56A* of *Schedule 4* to the *CA 1985*, if (but only if) profit for the LLP for the year in question exceeds £200,000. If so, then the amount payable to the member receiving the highest share of profit needs to be stated.

Two principles have to be applied in making all calculations for the purposes of this section (i.e. does profit exceed the threshold, who is the highest earner, and how much has that member received). The first is that 'profit' includes all remuneration and all specified classes of 'emoluments', whether they are received from the LLP itself, any subsidiary undertakings (whether incorporated or not, and therefore including partnerships) or indeed 'any other person'.

The second principle is that those 'emoluments' (which are defined by a cross-reference to *Schedule 6* of the *CA 1985*) comprise all:

- emoluments paid to or receivable by members for qualifying services (i.e. services to the LLP or associated undertakings);

- money (or the value of assets – other than share option schemes) paid to or received or receivable by members under long-term incentive schemes in respect of qualifying services;

- pension contributions for members' qualifying services in relation to money purchase schemes.

Information not needing disclosure 11.12

It may also be worth considering, before getting too hot under the collar as to the burden of disclosure (see 11.1 and 11.2 above), some areas where the *CA 1985* requires individual disclosure by company directors, but not members of LLPs.

By a combination of *section 330* of and *Schedule 6* to the *CA 1985*, this disclosure by directors would include individual details of:

- pension scheme benefits;
- compensation for loss of office;
- sums paid to third parties;
- loans, quasi-loans etc;
- guarantees.

Exemption for small LLPs 11.13

Although there are no different provisions for medium-sized LLPs in relation to the disclosure of members' interests, there are exemptions from some of the above disclosure requirements available for those LLPs which fit within the 'small' category (see 10.38 above as to the criteria) and which do not fall foul of the exclusion from the small LLP benefits which applies to ineligible businesses (e.g. authorised persons under the *Financial Services Act 1986* – see 10.42 above).

Such LLPs are referred to in the following paragraphs as 'qualifying small LLPs'. They need only prepare the simpler accounts required by the modified *Schedule 8* to the *CA 1985*. There is no change as to the information required for the balance sheet, or the way the profit and loss account is structured, or the additional information needed under *paragraph 37A* (see 11.9 above). However, there is no equivalent to the requirements of *paragraph 56A* (see 11.10 and 11.11 above) in relation to members' profit entitlements. It is worth remembering the Steering Group's recommendations for the expansion of the class of small LLPs, referred to in 10.51 above.

Exemption for qualifying small LLPs with abbreviated balance sheets 11.14

Finally, there is a further exemption for those qualifying small LLPs which opt under *section 246* of the *CA 1985* (as modified) to deliver only an abbreviated balance sheet to the Registrar, in compliance with the modified *Schedule 8A*. That balance sheet will have the same information as to members' debts and capital, but there is of course no profit and loss account, and there is no requirement for either the *paragraph 37A* information as to the movement of funds (see 11.9 above), or the *paragraph 56A* information as to profit entitlements (see 11.10 and 11.11 above).

Note however that this only applies to the information deliverable to the Registrar, and thus to become public: it does not apply to the accounts to be distributed to members and debenture holders, which have to be prepared as in 11.13 above. Note also for the future that this classification is under threat from the DTI Company Law Steering Group's final report, which recommends the abolition of the right for such undertakings to deliver only an abbreviated balance sheet.

Summary of disclosure requirements   **11.15**

To sum up, the disclosure requirements look like this:

Statutory requirement	Application
Balance sheet information as to members' debts and capital	All LLPs
Profit & loss account excluding members' remuneration	All LLPs, save for the registrar's copy where a qualifying small LLP has opted to deliver only an abbreviated balance sheet
Paragraph 37A information on the movement of funds	Ditto
Paragraph 56A information on average member numbers	All LLPs other than qualifying small LLPs
Paragraph 56A information on highest earning member's remuneration	All LLPs except qualifying small LLPs, or those LLPs with profit less than £200,000

12 – Miscellaneous Provisions

> This chapter considers the miscellany of items, other than in respect of accounts and auditing requirements (covered in Chapters 10 and 11), which are applied to LLPs by *SI 2001/1090, Sch 2* (see 1.14 above), importing provisions from the *Companies Act 1985*.
>
> The consequences for an LLP whose membership falls below two are considered. The requirements for the making of contracts by an LLP, and entry by it into deeds, are then reviewed. Next come the interlinked topics of the creation and registration of debentures; and the registration of charges created by an LLP. The powers of the Secretary of State to appoint inspectors, and conduct investigations, into an LLP's affairs are set out. The law concerning the possibility of LLPs entering into arrangements and reconstructions is covered, and finally the potentially thorny problems of petitions alleging unfair prejudice, under *section 459* of the *CA 1985*, are examined.

Introduction   12.1

As explained previously (see 10.3 above), *SI 2001/1090, Sch 2* works differently from *SI 2001/1090, Sch 1*. It specifies certain selected provisions from the *CA 1985* which are to have effect with regard to LLPs, and then indicates whether they are to be incorporated with only normal modifications (e.g. 'member' for 'director'), or are to be given specific modification. The provisions thus included follow no particular pattern.

The *CA 1985*, as before, is referred to as modified.

Minimum membership   12.2

Section 2 of the *LLPA 2000* itself requires that an LLP shall initially have at least two members (see 2.6). It leaves it to the modified *section 24* of the *CA 1985*, however, to deal with the circumstances where membership subsequently falls below the minimum required number of two.

The position is then as interesting for what does not happen, as what does. The first point is that, for six months after the situation has arisen where there is only one member, nothing at all happens. The LLP can continue to trade under that member's direction, and he incurs no penalty or added potential liability. After that six months, if it is still continuing with just one member, it still continues to exist, and can still continue to trade. However that member (providing he knows that the LLP is carrying on business with just him as member) becomes jointly and severally liable for such of the debts of the LLP as are incurred after the end of that six-month period. (It is possible to imagine a scenario where even this liability might not attach. Imagine an LLP where two elderly brothers are the sole members, but have delegated all responsibility for the actual carrying on of the business to the next generation, without making them members. One dies, and some months later the other suffers the onset of senile dementia. The business could then be carried on by others in the family, without the surviving member's knowledge, so presumably no personal liability would attach.)

It is not therefore until someone takes some active steps to remedy the situation, e.g. by petitioning for the winding up of the LLP, that it, as a legal entity, with unlimited capacity, ceases to exist.

Contractual requirements

Formalities for entering into contracts 12.3

There are two basic requirements for a contract to which an LLP is a party. Under *section 36* of the *CA 1985* (as modified), either the contract, if 'by' the LLP, may be made in writing under the common seal of the LLP (assuming it has opted to have such a seal) or, if it is 'on behalf of' the LLP, may be made by any party acting under its express or implied authority.

Further, if the general law applies any overlay of requirements as to formality (e.g. that a contract for the sale of land must be in writing) then that will apply to an LLP's contacts as well as to any others.

Execution of documents 12.4

Reference was made in 12.3 above to the fact that an LLP may choose whether to have a common seal or not. *Section 36A(3)* of the *CA 1985* (as modified) specifies that. If it does opt for a seal, an LLP may execute a document by affixing the seal to it. If not, then any document signed by two members, and expressed in some way to be executed by the LLP has exactly the same effect as if executed under seal. It is hard therefore to see the advantage of opting to have a seal, unless potential overseas use makes this desirable (see 12.7 below).

Such a document as above, whichever method of execution is chosen, will be regarded as a deed if it is clear on the face of it that it is intended to be. It will have effect on delivery, and will be presumed to be delivered upon execution unless a contrary intention is proved, e.g. by a statement that it is delivered in escrow. In favour of a purchaser acting in good faith and for valuable consideration (including a lessee, mortgagee or other person taking an interest in property), there are presumptions:

- of due execution, if the document purports to be signed by two members; and

- of delivery upon execution, if it purports to be a deed.

Pre-incorporation contracts 12.5

Pre-incorporation contracts are a danger for the person making them on behalf of the prospective LLP. The reason is that, by the modified *section 36C* of the *CA 1985*, any such contract takes effect not as a contract between the third party and the LLP, but between the third party and the person purporting to act on behalf of or as agent for the LLP, and that person becomes personally liable. This applies to deeds just as it does to contracts.

It is however capable of being displaced by agreement, so if the third party can be persuaded to accept the liability of the as yet unformed LLP, all well and good. More likely, however, is that the third party will wish to adhere to his statutory rights, and that it will be incumbent on the person dealing on the LLP's behalf to ensure that he takes advantage of *section 5(2)* of the *LLPA 2000*, and puts in place a pre-incorporation agreement between the members and the LLP, which binds the LLP to ratify and accept liability for such pre-incorporation agreements, so that even though he may be primarily liable to the third party, he has the benefit of an indemnity from the LLP.

Bills of exchange etc. 12.6

By *section 37* of the *CA 1985* (as modified), a bill of exchange, or a promissory note, is deemed to have been made, accepted or endorsed on behalf of an LLP if this is done in its name, or by or on behalf or on account of, the LLP, by someone acting under its authority.

Bear in mind also that, by *section 349* of the *CA 1985* (as modified), the LLP's name must be stated on all such documents, such as on cheques, and that if not it and anyone (member or not) who issues and/or signs such a document is liable to a fine and, in the case of the signatory, is personally liable under the document.

Sundry other documentary provisions 12.7

An LLP may, by writing under its common seal, appoint someone to execute deeds on its behalf outside the UK, and a deed executed by such an attorney has the same effect as if under the LLP's seal (*CA 1985, s 38*, as modified)).

Further, if the LLP has a common seal, it may create facsimiles for use in specified overseas countries etc, and authorise someone to affix the same, which authority a third party may rely on (*CA 1985, s 39*, as modified) unless it appears from the face of the authority that it was for a limited and expired period, or unless the third party has notice of revocation or determination. Any member of an LLP may, by his signature, authenticate a document on the LLP's behalf (*CA 1985, s 41*, as modified).

Events affecting an LLP's status 12.8

There may be certain events in an LLP's lifetime which it wishes to be able to rely on as having happened, and as binding a third party which it is dealing with. It may however be unable to do so if notice of that event has not been properly dealt with. This can apply to:

- the making of a winding up order for the LLP;

- the appointment of a liquidator in the voluntary winding up of the LLP;

- any alteration of the LLP's incorporation document;

- any change in the LLP's registered office (in connection with the service of any document upon it).

It will be unable, in accordance with *section 42* of the *CA 1985* (as modified), to rely upon such an event having happened, unless that event has been officially notified by it to the Registrar at the material time, or can be shown by the LLP to have been known at that time to the person concerned. Even if the official notification has been given, it cannot rely upon that if the material time is on or before the fifteenth day after official notification (or, if that fifteenth day is not a business day, the next business day after that) if the third party can be shown to have been unavoidably prevented from knowing of it.

In other words, if the LLP seeks to rely on such an event, it will, regardless of official notification, be in its interests specifically to draw the third party's attention to it at the material time, and it will not really be safe to rely upon official notification alone until the 15-day period has passed.

Debentures

Creation of debentures 12.9

One major potential advantage of the corporate status of LLPs is their ability, unlike partnerships, to create and issue debentures. Prospective providers of finance to LLPs will have, for the first time, the ability thus to take floating charges on the assets – and in particular on the book debts – of the business.

This may seem a one-sided benefit, but it may in practice work very much in members' favour, if such security can be offered in place of any personal guarantees, or security over the members' private properties, which banks and others may well otherwise require. It may even offer the only form of security which an LLP can find for its borrowing.

Certain professional LLPs may have to check their profession's rules, to see whether this may be thought to cause any problem with the consequent possibility of finance providers being entitled to receive fees direct from clients.

The development of floating charges 12.10

There is no statutory provision saying that an LLP can create floating charges – nor is there for companies.

The concept of a charge which does not attach to specific assets until a defined event causes it to crystallise is a creation of Victorian ingenuity and common law, having been first accepted as a principle in *Re Panama, New Zealand & Australia Royal Mail Co (1870) 5 Ch App 318*. The development of the floating charge, and its interplay with other forms of security, is likewise largely a matter of case law. In more recent times, the relationship between floating charges and various insolvency provisions, such as administration orders, has been the subject of legislative development. These areas are beyond the scope of this work, and the reader who needs to get to grips with such detail is referred to the major company law texts, such as *Tolley's Company Law* (in particular, the 'Company Charges' chapter).

Areas of legislative provision 12.11

Although the floating charge, and hence the debenture, may be largely creatures of common law, there is much statutory provision for their administration, and this will apply as much to LLPs as to companies.

The right of debenture holders to receive copies of the LLPs accounts has already been examined in Chapter 10 above. *Part XII* of the *CA 1985* provides for the registration of charges by LLPs, which will apply to both fixed and floating charges created by LLPs, and this is dealt with from 12.21 below. There is also a group of miscellaneous provisions found in *Chapter VIII* of *Part V* of the *CA 1985* relating to debentures, and those are examined below.

Transfer and registration 12.12

Debentures are, ordinarily, assignable securities. By *section 183* of the *CA 1985* (as modified), any transfer must be by means of a proper written transfer, to be delivered to the LLP, in order for the transfer to be registered by the LLP (unless the transfer is by operation of law). The CREST system does not apply to transfers of debentures.

If for any reason the LLP declines to register the transfer, it must, within two months of that refusal, send notice to the prospective transferee of that refusal, and if it does not then it, and every member in default, will be guilty of an offence. It is worth noting that this provision does however specifically incorporate reference to *section 207* of the *Companies Act 1989*, and the ability of the Secretary of State to make regulations under that section providing for title to securities (including debentures) to be evidenced and transferred without written instrument, so although there are no currently relevant regulations, the possibility for a future regime of electronic transfer exists.

Certification of transfer 12.13

An LLP may certify the transfer of a debenture by marking the transfer with 'copy lodged' or something similar. If it does, it is taken to have certified not that the transferor has actual title to the debenture, but that there have been produced to it documents which on the face of it show a prima facie title (*CA 1985, s 184*, as modified).

The LLP must be careful in the exercise of this function, since third parties may rely upon the faith of the certification and, if the certification is negligently wrong, the LLP becomes as liable to that third party as if the wrong certification had been fraudulent. There are detailed provisions in *section 184* as to the process for certification and signing of the certificate.

Issue of certificates   12.14

It is the task of the LLP to issue debenture certificates. It has a period of two months to do so from the time of an event which triggers that obligation. That event may, by *section 185* of the *CA 1985* (as modified), be either the allotment of any debentures, or the lodgement of any (properly stamped) transfer, other than one which is refused. If it fails to issue the necessary certificates, it and every member in default is guilty of an offence, and daily default fines can be levied.

Further if a third party who is entitled to receive a certificate serves notice on the LLP requiring it to fulfil its obligations, and it does not do so within ten days, then that person can apply to the court for an order directing the LLP and any member in default to perform its obligations, and to pay the application's costs. There is an exception for dealings through a 'recognised clearing house' etc.

Register of debenture holders   12.15

Section 190 of the *CA 1985* (as modified) provides for the keeping of a register of debenture holders. (The provisions also apply to any duplicate, kept in the UK, of any such register the original of which is kept overseas.)

LLPs registered in England and Wales must not keep such a register in Scotland (and vice versa). The register may only be kept at the LLP's registered office, or at any other office of the LLP where it is made up, or at the office of a third party to whom the making up function is delegated. Unless the register is, and always has been, kept at the LLP's registered office, then notice of where it is kept, and any change in those arrangements, must be sent to the Registrar in Form LLP190 (although, curiously, there does not seem to be the usual criminal sanction for failure to file this notice).

Inspection of register   12.16

The register is a public document. It may be inspected by anyone, under *section 191* of the *CA 1985* (as modified). Further, anyone may require a copy. Similarly, if there is a trust deed relating to an issue of debentures, a copy of that deed may be requested by any holder of a debenture within that issue, and the LLP must send him a copy. All of the above are dependent on payment of a prescribed fee (except for a registered debenture holder who need not pay to inspect the register).

If the LLP does not comply with any of these provisions, the LLP and any member in default is guilty of an offence, and a daily default fine may be levied. Further, the court may by order compel immediate compliance. These provisions do not apply, however, if the register is closed, in accordance with the original debenture documentation, and such closure lasts for not more than an aggregate 30 days in any year. There is a specific provision that the LLP shall not be liable for any error in the register more than 20 years after the error occurred.

Liability of debenture trustees   12.17

It is not uncommon for there to be a trust deed for an issue of debentures, with trustees appointed to secure the interests of the debenture holders.

By *section 192* of the *CA 1985* (as modified), any provision in the trust deed which purports to grant a trustee an exemption from, or an indemnity against, his potential liability for breach of trust where he fails to show the degree of care and diligence which is required of him as a trustee, is void. That does not however prevent a specific retrospective release being given to a trustee for anything done or omitted by him. Nor does it preclude a provision allowing a retrospective release to be given, if supported by not less than 75 per cent of the debenture holders, which has effect:

- in relation to specific acts or omissions; or
- if the trustee dies; or
- if the trustee ceases to act.

If such a provision is to be incorporated, it will need to have detailed provisions for the calling of a meeting of the debenture holders, and for proxy voting if this is desired.

Redemption of debentures   12.18

It is usual for debentures to be redeemable under specific circumstances, i.e. for the monies originally advanced by the debenture holder to the LLP to be repayable on a specific date, or on the happening of a specific event. This is not however necessary, and *section 193* of the *CA 1985* (as modified) specifically allows for debentures either to be irredeemable, or redeemable upon a contingency or a date, however remote those events may be.

Further, by *section 194* of the *CA 1985* (as modified), if debentures are redeemed, there is nothing to stop the LLP from re-issuing them or replacing them, unless there is any contractual bar to this or the LLP has somehow determined to cancel them. If the debentures are reissued, the position is the same as if the redemption had never taken place, as far as the holder's rights are concerned, but the reissue is treated as a new issue for stamp duty purposes.

Finally, if a debenture is for the purpose of securing a current account, there is no deemed redemption merely because that account, for a time, goes into credit.

Specific performance of contract to issue debentures   12.19

Section 195 of the *CA 1985* (as modified) states, very simply, that if the LLP has entered into a contract with a third party to issue debentures, that third party can enforce the contract by means of an action for specific performance.

Floating charges and preferential debts   12.20

Almost invariably, debentures will be secured by a floating charge. For any such debenture, *section 196* of the *CA 1985* lays down the rules which apply as between the debenture holders, and those entitled to the payment of 'preferential debts', in the event that the debenture holders go into possession of assets subject to the floating charge, at a time when the LLP is not in the course of being wound up. Preferential debts are defined by *Schedule 6* to the *Insolvency Act 1986*, and consist essentially of PAYE, VAT and sundry other government debts, and some monies payable to staff in respect of pension contributions and recently due remuneration.

The *IA 1986* provides that the preferential debts are payable, by the person taking possession, in priority to any monies due under the debenture. The debenture holders must rely on a claim as an ordinary creditor for any shortfall which consequently arises. This could well seriously detract from the desirability of attempting to enforce a debenture, since not only does it possibly bring forward the payment of preferential debts at the expense of the debenture holder, but it places a large administrative burden on those attempting to enforce, since they will need to take all appropriate steps to discover what preferential debts are due, which may in practice involve appointing an insolvency practitioner.

No doubt debenture holders will therefore be hoping that a proposal is implemented, which is currently being discussed as part of a review of insolvency law, namely that the concept of preferential debts in favour of the Crown should be abolished. Since however it would require Government determination to implement such a proposal, that may be an over-optimistic hope!

Registration of charges

Registration generally   **12.21**

Following on from looking at the provisions for debentures created by LLPs, it seems logical to move on to look at the provisions of the *CA 1985* which deal generally with the registration of charges created by LLPs, which are to be found in *Chapter I* of *Part XII* of that Act, i.e. *sections 395* to *408* as modified.

These provisions have, over the years, caused many problems to the companies who have had to operate them, and there seems no reason to believe that they will not cause just as many difficulties for LLPs. The difficulties are on two levels. Firstly, there is the question of what is or is not a 'charge' caught by the statutory provisions. An example is the line of cases which ran through the 1980s which concerned retention of title clauses in conditions for the sale of goods, and the often raised question of whether the various draftsmen's attempts to retain security over unpaid-for goods created a registrable charge (e.g. *Re Bond Worth Limited [1980] Ch 228*, or *Clough Mill Limited v Martin [1984] 3 All ER 982*).

The second difficulty is the draconian consequences of failing correctly to recognise a charge or, having recognised it, failing punctually to register it, namely that it is rendered void against creditors etc, as below. The professions abound with apocryphal stories of massive negligence claims due to failure to register a charge within time. Detailed consideration of what may or may not constitute a charge is beyond the scope of this work, and readers are referred to standard company texts, such as *Tolley's Company Law* ('Company Charges' chapter, C5004/1 onwards). What this part of the current chapter will do is to look at the procedural requirements as to charges created by LLPs.

The consequences of failure to register   **12.22**

If an LLP creates a charge to which *section 395* of the *CA 1985* (as modified) applies then it must, within 21 days after date of the charge's creation, deliver to the Registrar for registration the required particulars of the charge in Form LLP395, together with the original instrument (if any) by which the charge is evidenced or created.

If the LLP does not, then any security conferred by the charge is wholly void as against any liquidator, administrator or creditor of the LLP. It is not that the contract between the chargor LLP and the chargee creditor is invalidated, merely that the security is adversely affected. Indeed, it is specifically provided that, when a charge becomes void by reason of the provision, the money due under the contract which created the charge becomes immediately due and payable.

Charges which have to be registered   12.23

The following are the categories of charge (for which 'mortgage' is expressly stated to be synonymous) which, under *section 396* of the *CA 1985* (as modified), have to be registered, namely:

- a charge for the purpose of securing any issue of debentures;
- a charge created or evidenced by an instrument which, if executed by an individual, would require registration as a bill of sale;
- a charge on land (wherever situated) or any interest in it;
- a charge on the LLP's book debts;
- a floating charge on the LLPs undertaking or property;
- a charge on a ship (or any share in one) or an aircraft;
- a charge on goodwill, or on any intellectual property.

Supplemental provisions   12.24

Section 396 of the *CA 1985* also contains a number of supplemental provisions which amplify the above categories. These are:

- a charge for rent, or any other periodical sum issuing out of land, does not require registration;
- if an LLP gives a negotiable instrument to secure the payment of book debts, depositing that instrument in order to secure an advance to the LLP is not to be regarded as a charge on the book debts;
- the holding of debentures, which entitle to the holder to a charge on land, is not itself deemed to be an interest in land;

- 'intellectual property' is defined to include any patent, trade mark, registered design, copyright or design right; or any licence under or in respect of any such right.

Registration of debentures 12.25

There are specific provisions which apply to the registration of a series of debentures, i.e. where the benefits of the debentures apply to a number of debenture holders ranking *pari passu*. Here, it is sufficient if, within the same 21-day period as is referred to in 12.26 above, the Registrar is given, in Form LLP397, the following particulars:

- the total amount secured by the series;
- the dates of:
  - the LLP's determination(s) to issue the series; and
  - the covering deed (if any) by which the security is created or defined;
- a general description of the property charged;
- the names of the trustees (if any) for the debenture holders.

In addition, the LLP needs to send the Registrar the deed which created the series. If it did not have such a deed, then a sample one of the series of debentures must be produced. If the issue of the debentures in the series is staggered, then each time there is an issue particulars of the date and amount of each issue must be sent to the registrar in Form LLP397A (though if this is not done it does not invalidate the debentures).

Notification of discount etc. 12.26

Either Form LLP397 or Form LLP397A, as the case may be (see 12.25 above), also needs to give a further set of details, under *section 397(2)* of the *CA 1985* (as modified).

These relate to any discount, allowance or commission which may have been paid or made (directly or indirectly) by the LLP to anyone, in relation to his taking or procuring anyone else to take such debentures. The form in question must disclose the amount or rate of any such payment etc. It does not count as a discount if the LLP deposits any of the debentures with anyone to secure its debt. If the details of discount etc. are not given, it does not invalidate the debentures.

Overseas charges   **12.27**

A charge needs to be registered even if it is created abroad, and is secured on property situated abroad. In that situation, however, it is sufficient if a verified copy, rather than the original, is delivered to the Registrar (*CA 1985, s 398*, as modified).

The time for compliance in such a case is also extended, to 21 days after the copy could, in due course of post and if sent promptly, have been received in the UK. If however the charge is taken over property situated overseas, but it is actually created in the UK, the original is still needed by the Registrar, even though there may be further steps, to be taken abroad, to validate the charge.

Finally, if the property charged is in Scotland or Northern Ireland, and further action is needed in the appropriate one of those jurisdictions to validate it, it will be sufficient to produce to the Registrar in place of the original charge document:

● a verified copy of the charge; and

● a certificate in Form LLP398 to the effect that the charge has been presented for registration in the appropriate jurisdiction.

The duty to register charges   **12.28**

The primary duty to register charges created by an LLP is that of the LLP itself, under *section 399 of the CA 1985* (as modified).

However, such registration can be effected on the application of any person interested in it. In other words, if the chargee does not trust the LLP to register the charge, and hence to protect his security, he can do it himself. In practice, that is common, and banks etc. will almost always insist on dealing with the registration formalities themselves. Anyone so registering a charge is entitled to recover the fee paid to the Registrar from the LLP.

If the LLP fails to register a charge, and no-one else steps into the breach and does it for them, then the LLP, and every member in default, is guilty of an offence, and a daily default fine can be levied.

Charges existing on property acquired   **12.29**

An LLP may, of course, acquire property which is already subject to a charge (*CA 1985, s 400*, as modified). This might, for instance, arise on the transfer of a partnership's business to an LLP, where the LLP could take over premises already subject to a mortgage. In such circumstances, the LLP has 21 days from the completion of the acquisition to send to the Registrar a certified copy of the charge, and the necessary particulars, in Form LLP400.

If however that property is outside the UK, and the charge was created outside the UK, then the compliance period is extended to 21 days after a promptly posted copy of the charge should have arrived in the UK. The penalties for failure to comply with these requirements are the same as for failure to register a new charge, as above (see 12.28 above).

The register of charges 12.30

The Registrar's duty is to keep the register of charges, under the modified *section 401* of the *CA 1985*, for each LLP, in Form LLP401. The register thus created is public, and open to inspection by anyone. This will therefore show:

- details of any series of debentures (see 12.25 above);
- the date of:
  - ○ creation of the charge by the LLP; or
  - ○ acquisition of any already charged property;
- the amount secured by the charge;
- short particulars of the property charged;
- who is entitled to the charge.

Upon registration of any charge, the Registrar shall give a certificate of registration, stating the amount secured, which shall be conclusive evidence of the satisfaction of the requirements as to registration. It is common practice to attach such a certificate to the original charge document and indeed, by *section 402* of the *CA 1985* (as modified), it is obligatory to endorse a copy of the appropriate certificate of registration upon any debenture, or certificate of debenture stock, which is secured by the charge, and which was issued on or after the creation of the charge.

Entries of satisfaction and release 12.31

A feature of the system of registration of company, and hence LLP, charges, which always seems odd to those who are used to the procedures for dealing with individuals' mortgages, is that it is the borrower, not the lender, who is entitled to say that a charge has been paid off, and to inform the Registrar accordingly, without verification from the lender.

Section 403 of the *CA 1985* (as modified) requires that a statutory declaration shall be made in support of such information, to the effect that either the debt for which the charge was given has been paid or satisfied wholly or partly (in which case Form LLP403a is appropriate); or that part of the property charged has either ceased to be charged, or ceased to belong to the LLP (for which Form LLP403b is used).

Further, there is now the option of dealing with such matters by means of electronic communication, in that the Registrar may accept such communication from any designated member of the LLP (or an administrator or administrative receiver) if it verifies the information relevant for either of the above forms, and gives:

- a description of the charge;

- the date of its creation;

- the date of its registration;

- the name and address of the chargee (or trustee, for a debenture);

- details of the property no longer charged, if it is the case that the charge continues, but the property charged has altered.

Since, unlike a statutory declaration, the truthfulness of such an electronic communication would not be protected by the law of perjury, there is a specific offence created of making a false statement in connection with such a communication. When the Registrar completely discharges a register entry, he may be required by the LLP to provide it with a copy of the appropriate memorandum of satisfaction.

Rectification of register   12.32

Mention was made above of the strict time limits which apply to the registration of charges, and the potentially dire consequences of failure to comply (see 12.22). There is however power, in *section 404* of the *CA 1985* (as modified), for the court to act to alleviate the consequences of this.

Under the above provision the court must be satisfied that the omission to register, or to provide correctly a required particular, was accidental or for other reasonable cause, or did not prejudice creditors, or that it is otherwise just and equitable to grant relief. In those circumstances, either the LLP or a person interested (e.g. the chargee) may apply for an order that the time for registration be extended, or that any omission or misstatement be rectified. It may impose such terms and conditions as it believes are just and expedient. The court's discretion is wide, but it is unlikely to be exercised in the LLP's favour if it has already gone into administration, and only exceptionally (e.g. if there has been fraud) will it be exercised if the LLP is in liquidation.

Further, any order for relief is likely to contain a provision that it shall not prejudice the position of any creditor in respect of the interim period, between the time when registration should have been effected and the date of order, so that the position of, for instance, a subsequent and properly registered charge would not be adversely affected (*In Re Ashpurton Estates Limited [1983] Ch 110*).

Appointments of receivers or managers   12.33

If any chargee appoints a receiver or manager of an LLP's property, he must under *section 405* of the *CA 1985* (as modified) notify the Registrar within seven days of appointment, in Form LLP405(1).

Further, the receiver or manager so appointed must notify the Registrar when he ceases to act, in Form LLP405(2). Anyone not complying with these obligations is guilty of an offence, and a daily default fine may be levied.

The LLP's own charges records   12.34

In addition to the Registrar's records, an LLP has its own obligations under *sections 406* and *407* of the *CA 1985* (both as modified). It must keep a copy of every registrable charge which it creates at its registered office. In the case of a series of uniform debentures, a copy of one will suffice.

It must also keep at its registered office a register of charges, on which it must enter all fixed or floating charges, giving a short description of the property charged, the amount secured, and the name(s) of the chargee. Accidental failure to comply is not punishable, but any member knowingly and wilfully authorising or permitting an omission from the register will be guilty of an offence.

These records are public and, under *section 408* of the *CA 1985*, they must be kept open for not less than two hours in each business day and may be inspected by any member or creditor (free) or by any member of the public (who can be made to pay a fee, but not more than the princely sum of five pence). If inspection is refused, every member in default is guilty of an offence, and the court may order immediate inspection.

Investigations of an LLP's affairs

The concept of investigations   **12.35**

One area of the LLP legislation which will be totally new to those who have come from a partnership background is the ability of the Secretary of State to conduct far-reaching investigations into an LLP's affairs.

The privacy of partnership, which could only be disturbed by possible criminal investigation, or on application by a partner to a court, does not protect LLPs. They are subject to the same potentially stringent regime of inspection as any company. The vast majority of LLPs, like the majority of companies, will never encounter anything to do with these provisions, but if things are going wrong for the business the members need to be aware of these powers. Indeed, they themselves may wish to invoke them, if they believe the affairs of the LLP are being wrongly administered, against the law and against their interests.

Application for investigation by the LLP or its members   **12.36**

It is for the above reason (see last sentence of 12.35 above) that the first power of application for an investigation is given, by the modified *section 431* of the *CA 1985*, to the LLP itself, or to not less than one-fifth of those notified to the Registrar as members. There is no minimum number, so that in a five-member LLP it would be open to one member to make such application. In a proper case, this is therefore a powerful weapon in an aggrieved member's hands.

The application to the Secretary of State must be supported by such evidence as he requests, to show that there is good reason for investigation, and by a deposit of not more than (currently) £5,000, for the costs of the investigation. If he is sufficiently persuaded, he may appoint one or more inspectors to report to him, by such means as he thinks fit. Note that the report is to the Secretary of State, not the applicant. How he deals with it is a matter for him, as shown in 12.39 below.

Other causes of commencement of investigation   **12.37**

There are two other routes, under the modified *section 432* of the *CA 1985*, to the commencement of an investigation. One is if a court orders the Secretary of State to undertake the task.

The other route is if he himself is satisfied that he should, on the basis that:

- the LLP's affairs are being, or have been, conducted:
  - ○ fraudulently; or
  - ○ in a manner unfairly prejudicial to some members or their successors in title;
- any particular act or omission is or would be so prejudicial;
- the LLP was formed for a fraudulent or unlawful purpose;
- those who formed or are managing it have been guilty of fraud, misfeasance or misconduct towards the LLP or its members;
- the members have not been given all reasonably expected information.

Inspectors' powers 12.38

The powers given to the appointed inspectors are wide, in accordance with *sections 433* and *434* of the *CA 1985* (as modified).

They may themselves determine to widen the scope of their investigations to any other body corporate (whether LLP or company) in the same group as the LLP. They can require assistance from anyone, and such assistance can include a requirement to attend before them, and /or to produce any documentation of or relating to the LLP or to their investigations. For this purpose documentation will include any form of records, e.g. computer data and records. They may decide to take evidence on oath from any person. Those whose help they may seek specifically include the LLPs past and present members and agents; and its bankers, solicitors and auditors.

Any answers given by anyone may be used against them in civil proceedings, but generally not in criminal proceedings (save in certain specified circumstances in a perjury prosecution). If anyone fails to comply with any requirement of the inspectors, or to reply to their questions, then the inspectors may certify that to the court, with a view to the court's investigating the non-compliance and, if appropriate, holding the person in question liable for contempt of court (*CA 1985, s 436*, as modified).

Inspectors' reports 12.39

The inspectors' report, under the modified *section 437* of the *CA 1985*, to the Secretary of State. They may submit interim reports, or bring particular matters to his attention, or be required to do so.

If, during the investigation, it appears that criminal offences may have been committed, and the relevant prosecuting authorities have been informed, the Secretary of State may call a halt to the investigation or a defined part of it, in which case the inspectors shall only report if their original appointment was by the court, or if the Secretary of State directs them to do so.

The inspectors' reports are, under the modified *section 441* of the *CA 1985*, admissible in any proceedings as evidence of their opinion and, in proceedings under the *Company Directors Disqualification Act 1986*, as evidence of fact. If their appointment was initially by the court, a copy of their report must be given to that court. Otherwise, the Secretary of State normally has a discretion as to how (if at all) he wishes to make the report known to anyone, unless the original appointment was directed by him of his own volition, and on terms that the report was not for publication. He may decide to:

- forward a copy to the LLP's registered office; or

- publish the report; or

- provide copies, on request and on payment, to:

  - any member;

  - anyone whose conduct is referred to in the report;

  - the auditors;

  - the original applicants for the investigation;

  - anyone else whose financial interests appear affected, whether as a creditor or otherwise.

Power to sue on the LLP's behalf   12.40

If, as a result of any investigations as above, the Secretary of State concludes that it is in the public interest for any civil proceedings to be brought by him on the LLP's behalf, he may under *section 438* of the *CA 1985* (as modified) take such proceedings in the LLP's name.

He must however indemnify the LLP against any costs and expenses related to the litigation.

Costs of investigations   12.41

The Secretary of State is initially liable for all of an investigation's costs, but he can in certain circumstances seek under *section 439* of the *CA 1985* (as modified) to recover those costs, which will include general staff costs and overheads, and the costs of such civil proceedings as above.

Recovery may be effected against anyone convicted in proceedings brought as a result of the investigation, or against whom an order for costs is made in any such civil proceedings as above. Further, if such civil proceedings result in a payment to or a recovery of property by the LLP, then the costs of the investigation are a first charge on the sums payable or money recovered.

The LLP itself may have to pay the expenses (though the Secretary of State may grant relief against this) if the original application was made neither by it, nor by the Secretary of State. If the original application was by the LLP or its members, the emphasis is slightly different, in that the applicants are liable, to such extent as the Secretary of State directs. (In the exercise of this discretion, the Secretary of State may be guided by any comments made by the inspectors.)

Power to require production of documents   **12.42**

There is also a lesser power available to the Secretary of State, if he is concerned about an LLP's affairs, but does not want to launch a full scale investigation. He may, instead, exercise the power given to him under *section 447* of the *CA 1985* (as modified) to require the LLP to produce such documents as he may specify to him or an appointed officer. ('Documents' has the same wide interpretation as in 12.38 above.) He merely needs to conclude that he has good reason to make such a demand.

The power extends to anyone in possession of the appropriate documents (but without prejudice to any lien on them). The power includes the right to copy documents as produced, and to require an explanation for them. If the documents are not produced, the person to whom the requirement was directed must state where he believes them to be. Failure to comply with such a requirement is an offence, though it is a defence to prove that the documents were not in the defendant's power or possession, and that it was not reasonably practical for him to comply with the requirement. Any statement made may be used in proceedings, as in 12.38 above (but with the same restrictions on their use in criminal proceedings as are mentioned there).

Entry and search of premises   **12.43**

All of these powers discussed above are of course subject to efforts to circumvent them, and as a back-up it is necessary for there to be powers to enter and search premises. Those powers, under *section 448* of the *CA 1985* (as modified), are however exercisable only on obtaining of a warrant from a justice of the peace, who is satisfied by evidence on oath given by or on behalf of the Secretary of State or his appointees, as to the relevant circumstances. A warrant is effective for a month.

There are two distinct possibilities. One is where there has already been a demand for the production of documents, which has not been complied with. The other is a pre-emptive strike, where it can be shown to the JP that:

- there are reasonable grounds for believing that a serious offence has been committed;

- there are documents relevant to that offence upon the premises;

- there is power to demand the production of the documents;

- there are reasonable grounds for belief that, if the warrant is not granted, the documents would be removed, hidden, tampered with or destroyed.

The offence in question must be one which is punishable, on indictment, by at least two years' imprisonment.

Undertaking the search   12.44

The warrant (see 12.43 above) grants authorisation to the police and to any other named person, such as the investigating inspector. Such persons may use reasonable force to enter the premises in question. They may search for, take possession of, and copy any of the appropriate documents, which again are widely defined and could include computer data.

They may also ask any person named in the warrant for an explanation of the documents or, if they are not found, to state where they are. Any documents found can be kept for three months or, if consequent criminal proceedings are taken, until the end of those proceedings. Note this extended period does not apply in the event that the proceedings commenced are civil proceedings (as per 12.40 above). Anyone intentionally obstructing the exercise of these rights, or failing without reasonable excuse to give a requested explanation, is guilty of an offence.

Handling information received   12.45

Naturally, information obtained under these procedures may be extremely sensitive. Unless therefore it is required for official purposes, it must not be published or disclosed without the LLP's prior written consent, and anyone who does disclose or publish such information is guilty of an offence under *section 449* of the *CA 1985* (as modified).

For this purpose there are however a wide range of possible official purposes, which can range from a conventional prosecution to professional disciplinary proceedings. In the legislation there 20 instances are stipulated, and 16 possible prosecutors are listed. This applies not only to information obtained under the *section 447* procedure, but also, by *section 451A* of the *CA 1985* (as modified), to information obtained during an investigation.

Destruction etc. of an LLP's documents 12.46

It may of course be that even a pre-emptive strike is too late, and that the relevant documents (again including computer records) have been got at before the authorities get to them. It is therefore an offence, under *section 450* of the *CA 1985* (as modified), for any person to destroy, mutilate, falsify or make a false entry in any document affecting or relating to the LLP's property or affairs, or to be privy to any such act. It is however a defence to be able to prove that the defendant had no intention to conceal the state of affairs or to defeat the law.

Similarly, it is an offence fraudulently to part with, alter, or create an omission in any such document, or to be privy thereto. (The statutory defence mentioned is not appropriate here as fraudulent intent is a constituent of the charge.)

Giving false information 12.47

Another natural risk is that any statement made, or explanation given, will be false. Accordingly, it is an offence under *section 451* of the *CA 1985* (as modified) knowingly or recklessly to make or give a statement or explanation which is false in a material particular.

Privileged information 12.48

There are, under *section 452* of the *CA 1985*, two specific exceptions to the obligation to co-operate in an investigation, or to produce documents demanded or an explanation of them.

The first exception applies if the information of which disclosure is sought would, in High Court proceedings, be subject to legal professional privilege. (One exception is that a lawyer must, if asked, disclose the name and address of his client.)

The other exception is if the information is held by bankers who owe, in respect of it, an obligation of confidence to someone other than the LLP. In that instance the bankers are only obliged to disclose if either the person to whom the duty of confidence is owed consents, or the Secretary of State specifically so directs. In the case of the production of documents, the bankers must produce the document only if the demand for its production relates to an investigation into the customer's affairs, or the customer is someone of whom a demand under *section 447* has been made (see 12.42 above).

Order for production and inspection of books   **12.49**

The last provision in the *CA 1985*, with regard to the investigation of an LLP's affairs, is tucked away right at the end, in the modified *section 721*. There, it is provided that a court has power to make an order for the production and inspection of an LLP's books.

Application must be made to the High Court, by the Director of Public Prosecutions, or a chief officer of police. He has to show to the court that there is reasonable cause to believe that someone has, whilst a member of an LLP, committed an offence in connection with the management of the LLP's affairs, and that evidence thereof is to be found in any books or papers of the LLP. If so satisfied, the court may authorise any person named in its order to inspect the books and papers in question for the purpose of investigating the alleged offence. It may also require any named member of the LLP to produce the books and papers to a named person at a named place.

Such an order can also be made in respect of any bankers' books and papers so far as they relate to the LLP's affairs, save that no order can be made for the production of the documents, as distinct from requiring inspection of them.

No order made under this section is appealable. The ambit of this section seems not to be as wide as the provisions of *section 431 et seq*, (see 12.36 *et seq.* above), as those refer to 'documents' which are defined as including 'information recorded in any form'; whereas this section refers consistently to 'books and papers', which expression is, in turn, defined by the modified *section 744* of the *CA 1985* to include 'accounts deeds, writings and documents', whilst the definition of 'documents' later in that section does not make any reference to non-paper records. In other words, it seems as if the court, under this section, does not have the power to order inspection or production of computer records.

Financial Services Act 1986 investigations   **12.50**

Investigations may of course also be conducted into an LLP's affairs under other, more specific, statutes. One is the *Insolvency Act 1986*, and reference is made in the chapter on insolvency to these (see Chapter 16).

Chief amongst the other statutes is the *Financial Services Act 1986*. There are a number of sets of provisions in the *FSA 1986*, some of which link in with the *CA 1985* investigation procedure examined in the previous paragraphs above. These, briefly, are:

- investigation by the Secretary of State into the affairs of the managers of unit trusts or other collective investment schemes under *section 94* of the *FSA 1986*, where the procedure is similar to the provisions of *sections 434* and *436* of the *CA 1985*, and similar exclusions apply in relation to legal privilege or bankers' duty of confidence;

- investigative powers under *sections 105* and *106* of the *FSA 1986* in relation to any investment business, with powers for requiring the production of documents;

- investigations into possible insider dealing under *sections 177* and *178* of the *FSA 1986*;

- powers of entry under *section 199* of the *FSA 1986*.

Facing an investigation   **12.51**

In a number of cases above, reference has been made to the forms of investigation etc., and to the position facing the individual of whom questions may be raised. Has that person, such as a member in an LLP, any way out?

One option is to challenge, by way of judicial review, the decision to launch the investigation in the first place. Such a challenge is however unlikely to succeed, in the light of the decision in *Norwest Holst Limited v Secretary of State for Trade [1978] Ch 201*, to the effect that the decision to start an investigation is a purely administrative one to which the rules of natural justice do not apply. Further, the Secretary of State may not be obliged even to disclose his source, or his reasons. (In passing, any LLP suspicious that the source of information leading to any investigation may be a member of staff will need to bear in mind the effect of the 'Whistleblowers Act', i.e. the *Public Interest Disclosure Act 1998*, which may well give protection to the staff member in question.)

Another possibility, especially if proceedings have already been commenced against the individual of whom questions are being posed, is attempting to justify refusal on the grounds of self-incrimination. This may or may not help in any given circumstance, but at least it should go to the 'reasonableness' of any refusal to co-operate where that is necessary. The potential impact of the *Human Rights Act 1998* on this area of law is also an area which will need future investigation by the courts.

Arrangements and reconstructions

Available remedies   **12.52**

The various subsequent chapters on insolvency (see Chapter 13 to 17) deal with the more formal ways of an LLP dealing with difficult financial situations, including voluntary arrangements under the *Insolvency Act 1986.*

However, there is also power under the *CA 1985* for an LLP to effect a compromise with either its creditors, or its members; and power to carry out a reconstruction or amalgamation. These provisions are contained in *sections 425* to *427* of the *CA 1985* (as modified). Compromises and arrangements are widely construed, and are much wider than reconstructions and amalgamations. The LLP must however be a party to any such new terms, and in an 'arrangement' there must be some real degree of give and take between the interested parties. There is a major body of case law in respect of these provisions, and reference should be made to any of the standard company law texts, such as *Tolley's Company Law* (in particular 'Reconstructions and Amalgamations', R2001 onwards) for detailed guidance as to the parameters of the provisions, and the method of their implementation. This text will simply give an overview.

Summoning meetings to consider compromises **12.53**

A compromise can be between the LLP and either its creditors, or its members (or, in either case, any class of them). If a compromise is proposed, an application can be made to the court by anyone prospectively affected, i.e. the LLP itself, or any creditor or member.

Further, if the LLP is in the course of being wound up, or if an administration order has been made, the liquidator or administrator also has power to apply. The court may direct a meeting of the creditors, or the members, or the affected class of either. The court directs the manner of summoning the meeting (which, in the light of the voting provisions below, presumably needs to include provision for proxy voting).

Proceedings at meetings to consider compromises 12.54

To be effective, a compromise or arrangement needs approval from two sources. First, it needs the sanction of the court. Broadly, that sanction is likely to be based on the objective test approved in *Re Dorman Long & Company Limited [1934] 1 Ch 635*, to the effect that the court will grant sanction if the proposals are something that an 'intelligent and honest' person considering their interest 'might reasonably approve'.

Secondly, it needs the approval of at least 75 per cent of those voting either in person or by proxy at the meeting (i.e., as the case may be, the creditors, or the members, or the appropriate class of them). (Confusingly, the statute refers to 'a majority in number representing three-fourths in value of the creditors . . . or members . . .'. The expression 'in value' is easy enough to understand in the case of creditors, but it is difficult in the case of members. Presumably, if it is intended to apply to members, it has to refer to their investment in the LLP, but there is no guidance as to whether that might only be initially invested capital, or would for instance include retained profit. However, it does seem to rule out a one-member-one-vote arrangement in this scenario.)

If thus dually sanctioned, the compromise is binding on all those for whom the meeting was called, i.e. creditors or members etc. It is also binding on the LLP itself, and, if the LLP is being wound up, on the liquidators and contributories. The order only takes effect upon an office copy thereof being delivered to the registrar. If the LLP fails to deliver that office copy it, and every member in default, is guilty of an offence.

Information as to the compromise 12.55

When any such meeting as is referred to the three previous paragraphs above is called, each creditor or member entitled to attend has to be sent notice of the meeting. That must be accompanied by a statement explaining what the effect of the compromise would be, and in particular whether it would have any distinct effect on members because of their material interests.

If the meeting is to be advertised, there needs to be either a statement as above published with it, or an indication of where and how creditors or members could access without charge a copy of such a statement. Additionally, if the rights of debenture holders would be affected, information as to that must be given.

If the LLP defaults in any of these procedural conditions, an offence is committed by it and by any member (which for this purpose includes any liquidator and any debenture trustee) in default. It is however a defence for any person to show that the default was due to the refusal of a member or debenture holder to supply to him the necessary details of that person's material interest in the compromise. Such persons in turn are under a duty to supply those details, and commit an offence if they do not.

Reconstructions and amalgamations   12.56

Amongst the circumstances in which such compromises or arrangements may be proposed is where the idea is for either a reconstruction of any LLP(s); or the amalgamation of any two or more LLPs.

There is guidance in the body of case law which has developed in the company context as to what may fall within the terms 'reconstruction' or 'amalgamation'. Essentially, the former will normally require some degree of restructuring, and involves the passing of most of business A's undertaking to business B, where both businesses are controlled by substantially the same group of people – *Re South African Supply and Cold Storage Co [1904] 2 Ch 268*. It may apply to a partition of a business, or a demerger. It may be important to establish whether any proposals do fall within the definition, as it may have tax and stamp duty purposes. Amalgamations are simpler to consider, and can include the absorption of one business within another, rather than needing the creation of a wholly new entity.

Detailed orders   12.57

If, in any such scenario, all or any part of the undertaking or property of an LLP ('the transferor') is to be transferred to another LLP ('the transferee'), then there are certain specific matters which the court may rule upon, either when giving the sanction for proposals, or at any subsequent time. These are:

- the transfer of all or any part of the undertaking, property and liabilities of the transferor;

- the appropriation to any person of any of the LLP's property or interest;

- the continuation by or against the transferee of any pending litigation;

- the dissolution (without winding up) of the transferor;

- provisions for what is to happen in regard to dissenters;

- incidental and supplemental matters needed to effect the changes.

The order itself effects the vesting of any property or liabilities ordered to be transferred, and it can, if the arrangements so provide, free the property of any charge. An office copy of any such order made, whether in relation to the sanction and meeting, or the detailed provisions, must be deposited by the LLP with the Registrar within seven days of its making. If this is not done, the LLP, and every member in default, is guilty of an offence and a daily default fine may be levied.

The use of the compromise provisions 12.58

To an extent, these provisions may have had their day, except for reconstructions or amalgamations of solvent LLPs. The relevant provisions in the *IA 1986* for voluntary arrangements (when brought into force) may be more attractive for insolvent LLPs, insofar as they will introduce to company voluntary arrangements (or CVAs) (and hence those for LLPs) a moratorium such as that which has always been available for individual voluntary arrangements (or IVAs). There are however snags – see 13.26 to 13.29 below.

There may therefore still be advantages in an insolvency context in following the arrangement and reconstruction route, such as the fact that there is no requirement for a nominee/supervisor, so that the operational costs of a compromise may be less. Otherwise, the likely area for their use will be where LLPs can seek to overcome unreasonable minority dissent to sensible and financially viable restructuring.

Protection from unfair prejudice

The remedy in CA 1985, section 459 12.59

Having dealt with the position where an uncooperative minority may be overcome (see 12.52 onwards), it is perhaps appropriate to turn to the opposite side of the coin, i.e. where there is unfair action being taken against the minority by the majority.

During the progress of the LLP legislation through Parliament, one much debated topic was whether it was appropriate for there to be any protection for a minority or whether, since the basic philosophy of the legislation was to leave members to sort out their own arrangements by their partnership agreement, this would be inappropriate. This was chiefly considered in the context of an individual member seeking to get his investment out of the LLP. The Government eventually took the stance that it would not legislate at all for the removal of capital etc, but that it would permit the same degree of protection for a member as for a shareholder, under *section 459* of the *CA 1985*.

Excluding the section

12.60

One important proviso, however, was that the LLP's members were to be able to exclude the section. Hence, by the modified *section 459(1A)* of the *CA 1985*, it is provided that the members of an LLP may, by unanimous agreement, exclude the rights in the section, for such period as they may agree. Presumably, that period can be indefinite.

The agreement need not be in writing, but it must be recorded in writing, so presumably properly written-up minutes of a members' meeting would suffice. There is nothing to say that this cannot be dealt with in the initial LLP partnership agreement, and indeed it is recommended that it should be, as that is the time the members, and the agreement's draftsman, will be considering the issue of future capital withdrawal, and hence this would be the sensible time for this issue to be aired and determined. There is no halfway house – either the section applies in its totality or it does not.

The nature of the right

12.61

The essential right is for a member of an LLP to petition the court, on the grounds that the LLP's affairs are being, or have been, conducted in a manner which is unfairly prejudicial. The prejudice can be either to all members, or some part of the membership, including the petitioner at least.

The petition may also apply to any specific act or omission, whether actual or proposed. The procedure for any petition is laid down in the *Companies (Unfair Prejudice Applications) Proceedings Rules 1986 (SI 1986/2000)*, and the *Insolvency Rules 1986 (SI 1986/1925)*.

An alternative route to the court, however, is that the Secretary of State may, under *section 460* of the *CA 1985* (as modified), apply to the court if he believes there is or has been any such prejudicial conduct, or that any actual or proposed act or omission would be so prejudicial, if he is drawn to that conclusion by any investigations etc. which he has conducted, or any inspector's report which has been presented to him. Such an application may be in addition to, or in place of, a petition by the Secretary of State for the winding up of the LLP.

Available remedies   **12.62**

The court's available remedies are very wide, in that under *section 461* of the *CA 1985*, it may, if it is satisfied that the petition is well founded, 'make such order as it thinks fit for giving relief in respect of the matters complained of'.

Without prejudice to the breadth of the above power, there are certain specific provisions which may be included in the list of remedies, namely orders to:

- regulate the future conduct of the LLP's affairs;

- stop the LLP from doing or continuing an act complained of;

- require the LLP to do an act it has omitted to do;

- authorise civil proceedings to be brought in the LLP's name, and on its behalf, on such terms as the court may direct;

- provide for any member's interest in the LLP to be bought out by other members, or by the LLP itself;

- restrain the LLP from generally or specifically altering the LLP's partnership agreement without leave;

- make any alteration to the LLP's partnership agreement.

Judicial application of section 459   **12.63**

There is a large body of case law concerning *section 459* in general, and the derivative remedy (i.e. the taking of action in the LLP's name) in particular. Readers are referred to the standard company law texts, such as *Tolley's Company Law* ('Shareholders', S4001 onwards).

It has been very difficult to draw principles out of this body of law, as courts have often indicated that their judgments are related only to the facts before them. There is however one major recent case which is of considerable importance to an understanding of the position, especially since the DTI's Company Law Review Steering Group in its final report has come down on the side of preserving, rather than overturning, the ruling in that case. This is *O'Neill v Phillips [1999] 2 All ER 961*, where the House of Lords attempted to strike a balance between the apparent breadth of discretion given to the courts by the section, and the desirability of legal certainty. Their view was that 'fairness' had to be judged in the context of the commercial structure within which people had chosen to work. In the company context that related to the memorandum and articles of association, and any shareholders' agreement. In the LLP context, it would presumably relate to the partnership agreement and such of the default provisions as are applicable. Nonetheless, 'unfairness' did not have to relate to a breach of the duties imposed by those agreements, but could consist of 'using the rules in a manner which equity would regard as contrary to good faith'.

Practical application to LLPs   12.64

The result of the comparatively narrow approach in *O'Neill v Phillips* (see 12.63 above) would seem to be that it will be difficult for members to seek the remedy of a *section 459* petition. They have the opportunity to select either to rely upon the default provisions in *regulations* 7 and 8, or to formulate their own rules under a partnership agreement.

Members could be said to have more opportunity than company shareholders to choose the rules by which they will conduct their business. That being so, the instances where, in the absence of a breach of those rules, equity will permit the courts to step in will seemingly be limited. This could occur in the context of a situation which is provided for neither in the default provisions nor in an agreement. There might be instances where the majority was acting to frustrate the minority's 'legitimate expectations' derived from the conduct of the parties, a concept espoused in *Re Saul D Harrison & Sons plc [1994] BCC 475* – but it was specifically stated in *O'Neill v Phillips* that that was itself a doctrine which was limited and should not be allowed to expand too freely.

The courts, which acknowledge the undesirable cost and complexity of *section 459* proceedings (even in the days of proactive case management under the *Civil Procedure Rules*) will presumably not encourage applications. All of this indicates once again how important it is that the LLP should, at the outset, have a properly formed partnership agreement which accurately reflects the members' wishes, and should regularly review that agreement.

Orders under section 459   12.65

There were however also some guidelines in *O'Neill v Phillips* (see 12.63 above) as to the nature of an order which might be made, in the typical situation where a minority shareholder was trying to compel the purchase of his shareholding, where the 'unfairness' underlying his claim was his exclusion from the affairs of the business without a fair offer being made for his shares.

The principles which applied to a reasonable offer, which presumably would apply to a member of an LLP with little adjustment, were:

- the offer should be without any minority shareholding discount;

- if not agreed, the value should be determined by an expert;

- the offeror should agree to such expert determination;

- both parties should have equal access to the expert and equal opportunity to pass information to him about the company;

- the offeror should not automatically have to pay costs, if not given a reasonable time to make an offer before the petition was issued.

Unilateral withdrawal 12.66

The legislation provides that a member may unilaterally withdraw from membership by notice. There is however no statutory provision for his right to withdraw his capital. There may of course be a mechanism in an express agreement for him to do so, either because it gives other members the right to acquire his share, and they choose to do; or because they are required by the agreement to do so.

What then of the situation where ether there is no agreement, or where the remaining members choose not to exercise an option to buy out the retiring member? He has of course the possibility of applying for the winding up of the LLP, on the grounds that it would be just and equitable (see 16.6 and 16.7 below), but this will not necessarily be readily granted. Will he, just because he has decided to go, have the right to a remedy under *section 459* of the *CA 1985*? *O'Neill v Phillips* suggests not. It was there stated that it was not the case that 'a member who has not been dismissed or excluded can demand that his shares be purchased simply because he feels that he has lost trust and confidence in the others'.

There seems no reason to think that the above would not be applied to LLPs, and any member considering unilateral withdrawal should therefore consider very carefully, before giving his notice, what rights the partnership agreement gives him.

The Registrar 12.67

The Registrar of Companies is referred to throughout this work as 'the Registrar' (or occasionally and colloquially as 'Companies House'). His position, establishment and powers in relation to LLPs are set out in *sections 705 to 714* of the *CA 1985* (as modified). They are effectively exactly the same as for companies, and so are not examined in detail here.

Miscellaneous and supplementary provisions   **12.68**

In similar fashion to provisions about the Registrar (see 12.67above), the miscellaneous and supplementary provisions contained in *sections 722 to 734* of the *CA 1985* are applied to LLPs, without any substantive variations.

13 – Voluntary Arrangements

> This chapter looks at the first set of provisions under the *Insolvency Act 1986*, as applied to LLPs, namely voluntary arrangements. These are provisions designed to allow insolvent LLPs, which believe they can custom-design a set of proposals which will offer their creditors a better outcome than a winding up, and which will allow the LLP to survive, to seek the sanction of statute and the courts for those proposals.
>
> The chapter looks at the ways of creating such arrangements, and the advantages and drawbacks of them from the perspectives of both the LLP and the body of creditors.

Applying the 1986 Act   13.1

The *IA 1986* is applied to LLPs by virtue of *SI 2001/1090, reg 5* (see 1.14 above). This applies six of the first seven Parts of the First Group of Parts of the *IA 1986* (*Part V* being the exception) and the Third Group of Parts. Further, *regulation 10* of and *Schedule 6* to *SI 2001/1090* apply the *Insolvency Rules 1986* (and various other ancillary insolvency-related statutory instruments) so that references in this chapter and in Chapters 14 to 17 to 'Rules' are to the Insolvency Rules.

In effect the legislation equates LLPs to companies in the insolvency context. It applies the provisions with some standard modifications, e.g. that references to a director or officer of a company are to be taken to include reference to a member of an LLP, and that (importantly) references to a 'shadow director' shall include references to a 'shadow member'. It also equates an LLP's partnership agreement to the memorandum and articles of association of a company. Certain more detailed adaptations are however needed, and it therefore goes on, in the by now familiar columnar form, to set these out in *SI 2001/1090, Sch 3*. All references in this chapter and in Chapters 14 to 17 which also deal with insolvency issues, are to the *IA 1986* as so applied.

The concept of voluntary arrangements   **13.2**

The underlying basis of an arrangement is that of the law of contract, i.e. that it is a deal struck between an LLP and its then creditors as to a partial and/or delayed settlement of its debts, which becomes binding on the creditors. The non-contractual overlay is that it only needs 75 per cent (by value) of the creditors to approve the arrangement for it to become binding upon all, i.e. it is a species of contract to which a creditor may become bound despite never having agreed to it.

The idea is not normally that, as in a receivership, the 'supervisor' of the voluntary arrangement shall actually take over the running of the LLP's business and be entitled to collect its book debts directly; but rather that the LLP will be allowed to continue to run its own affairs, provided that it hands over to the supervisor any assets specified in the proposals as being for the benefit of the arrangement creditors, whether those be tangible assets for sale, lump sums, or periodical payments from the LLP's revenue.

Once in the hands of the supervisor, these sums become subject to a trust in favour of the arrangement's creditors, which may be implicit, but is spelt out in the better drafted sets of proposals, for the avoidance of doubt. Arrangements may however even go beyond that pattern, and the Court of Appeal has held that it is possible for a voluntary arrangement to contemplate that no funds will be paid to unsecured creditors during the period of the arrangement, if they have the right to prosecute their claims after it comes to an end – *Commissioners of Inland Revenue v Adam & Partners Limited [2000] BPIR 986.*

The role of the nominee/supervisor   **13.3**

Another difference from the straightforward concept of a contract is that a third party is introduced into the equation. An independent professional is called upon to act firstly as the nominee, in the framing of the proposals for the arrangement, and then, if they are approved, as supervisor of the arrangement, with his fees being provided for in the arrangement. (Hitherto, the role has been confined to licensed insolvency practitioners, but the *Insolvency Act 2000 (IA 2000)* when brought fully into force, will allow the Government to nominate other professional bodies, from amongst the ranks of those dealing generally with business recovery and turn-round.)

As such, the nominee/supervisor owes duties to the creditors and the court, as well as to the LLP. This can lead to some difficult situations, and the members of an LLP which fails to fulfil its obligations under an arrangement may find that the friendly supervisor who helped them out of their problems in the first place by framing the proposals ends up petitioning for the winding up of the LLP, in order to fulfil the duties placed upon him. A supervisor's duty is essentially only to the creditors of the arrangement, as distinct from post-arrangement creditors, and he is not generally under a duty of care to the latter group – *Heritage Joinery v Krasner [1999] BPIR 683.*

Framing the proposals   13.4

In the 15 years since arrangements became a possibility, certain principles surrounding the framing of proposals have become evident. The first such principle is that they need above all to be practical. In the early years, all too many proposals were submitted which put forward unrealistic dividends of ten per cent or less for unsecured creditors, and which ended up benefiting those insolvency practitioners who had lent their names to them more than anyone else.

Another of these principles is that, since the *IA 1986* is quite deliberately silent as to what needs to go into proposals, they should be sufficiently broadly drawn as to cover every contingency that can reasonably be foreseen. An example of this is the case of *Pitt v Mond [2001] BPIR 624,* which held that in 1990 (when arrangements were in their infancy) it was not negligence on the part of a nominee/supervisor to have failed to have provided for what the consequences might be if there was a steep fall in property prices, but hinted that in the more developed climate of 2000 more might be expected of the proposals' draftsman.

The proposals should be sufficiently precise to allow all parties to under-stand what is required of them. Perhaps most important of all (since almost by definition the small print will need most closely examining when things are going wrong) they need to define carefully what may constitute the failure of an arrangement, and what the consequences of failure should be. (One practical point is that the provisions of an insolvency practitioner's standard conditions, which are often annexed to the proposals, should be carefully checked, as they may contain provisions which have been tacked on since the standard was originally drafted, and which may be inconsistent either with the main proposals, or even with each other.)

Practical difficulties of LLP arrangements   13.5

There are two practical difficulties which may afflict those seeking to put proposals together for an arrangement for an LLP. The first is one which LLPs will share with partnerships, namely that in many cases where the LLP hits difficulties, its members as individuals will also be having difficulties, which will include failure to pay their Schedule D income tax. Such tax is now, under the self-assessment regime, a personal debt, and not a debt of the LLP, and so it will not be affected by the LLP's arrangement. If the members are not to end up being bankrupted personally, and thus unable to fulfil the roles needed of them in order for the LLP's arrangement to work, then there will need to be interlocking personal voluntary arrangements, which adds to the cost and complexity of the operation.

The other practical difficulty is the lack (at present) of any period of moratorium, and this is returned to in detail at the end of this chapter (see 13.26 below).

Proposing the arrangement   13.6

There are two ways in which an arrangement for an LLP may be proposed. Firstly, if the LLP is not already the subject of insolvency proceedings, it may itself propose the arrangement to its creditors (*IA 1986, s 1(1)*, as modified).

The other way is that, if the LLP already has an administrator or a liquidator in charge of its affairs, that person may also propose such an arrangement (often as a means of closure to the formal insolvency proceedings). In the latter case the proposal is not only to the creditors, but to the LLP as well (*IA 1986, s 1(3)*, as modified).

In either case, whether by making the proposal, or by considering an administrator's or liquidator's proposal, the LLP has to make a decision of fundamental importance. The partnership agreement should therefore contain provision for how this is to be considered, e.g. is a meeting necessary and, if so, what rules apply to it.

The LLP's proposal   13.7

Where the proposal is that of the LLP itself, it is for the designated members to submit to the nominee the proposals for the arrangement, followed within seven days by a statement of affairs (though in practice these will both be drafted by the nominee with the aid of information given to him) (*IA 1986, s 2(3)*, as modified). (*Rules 1.3* and *1.5* respectively govern the minimum contents of the proposals and the statement of affairs.)

The nominee then first has to endorse a copy of the notice with his willingness to act, and return the endorsed copy to the LLP (*Rule 1.4*). Next, he submits a report to the court (within 28 days, or such longer period as the court may allow, after he is given notice of the proposal) stating whether in his opinion, a meeting of creditors should be called to consider the proposals and, if so, where and when (*IA 1986, s 2(2)*, as modified). He then summons that meeting by notifying all creditors of whom he is aware (*IA 1986, s 3*, as modified).

The date of the meeting must be not less than 14, nor more than 28 days from the date of the filing of his report, and notice must be given as above not less than 14 days before the meeting, accompanied by copies of the proposal, the statement of affairs, a note of the nominee's comments, and information as to the court in which the proposals were lodged (*Rule 1.9*). Notice of the creditors' meeting should be given not only to all members, but also to all those who have been members in the immediately preceding two years, if the convenor thinks their presence needed (*Rule 1.16*). The convenor may however exclude any such member or former member from the meeting (whether or not previously notified) – this provision being inserted to prevent disruption of the meeting by a dissatisfied member.

The creditors' meeting 13.8

The purpose of the meeting referred to in 13.7 above, which is governed by *section 4* of the *IA 1986*, is to consider whether to approve the proposals, with or without modifications, amongst which may be the substitution of another suitably qualified practitioner for the initially proposed supervisor.

Modifications are often proposed by Crown and other major creditors, e.g. banks, and they inevitably tighten the conditions of the proposals, e.g. by introducing tougher criteria for defining the failure of the proposals. Often they are only put forward at the last minute. Care needs to be taken that they are not contradictory to or inconsistent with other provisions in the proposals, which are not directly affected by the modifications, or there can be later difficulties in interpretation of the amended proposals. Certain proposals or modifications may not be accepted without the approval of anyone adversely affected, i.e:

- those which affect the rights of a secured creditor to enforce his security;

- those whereby any preferential debt is not to be given its proper priority over other debts;

- those whereby there is any difference between the proportional dividends payable to creditors in respect of different preferential debts.

Conduct of the meeting 13.9

When notice of meetings is sent out, a form of proxy must be enclosed (*Rule 1.13*). Whoever convenes the meeting must act as chairman or, if he cannot be present, must nominate someone from within his firm who is either a licensed insolvency practitioner in his own right, or an employee of the convenor's firm experienced in insolvency matters (*Rule 1.14*).

In practice, the senior manager who has the day-to-day conduct of the file in the nominee's office will often be so appointed. Frequently, the chairman will hold proxy votes, but must not use such proxies to increase his firm's remuneration unless specifically so directed (*Rule 1.15*).

Voting at creditors' meetings 13.10

Any notified creditor is entitled to vote at the creditors' meeting, in person or by proxy. His vote is governed by the size of his debt as at the date of the meeting (or, if the LLP is already in administration or being wound up, as at the date of commencement of the relevant proceedings).

If the debt is unascertained or unliquidated, the only way it can be admitted to vote is if the chairman puts a minimum agreed figure on it. Decisions on how much debt is to be admitted, or whether a claim is to be rejected, are left to the chairman of the meeting, though an aggrieved creditor can appeal to the court. A cautious chairman may decide to admit a contested claim, but mark it as objected to, on the basis that a successful objector can then seek to have that creditor's vote declared invalid. Any application to the court must be commenced within 28 days of the chairman's report to the court of the outcome of the meeting, and the court has no discretion to extend that period – *Re Bournemouth & Boscombe AFC Co Ltd [1998] BPIR 183*. The chairman cannot become personally liable for the costs of any successful objection. If a court disapproves of a chairman's decision it may – but only if it considers that the issue complained of gave rise to unfair prejudice or material irregularity – reverse or vary the decision, or summon another meeting, or may such order as it thinks fit.

All the above procedures are laid down in *Rule 1.17*.

Voting at members' meetings 13.11

What is less clear is what the procedures are to be for voting at members' meetings, if requisite, i.e. if the proposals are made by an administrator or liquidator (see 13.21 below).

Rule 1.18, in the company context, gives members of a company votes equivalent to the voting rights represented by their shares. No such concept is of course applicable to members of an LLP. The rule goes on to say that references to a member's shares include 'any other interest which he may have as a member of the company'. It might be suggested therefore that members of an LLP should have votes equivalent to their proportionate interests in the capital of the LLP. The problem is defining what such capital might be, e.g. should it be considered to include a member's share of retained and undrawn or unallocated profits.

This is an area where the draftsman of an LLP partnership agreement should attempt to lay down some clear principles, in the hope that these would be followed by the court, even though the rule itself is not adapted for the LLP scenario and therefore makes no reference to such agreements (even by reference to articles).

Majorities at creditors' meetings 13.12

The requisite majorities at a creditors' meeting are calculated under *Rule 1.19* by reference to the aggregate value of the creditors voting for or against any resolution, either in person or by proxy. In the case of a resolution to approve any proposal or modification, a majority in excess of 75 per cent is needed (i.e. exactly 75 per cent is not sufficient). For any other resolution a majority in excess of 50 per cent will do. Claims shall be omitted (wholly or partly as appropriate) if they are un-notified; or wholly or partly secured; or wholly or partly derived from a bill of exchange or promissory note (though there are exceptions to the latter).

A similar position to that set out above applies with regard to seeking relief from the court if aggrieved by any decision of the chairman. Further, if a claim is disputed, even if admitted for voting purposes, there is (unless the arrangements themselves say otherwise) nothing to prevent a claimant bringing and pursuing proceedings to establish the correctness of his claim – *Alman v Approach Housing Limited [2001] BPIR 203*.

Majorities at members' meetings 13.13

By contrast (see 13.12 above), at members' meetings called by a proposing administrator or liquidator (see 13.21 below), a majority in excess of 50 per cent will by *Rule 1.20* suffice for any resolution.

In this instance, however, this is expressed to be subject to any contrary provision in the partnership agreement.

Adjournments of meetings 13.14

The chairman has a fairly broad discretion to deal with necessary adjournments, under *Rule 1.21*.

He can, for instance, adjourn until later on in the originally designated day, and may even decide to combine the members' and creditors' meetings (if the former is needed – see 13.21 below). Alternatively, he may adjourn for up to 14 days. Notice of adjournment shall be given to the court.

Acceptance of modifications by the LLP 13.15

One specific addition to the modified provisions of *section 4* of the *IA 1986* is a new sub-section (*s 4(5A)*) requiring the chairman of the meeting to ascertain from the LLP, before the end of the meeting, whether it approves of any modifications. If the LLP is silent, it is presumed not to agree to them.

In practice, this means that there have to be some representatives of the LLP present at the meeting who are authorised by the LLP to give its consent to modifications, of which the LLP as a body may have had no prior notice. If it is not in a position to do this, then unless the chairman adjourns the meeting its dissent is presumed, creditors who would approve amended proposals may vote against the original version, and the proposals may fail. The partnership agreement should therefore clearly provide for who is to be so authorised, and how.

Passing of property 13.16

As soon as an arrangement is approved, i.e. without needing any court sanction, any assets which are due to go to the supervisor should be passed to him under *Rule 1.23* by the LLP (or the administrator or liquidator thereof if the proposals were made by him – see 13.21 below).

In the latter case the appropriate practitioner's fees (including any monies due to the Official Receiver) need to be discharged, or an undertaking given to discharge them out of the first tranche of monies received by the supervisor, since there is a charge over the assets to that effect.

Reporting the meeting 13.17

After the meeting, it is, under the modified *section 4(6)* of the *IA 1986* and *Rule 1.24*, the task of the chairman of the meeting to report the outcome, including any modifications, to the court within four days and to the LLP and all those originally entitled to notice of the meeting(s).

If the proposals were accepted, then the supervisor must also send a copy of the chairman's report to Companies House.

The effect of approval   13.18

If the proposals are approved, either with or without modifications, they take effect, under *section 5* of the *IA 1986* (as modified), as from the date of the creditors' meeting. The deal thus approved binds every person who had notice of the meeting and was entitled to vote at it, whether or not they were present at the meeting in person or by proxy.

Thus a creditor who was either silent, or who was in an unsuccessful minority of opposers, may nonetheless be bound to the arrangement. He (or, more improbably, a member of the LLP) may however apply to the court under *section 6* of the *IA 1986* (as modified), within 28 days of the chairman's report, if he considers that an arrangement unfairly prejudices his interests, or that there was some material irregularity at or in connection with the meeting.

In such circumstances, the court may revoke or suspend the approval of the arrangements, or give directions for further meetings to be summoned (failure to comply with which can in turn lead to a later order for suspension or revocation). It can also give such supplemental directions as may be necessary, related in particular to events which may have taken place between the meeting and its order. Irregularities which do not lead to such an application do not invalidate the meeting.

Subsequent court intervention   13.19

The court may also have a role to play during the course of the implementation of the arrangement, and various powers are given to it by *section 7* of the *IA 1986* (as modified).

Anyone, creditor or not, may apply to the court for relief if he is dissatisfied by any act or omission of the supervisor. If the supervisor has been acting within the framework of the proposals, the court is unlikely to interfere. If it intervenes, the court has power to confirm, reverse or modify any act or decision of the supervisor; or to give directions to him; or to make any other order it thinks fit.

Equally, if the supervisor is himself unsure of what action he should take, he may apply to the court for directions. He is specifically included amongst the list of those who may apply, in suitable circumstances (e.g. failure of the arrangement according to its own designated criteria) for the winding up or administration of the LLP.

Appointment of a supervisor by the court 13.20

It may be that the court is itself called upon to appoint a supervisor. It may do so, under *section 7(5)* of the *IA 1986*, if it is satisfied that it is expedient for it to do so, and that in practice it is not feasible for the appointment to be otherwise made.

Such an appointment, of a suitably qualified practitioner, may be either to replace an original appointee, or to fill a vacancy. This can apply to multiple appointments as well, i.e. the court could appoint a second or subsequent supervisor, or replace one of joint appointees.

Proposals by administrator or liquidator 13.21

As mentioned above (see 13.6 above), it is possible for the proposals to be made by an administrator or liquidator of an LLP, rather than by the members. Differently modified versions of *sections 2* and *3* of the *IA 1986* cover this eventuality.

Within that possibility, there is then a further split of ways forward, in that the proposer may put forward a third party as the supervisor of the arrangement, or may suggest himself. In the former instance, the nominee's statement to the court must provide for the necessity of and arrangements for a meeting of the members of the LLP, as well as but separate from a meeting of its creditors, to consider the arrangement. The details necessary for the statement of affairs etc must be given to the nominee by the proposer. It is the duty of the nominee to summon the two meetings.

In the latter instance, i.e. if the administrator or liquidator is proposing himself as supervisor, then, presumably since his appointment already has court sanction, he may proceed to the summoning of the two meetings without the interim step of reporting on their advisability to the court.

Whoever is the proposed nominee, if the LLP is already in liquidation, notice of the proposals and the identity of the nominee must also be given to the Official Receiver (*Rules 1.10* and *1.12*).

Revocation or suspension of the arrangement 13.22

As mentioned above (see 13.18 above) the court has the power, in certain circumstances, to revoke or suspend the arrangement. *Rule 1.25* deals with the consequences.

The person who obtained the revocation etc. order must serve it upon the supervisor, and the proposer of the arrangement, and Companies House. If further meetings need to be called, whoever is responsible for that must also be notified. It is then the job of the proposers (i.e. the members of the LLP, or its administrator or liquidator) firstly to notify anyone who was originally notified of the initial meeting(s) or who they think may be affected by the order; and secondly to notify the court within seven days if it intends either to submit revised proposals, or to re-submit the original ones.

The supervisor's duties   13.23

The supervisor must of course keep full accounting records and, at least annually, send an account, together with a report on how the arrangement is going, to:

● the court;

● Companies House;

● the LLP;

● the arrangement creditors;

● the members (unless on application by the supervisor the court orders otherwise);

● the LLP's auditors.

He must also provide such information and documents to the Secretary of State as the latter may request. *Rules 1.26* and *1.27* relate to these obligations. His fees for the performance of his duties are, by *Rule 1.28*, such as are sanctioned by the arrangement, or such as would have been payable in an administration or winding up.

Completion of the arrangement   13.24

All concerned hope that the arrangement will proceed as normal to a conclusion. It may or may not be that the outcome is as originally predicted, but nonetheless in most cases it should be possible for conclusion to be reached.

At that stage, the supervisor must, under *Rule 1.29*, send all the arrangement's creditors, and all members, a notice of conclusion, and a final report and summary account, together with an explanation of any difference in the result from that envisaged in the initial proposals. He then has to send copies to the court and to Companies House as well.

Failure of an arrangement 13.25

It may however be that an arrangement may fail. What constitutes 'failure' should, as discussed above (see 13.4 above), normally be clearly designated in the original proposals or, if things start to go wrong, there can be awful confusion.

The most common cause of failure is a simple lack of the promised payments due to the supervisor, so that he cannot discharge the arrangement creditors' debts as planned. Normally, the proposals will have provided that, in that event, he may petition the court for the winding up of the LLP, and that, to cover that eventuality, he should at all times retain sufficient funds in hand to allow him to do this. If he does so, then a winding-up order granted on his petition will have the effect of bringing to an end the trusts created by the arrangement, so that he then holds any balance of funds in his possession for the eventual liquidator of the LLP. (For this reason, most supervisors in this position will wish to make a partial distribution to the arrangement creditors before seeking the winding up, so that the amounts passed to the liquidator, after the fees etc payable in respect of the winding up proceedings, are minimal.) This would not however be the case on a voluntary winding up or on a petition presented by someone other than the supervisor.

There has in recent times been a plethora of cases on the above subject – see for instance *Re Arthur Rathbone Kitchens Limited [1998] BPIR 1*; *Re Excalibur Airways Limited [1998] BPIR 598*; *Souster v Carman Construction Co Ltd [2000] BPIR 371*; *Re Brelec Installations Limited [2001] BPIR 210*; *Re Maple Environmental Services Limited [2001] BPIR 321* and *Re Kudos Glass Limited [2001] BPIR 517*.

Practical difficulties of LLP arrangements – a moratorium 13.26

One major problem with voluntary arrangements is that, since LLPs are treated under the *IA 1986* as companies, not individuals, there is at present no provision for a moratorium (brought about either automatically or by interim order) on court proceedings against the LLP between the submission of the proposals and the meeting at which they are hopefully to be approved. (It is however remarkable how many creditors, having got used to the concept of the effect of the interim order in individual voluntary arrangements, assume the same applies to company arrangements and refrain from taking proceedings once notified of the lodgement of proposals for a company arrangement with the court!).

This situation will be altered when the relevant provisions of the *Insolvency Act 2000* (*section 1* and *Schedule 1*, introducing a new *Schedule A1* to the *IA 1986*) are brought into force.

Obtaining a moratorium   13.27

The moratorium scheme is too complex to go into fully in this work, especially before it is even in force, and because it is not unlikely that the Secretary of State may in any event use the powers given to him in the above legislation to modify certain provisions of the 45 paragraphs of *Schedule A1* (see 13.26 above) which are required for the scheme.

Briefly, however, the provisions will allow most small LLPs (using the same definitions as for the 'small' accounting exemptions set out in 10.37 *et seq.* above) which are not already the subject of insolvency proceedings, and which have not recently taken advantage of these provisions, to seek a moratorium. To do so, it needs to file at court, with the proposals for the arrangement, a statement by the nominee that the arrangement has a reasonable chance of approval, and that the LLP has sufficient funds to trade through the period of the moratorium. The moratorium will last from the date upon which the papers are filed, to the sooner of the expiry of 28 days or the date of the meeting(s) of the creditors (and the LLP if appropriate) which are to consider approval of the arrangement. The nominee must, at both the start and end of the moratorium, advertise the fact, and notify the LLP and any creditor he knows of (save that at the start only creditors who have actually petitioned for the LLP's winding up need specifically be notified).

The effect of a moratorium   13.28

During the period of the moratorium, none of the following steps may be taken (except, in some cases, with the leave of the court):

- any petition for winding up or administration of the LLP;
- any appointment of an administrative receiver;
- any meeting of the LLP or its members;
- any forfeiture by a landlord;
- any enforcement of security or the taking of possession of goods on hire purchase;
- any commencement or continuation of any proceedings or execution;
- any crystallisation of a floating charge.

The nominee's responsibilities
13.29

It may be that in practice it will be difficult to find willing nominees, at least if the arrangements proposed are to be as non-interventionist as at present is the trend.

The reason for this is that the nominee's responsibilities are considerably increased. He is expected continually to monitor the progress of the LLP during the moratorium, to check the likely acceptability of approval of the proposals, and the likely ability of the LLP to fund its operations through the moratorium period. He (or a moratorium committee if appointed) is required to approve any disposal or payment by the LLP as being for the LLP's benefit. Anyone claiming that any act or omission of the nominee has led to loss to the LLP has the ability, if the LLP itself does not act against the nominee to recover such loss, to seek the sanction of the court to do so. Any nominee will therefore have to take a much more interventionist role in the running of the LLP during the moratorium than otherwise, with no doubt a consequent effect upon fee levels.

14 – Administration Orders etc.

The second option for an LLP which is insolvent is an administration order. This procedure gives more effective protection than a voluntary arrangement, but needs to be combined with a clear initial sense of the purposes of the administration, and an intended exit route. The procedures for obtaining an administration order, and the effects of the petition and the subsequent order will be considered. A prime task of the administrator is to arrange an appropriate statement of affairs, and to formulate proposals for the administration, and this area is also examined.

The administrator's powers and duties are described. The potential ability of objectors to the administrator's actions to seek redress for unfair prejudice are looked at. The procedures applying to the termination of the administration are set out. Lastly, brief mention is made of the position regarding receivers and administrative receivers.

Introduction 14.1

The purpose of an administration is to fill the gap between the relatively relaxed regime of a voluntary arrangement, and the finality of a liquidation, by providing a court-governed opportunity for a licensed insolvency practitioner to take over the running of the LLP in the hope that its fortunes can be turned round. The outcome will depend on the success of the revival attempt, and may vary from a return to members' control to the dissolution of the LLP.

The effect of an administration order, summarised in *section 8(2)* of the *Insolvency Act 1986* (as modified), is that whilst the order is in force the affairs, business and property of the LLP are managed by the administrator. This is therefore a much more forceful and involved role than that of a supervisor of a voluntary arrangement, as described in Chapter 13. It is not however the administrator's task actually to distribute the assets amongst the creditors, and if such distribution is to be carried out it must be through the medium of one of the intended outcomes of the administration, as set out below (see 14.2 below).

The purposes of an administration order 14.2

There are four purposes for which an administration order may be made, which are specified in *section 8(3)* of the *IA 1986* (as modified), which reflect the above range of possible outcomes. The order itself must state which one or more of the four reasons apply to it. Following the spectrum of optimism, they are as detailed below:

- To allow the survival of the LLP, and the whole or any part of its undertaking, as a going concern. In other words it is hoped that the administrator will, at some stage, be able to hand all or part of the enterprise back to the members, without any other intervening process.

- To facilitate the approval of a voluntary arrangement. This is to cover the situation where the LLP would not succeed in getting creditors' support to move straight to an arrangement; but the hope is that if the more rigorous regime of an administration is applied an arrangement may be a viable exit route, as a preliminary to the revival of the LLP's independence. It was indicated in 13.6 and 13.21 above that an administrator is one of those who may submit proposals for an arrangement.

- To bring about the sanctioning of a compromise or arrangement, under *section 425* of the *Companies Act 1985*, between the LLP and any of those mentioned in that section (see 12.57 et seq above).

- To bring about a more advantageous realisation of an LLP's assets than would be the result of a winding up. This is intended to give the freer range of an administration to an insolvency practitioner than the restricted duties of a liquidator, even if, once the assets have been so realised and distributed, a winding up needs to be commenced to administer the last rites. (For such a purpose, the administrator is both a potential petitioner and a potential liquidator.)

Applying for an administration order 14.3

The applicant for an administration order will need firstly to satisfy the court that it has the jurisdiction to make an order under *section 8(1)* of the *IA 1986* (as modified), namely that the LLP is insolvent, i.e. unable to pay its debts within the meaning of *section 123* of the *IA 1986*.

Next, it has to persuade the court that making an order would achieve one of the four purposes set out above. The application is presented in the form of a petition under *section 9* of the *IA 1986* (as modified).

Presentation of the petition 14.4

The petition may be presented by any one, or more, of the following:

- the LLP itself;

- any actual or contingent creditor(s);

- a magistrates' clerk enforcing fines;

- the Financial Services Authority, in respect of an LLP under its jurisdiction (*section 359* of the *Financial Services and Markets Act 2000*).

Once the petition is presented, it cannot be withdrawn without the leave of the court (*IA 1986, s 9(2)*, as modified)). The petition must be supported by evidence of the LLP's financial position, and the consent of the proposed administrator.

The petition may also be accompanied by a report from an independent person (who may include the proposed administrator) as to the advisability of the making of an order. It is generally regarded as good practice for there to be such a statement for the guidance of the court (though it is not compulsory), and the court has laid down guidelines as to how this can best be approached without over-complexity (*Practice Note [1994] 1 All ER 324*). *Rules 2.1* to *2.4* of the *Insolvency Rules 1986* govern this documentation.

Notification of petition 14.5

The application is essentially one where it is not appropriate to give general advance notice (e.g. to all creditors) but nonetheless notice of it, in the form of the petition and the supporting statements referred to above (see 14.4 above), must be given, forthwith upon its presentation to the court and in any event not less than five days before the hearing, to any prescribed person. *Rules 2.5* to *2.8* apply.

The period of five days may be abridged in exceptional circumstances, e.g. if the period of delay, and the possibility of public knowledge of the petition, might jeopardise the potential success of the administration, as in *Re Chancery plc [1991] BCLC 712*, where a banking institution applied successfully to abridge the period lest confidence be disastrously lost in the intervening period.

Those to whom notice must be given are:

- any administrative receiver already appointed;
- anyone entitled to appoint an administrative receiver;
- anyone who has already petitioned for a winding up;
- any provisional liquidator;
- the proposed administrator;
- the LLP itself (unless it is the petitioner);
- the Bank of England (if the LLP is a banking institution);
- any sheriff or other officer known to be attempting execution against the LLP or its property;
- anyone known to have distrained against the LLP or its property.

The LLP as petitioner   14.6

In the light of the fact of the LLP's ability to act as petitioner, the partnership agreement should provide the mechanism for the LLP to reach a determination to petition.

In the company context, the permissible petitioner is not the company, but its directors, and the question of whether resolutions have been properly passed for the purpose has been before the court on various occasions (e.g. *Re Emmadart Ltd [1979] 1 All ER 599* and *Re Equiticorp International Ltd (1989) 5 BCC 599*) so the clearer the position as to the LLP's formal determination the better.

One consequence of the apparent difference between an LLP's position and a company's is that in the former case the members of the LLP should avoid the fate which may befall petitioning directors if their petition is unsuccessful, namely that the costs may fall upon them personally, as in *Re WF Fearman Ltd (No 2) (1988) 4 BCC 141*.

Interaction with an administrative receiver   14.7

If a petition is issued at a time when an administrative receiver has already been appointed, then the court must ordinarily dismiss the petition, under *section 9(3)* of the *IA 1986* (as modified). This will not be the case, however, if the appointor of the administrative receiver consents to an order being made, or if the consequence of making the order, in relation to the security under which the administrative receiver was appointed, would be that it would:

- be liable to result in the security being released or discharged as a transaction at an undervalue or a preference; or

- result in the floating charge created by the security being avoided owing to its proximity in time to the onset of insolvency.

It is possible for an administrative receiver to be appointed (without needing the leave of the court) between the presentation of a petition for an administration order and its hearing, and for that receiver to commence his functions (*IA 1986, s 10(2)(b), (c)*).

Orders to be made   14.8

The court, on hearing a petition, has a range of options open to it. It may of course grant or dismiss the application. It may also adjourn the hearing either conditionally or unconditionally.

Lastly, it may make an interim order or any other order it thinks fit and, if it makes an interim order, it may restrict the powers of either the members of the LLP or the LLP itself. In doing so, it may make the exercise of any powers conditional upon consents, either of the court itself, or of any relevant insolvency practitioner. Reference should be made to *section 9(4)* and *(5)* of the *IA 1986* (as modified).

The effect of making the application   14.9

The effect of the presentation of a petition for an administration order is immediate, and gives to an LLP an effective regime of protection under *section 10(1)* of the *IA 1986* (as modified) preventing action being taken against it between then and the making of the final determination of the petition (referred to below as 'the interim period').

This protective effect may well – at least until the moratorium provisions of the *Insolvency Act 2000*, referred to in Chapter 12 (see 12.58; see also 13.26), are introduced and are shown to be practical and workable – be one of the prime motivations for seeking an administration order as opposed to proposing for a voluntary arrangement. (The one exception to the immediacy of the effect is if there is already an administrative receiver in place. In that event, under *section 10(3)* of the *IA 1986* (as modified), the interim period does not start until the appointor of the administrative receiver consents to the petition.)

Thus in the interim period:

- No determination may be made by the LLP that it should be voluntarily wound up.

- No order may be made that the LLP shall be compulsorily wound up.

- No landlord may forfeit a lease of an LLP's premises by peaceful re-entry for breach of the lease.

- No steps may be taken to enforce any security over the LLP's property.

- No steps may be taken to re-possess any goods in the LLP's possession under a hire purchase agreement etc., or a retention of title clause.

- No proceedings, execution or other legal process may be commenced or continued against the LLP or its property.

- No distress may be levied against the LLP or its property.

Qualification of the above prohibitions   14.10

The above provisions (except those relating to winding up) may however be subject to exceptions with the leave of the court and subject to any conditions it may impose. Guidance was given in *Re Atlantic Computer Systems plc [1992] 1 All ER 476* as to the circumstances in which leave is likely to be given.

The provisions as to winding up do not prohibit the presentation of a petition for the winding up of the LLP, merely an order being made on that petition before the petition for the administration order is resolved. Note that these provisions do not (save in relation to forfeiture) prevent a party from exercising a right to treat a contract as terminated by breach, so that e.g. a third party may, if the contract so allows, treat the presentation of the petition as an act justifying its withdrawal from a contract otherwise requiring future performance on its part. Also, the prohibitions do not remove third-party rights, but merely suspend them so that they may revive after the dismissal of the petition, or the conclusion of the administration, as the case may be.

Effect of an administration order   14.11

At the point of the making of an administration order, the tensions between this method of proceeding and other possible insolvency measures are automatically resolved under *section 11* of the *IA 1986* (as modified). Thus, any pending winding up petition is dismissed, and any previously appointed administrative receiver vacates his office.

Further, any other receiver may be required by the administrator to vacate his office. When any such vacation of office occurs, the departing administrative receiver or receiver may take his fees, and any proper indemnity, out of any assets of the LLP in his hands, in priority to the obligation to pass such monies to his appointor, and is absolved from any future liability to pay preferential debts. The several prohibitions referred to in 14.9 above continue to apply, with an additional possibility for exclusion being the consent of the administrator as an alternative to that of the court. No new administrative receiver may be appointed.

Notification of the order   14.12

After the making of an administration order, and for so long as it lasts, all relevant documents issued by or on behalf of the LLP or the administrator must give the administrator's name, and state that the affairs, business and property of the LLP are being managed by him. This applies to invoices, orders for goods, or letters. If this is not done, the LLP itself is liable to a fine, as also may be the administrator and/or any member of the LLP who, without reasonable excuse, has authorised or permitted the default (*IA 1986, s 12*, as modified).

Further provisions are also found in *section 21* of the *IA 1986*, which requires the administrator forthwith to notify the LLP of the order, and to advertise it in the *London Gazette* and whatever he deems to be the most suitable newspaper to bring it to the attention of the creditors.

The administrator must also send an office copy of the order to the Registrar within 14 days. He must, under *Rule 2.10*, notify forthwith any administrative receiver, any actual or potential appointor thereof, and any potential liquidator. He must notify all known creditors, within 28 days. He may also be ordered by the court to notify others. If he fails without reasonable excuse to carry out these functions, he is liable not only to a fine, but also to a daily default fine.

Appointment of the administrator   14.13

The prime method of appointment of the administrator is of course by means of the order itself.

Provision is also made, however, for appointment in the event of vacancy, whatever its cause (e.g. death, resignation, or disqualification of the incumbent from acting as a licensed insolvency practitioner). In that event, under *section 13* of the *IA 1986* (as modified), application may be made to the court for the necessary appointment by any of the following:

- any continuing administrator (where the original appointment was joint);

- by a creditors' committee if one is established;

- if neither of the above options can apply, then by:

  ○ the LLP itself; or

  ○ any creditor(s) of the LLP.

Submission of a statement of affairs   14.14

One of the first jobs of an administrator, under *section 22* of the *IA 1986* (as modified), is to require the submission to him of a statement of affairs, by one or more of those qualified to give such a statement. Those concerned may be:

- present or past members of the LLP;

- anyone participating in the formation of the LLP, if it was within the year before the making of the order;

- present employees of the LLP, or those who were employees within the last year, if the administrator thinks they can help;

- present members or employees of an LLP, or those who were in either of those categories during the previous year, where that LLP in turn is, or was within that year, a member of the subject LLP.

'Employee' in these circumstances is sufficiently widely defined to include someone acting under a contract for services.

Anyone so required to give a statement must do so within 21 days of being notified of the requirement to do so, unless the administrator releases them from the obligation, or agrees to extend the time limit. If an administrator is asked so to release a person, or to grant an extension of time, and refuses, the person concerned may apply to the court for a release or extension, which is within the discretion of the court.

If the person subject to the requirement fails without reasonable excuse to comply with it he will be liable to both a fine and a daily default fine for continued non-compliance. He is however able to recover from the administrator his reasonable expenses of preparing the statement, under *Rule 2.15*.

Contents of the statement of affairs 14.15

The statement, which must be verified by affidavit, needs to deal with the LLP's assets and liabilities, and to give details of its creditors and their respective securities. *Rules 2.11* and *2.12* apply to the requirements for the statement.

If its contents are deemed by the administrator to be commercially sensitive, he may apply to the court to restrict disclosure of all or any part of its contents (*Rule 2.13*).

General duties and powers of the administrator 14.16

The other immediate task of the administrator, under *section 17* of the *IA 1986*, is to take over custody and control of all the property of the LLP. It is then up to him to manage the affairs, business and property of the LLP. He is given wide powers under *sections 14* and *15* of the *IA 1986* to do all the things he needs to in order to carry out that latter task.

A list of 23 specific powers is contained in *Schedule 1* to the *IA 1986*, but they are merely examples of the general power. (Not only does he have power to manage, but he also has the power to stop anyone else (e.g. a member of the LLP) from doing so. Any powers vested in the LLP or its members, whatever their source, capable of interfering with the administrator's role, can only be so exercised with his general or specific consent.)

The administrator can appoint a manager to carry out these tasks on his behalf. If he considers a meeting of the members of the LLP, or of its creditors, is needed, he may summon such a meeting. Indeed, he must summon a creditors' meeting if required to do so either by the court, or by not less than a tenth (by value) of the LLP's creditors (*IA 1986, s 17(3)*). In the case of members' meetings, relevant procedures are imported from *section 92* of the *IA 1986*, so that the holding of the meeting shall be as per the procedure set out in the LLP's partnership agreement, with a quorum as provided therein (or a default quorum of two if the agreement is silent). If no provisions are made, then the administrator may apply to the court for directions. That in fact is merely an example of the administrator's broader power to apply to the court for directions in respect of any matter arising in connection with his duties.

As far as third parties are concerned, the administrator is acting as agent on behalf of the LLP (and, as such, he does of course owe to the LLP the same duties as any agent owes to his principal). If the third party is acting in good faith, and for value, he is not concerned to enquire whether the administrator is acting within his powers.

One power which is conspicuous by its absence is the ability to act like a liquidator in disclaiming a lease or other onerous contract.

Power to deal with property subject to floating charge   14.17

Specific provisions as to the administrator's powers to deal with property which is subject to some form of charge are contained in *section 15* of the *IA 1986* (as modified). He may without needing any consent dispose of or deal with any such property, if it is subject to what was – at the date of its creation – a floating charge, as if it were not subject to such security.

The holder of the security then acquires, however, such priority over any property which comes into the LLP's hands to replace the disposed of asset as he previously had over that asset. In other words, if it is prudent for a property subject to a floating charge to be sold, e.g. because it has high running costs, the original security holder takes substitute security over the proceeds of sale.

Power to deal with property subject to fixed charge   14.18

Section 15 of the *IA 1986* (see 14.17 above) also deals with the situation where the property in question is subject to a fixed charge, or to a hire purchase or similar agreement, or to a retention of title clause.

In such a case, if the administrator can show that the property's disposal would be likely to aid the purpose(s) of the administration order, he may apply to the court for permission to make the disposal free from the security. The holder of the security must be given notice of the application under *Rule 2.51*. If the court orders a disposal, the net proceeds of it must be paid to the secured creditor. If permission is sought to make a disposal at less than market value, the administrator has to make up the difference to the secured creditor. If such an order is obtained by the administrator, he has to notify the Registrar within 14 days, or face a fine and daily default fine in the absence of reasonable excuse for his default.

The administrator's proposals   14.19

It is the intention of the legislation that administrations should not be long-winded affairs. Thus the administrator has, under *section 23* of the *IA*

1986 (as modified), to present proposals within three months of appointment (though the court can extend this period), as to how he is to achieve the purpose(s) specified in the original order. He then has to deal with those proposals by:

- sending a copy to the Registrar;

- sending a copy to all creditors;

- laying a copy before a meeting of creditors convened by him for the purpose, on not less than 14 days' notice;

- sending a copy to all the LLP's members, or publishing in the *London Gazette*, and the newspaper in which the administration was first advertised, a notice telling members where they can write to get a copy of the statement.

If the administrator fails to comply with any of these requirements, he is liable to a fine and, potentially, to a daily default fine. In accordance with *Rule 2.16*, he must send with the proposals a statement giving details of the history of the administration and its present position, together with the statement of affairs referred to above (see 14.14 and 14.15), and any other information he thinks the creditors may need to make their minds up as to the proposals and their costs.

Consideration of proposals by creditors   14.20

It is the task of the creditors, at the meeting called as above (see 14.19), to decide whether to approve the administrator's proposals (*IA 1986, s 24* as modified). There are detailed provisions in *Rules 2.18* to *2.28* inclusive as to the calling and conduct of such meetings.

The creditors can suggest modifications, but can only incorporate these if the administrator approves. If they approve the proposals, they may also decide, under *section 26* of the *IA 1986* (as modified) to appoint three to five willing creditors as a creditors' committee, which may then require the administrator to give it such information as it may reasonably ask for, and to attend its meetings. (Detailed provisions about the creditors' committee meetings are found in *Rules 2.32* to *2.46*.)

After proposals, with or without modifications, are approved, and subject to any valid subsequent revisions, the administrator's powers must be exercised so as to enable him to put the proposals into effect. He must, under *Rule 2.30*, report to the court, the Registrar and the creditors on a six-monthly basis, as to the progress of his administration, with a receipts and payments account (for the requirements as to which, see *Rule 2.52*), and he must likewise report finally on vacating office (unless vacation results from a consequent winding up, the removal of the administrator by the court, or the administrator's ceasing to hold the necessary qualification as a licensed insolvency practitioner).

Notifying the outcome of the meeting   14.21

The result of the initial creditors' meeting must be notified by the administrator to the court, to the Registrar, and all known creditors (*section 24* of the *IA 1986*, as modified; *Rule 2.30*).

If that report is to the effect that the meeting had rejected the proposals (with or without modifications) the court has a number of options open to it. It may discharge the administration order altogether, and make any consequential orders it thinks fit. If it does so the administrator must send an office copy of the discharge order to the Registrar within 14 days, or risk a fine and possible daily default fine. Alternatively, it may adjourn the hearing either conditionally or unconditionally, or make an interim order, or make any other order it thinks fit.

Revision of proposals   14.22

If, after proposals have been approved, the administrator seeks their revision, he must go back to the creditors, under *section 25* of the *IA 1986* (as modified).

Thus he must send to all the creditors notice of the intended revisions, and convene another creditors' meeting for their consideration. He also has to send a copy of the intended revisions to all members of the LLP, or to publish a notice telling them where they can get copies. Consideration of the suggested revisions follows the same pattern as the original proposals (see 14.20 above), i.e. the creditors may reject them, or accept them with or without modifications, but they may be modified only on the basis that the administrator consents.

The administrator must notify the outcome of the meeting to the Registrar and all creditors (but not to the court). In exceptional cases, if revisions are commercially necessary, and simply cannot wait until the 14 days necessary for calling a creditors' meeting have elapsed, then the court has jurisdiction to fill in the gap by using its power to give directions effectively to grant consent to revisions, as in *Re Smallman Construction Ltd (1988) 4 BCC 784*.

Challenges to the administrator   14.23

Not all administrations can be expected to run smoothly. Often, that will not be the administrator's fault, but there are provisions in *section 27* of the

IA 1986 (as modified) designed to protect aggrieved creditors or members, in certain circumstances.

If any such person believes that the way in which the administrator is managing or has managed the affairs, business and property of the LLP has caused him unfair prejudice, or that any actual or proposed act or omission of the administrator would do so, then he can petition the court for aid. The alleged prejudice may be to creditors or members generally, or to any particular section which includes the petitioner.

The court's powers on such an application are broad, as below (see 14.24), but unless the application is made within 28 days of the passing of any proposals or any revisions thereto, no such order may prejudice or prevent the implementation of those proposals or revisions. Nor, in any event, may such an order prejudice or prevent the implementation of any voluntary arrangement which creditors have approved or any compromise or arrangement sanctioned by the court (see 12.52 et seq above).

Potential orders on an unfair prejudice application   14.24

In general terms, the court has its usual range of options on an application as described in 14.23. It may of course decline the application. It may adjourn the hearing conditionally or unconditionally. It may make an interim or any other order it thinks fit.

If it finds the alleged prejudice to have occurred, it may make such order for relief as it thinks fit and, in particular, may:

- regulate the administrator's future management of the LLP;

- require the administrator to cease to do something;

- require the administrator to remedy an omission;

- require the administrator to summon a meeting, of either creditors or members, to consider any point the court directs;

- discharge the administration order and make such consequential orders as it thinks fit (in which case the administrator must file an office copy of the discharge order with the Registrar within 14 days, or face a possible fine and daily default fine).

Discharge or variation of the administration order   14.25

Various references have been made above (see 14.24) to the possibility of the discharge of the administration order by the court. The administrator

213

himself may apply for such a discharge. Further, he may apply for the order to be varied, by specifying an additional purpose from amongst the list of those referred to in the original order (see 14.2 above). (*IA 1986, s 18*, as modified). (Since the proposals made by the administrator are intended to fulfil those purposes, any addition of a purpose after proposals have been approved may well in practice lead to the necessity of creditors' sanction for a revision of the proposals.)

It may be the administrator's own wish to apply for such a discharge or variation, if he believes that the original purpose(s) have either been achieved, or have proved incapable of achievement. Alternatively, he may be directed to so by a meeting of the creditors summoned under *section 17(3)*, as in 14.16 above. The court has the usual panoply of powers, i.e. it can grant or refuse, it can adjourn conditionally or unconditionally, or it can make an interim or any other order.

Where any order for variation or discharge is made, the administrator must send an office copy to the Registrar within 14 days, or face the possibility of a fine and daily default fine. He is however, perhaps surprisingly, under no obligation to notify the creditors or members of the order.

Vacation of office   14.26

The office of the administrator may be vacated, under the modified *section 19* of the *IA 1986*, in one of four ways, i.e.:

●   he may be removed by the court;

●   he may resign by giving notice to the court, the LLP and its creditors;

●   he may cease to be a registered insolvency practitioner;

●   the administration order may be discharged.

Rule 2.53, dealing with resignation, provides that it can only be effected (except with the leave of the court) on the grounds that the administrator is ill, intends to resign his insolvency practitioner's licence, has a conflict of interest, or has had a change in personal circumstances.

Presumably, the office may also be vacated by the administrator's death, but this is not specifically referred to. Since however the operative provisions of the section apply 'where at any time a person ceases to be administrator' this would seem to include cessation by reason of death.

On any cessation, then the administrator's remuneration and expenses are a charge upon any assets in his custody or control at the time of cessation.

That charge ranks ahead of any third-party security under a floating charge, but behind a charge which attaches to those assets in respect of any debt or liability incurred during his period of office under contracts entered into during the course of the administration.

Similar priority to such contractual debts is given to any 'qualifying liabilities' in respect of any contract of employment incurred during his period of office, where the contract of employment was adopted during the course of the administration. (There is a saving provision which stipulates that nothing an administrator does or omits to do during his first 14 days in post shall be taken as an adoption.)

A liability under a contract of employment counts as a qualifying liability if it is in respect of services rendered wholly or partly after the adoption of the contract, and relates to wages, salary, or occupational pension scheme contributions. Any part relating to pre-adoption services does not rank for the priority. Holiday and sickness payments are however included.

Release of the administrator   14.27

By virtue of *section 20* of the *IA 1986*, an administrator's release from his responsibilities occurs when the court so determines, save that in the event of his death it occurs when notice is given by his personal representatives to the court.

From the appropriate time onwards, the administrator is discharged from any liability for his acts and omissions whilst in office, and also in any other way relating to his conduct as an administrator. The only exception is that the court's powers under *section 212* of the *IA 1986* are preserved (see 17.13 below). These relate to:

- misapplying, retaining, or becoming accountable for the LLP's property;

- misfeasance or breach of fiduciary or other duty in relation to the LLP.

Leave of the court must be obtained, after the release, for such proceedings to be commenced. Orders may be made in such cases for the repayment or restoration of money or property, or for compensation to be paid.

Administrator's remuneration   14.28

Reference is made in various places above to the remuneration of the administrator. The assessment of that remuneration is governed by *Rule 2.47*.

It may be based upon either a percentage of the value of the property he has to deal with, or a time charge for him and his staff. The decision as to which approach is appropriate, and what percentage may be applied if that is held to be the right approach, is to be made by the creditors' committee, if there is one, or a meeting of the creditors generally if there is not. If not otherwise fixed, the court can intervene.

Similar provisions apply under *Rules 2.48* and *2.49* to any potential variation of the remuneration. If not less than 25 per cent of the creditors by value are aggrieved by what they consider to be excessive remuneration, they can apply to the court under *Rule 2.50* for it to be reduced, and the court has wide discretion to deal with the application.

Receivers and administrative receivers   14.29

At this point, mention should be made very briefly of the position regarding the appointment etc. of receivers or administrative receivers in the LLP context.

Quite simply, the provisions of *IA 1986, Part III*, which deal with this subject, apply to LLPs as they do to companies, with no modifications other than the general ones needed to make them referable to LLPs. Since, as stated elsewhere, this book does not set out to be one on insolvency, readers are simply referred to the standard texts on this subject, and can apply them easily to LLPs.

15 – Voluntary Winding Up

In this chapter the first of the two overall methods of winding up an LLP – a voluntary winding up – is considered. This encompasses both a member's voluntary winding up, where the LLP remains solvent; and a creditors' voluntary winding up where it does not. In neither case is the court necessarily involved, though it may make occasional interventions on procedural matters if called upon. The differences between the two methods, with the ability of the members to give a declaration of solvency being a key issue, and the possibility of converting from a members' to a creditors' winding up, are examined.

The appointment and role of the creditors' liquidation committee is described. Procedures for the appointment and removal of liquidators are explored, as are their powers and duties, particularly with regard to the possibility of transactions for consideration other than cash, and the distribution of the LLPs property.

General

Introduction   15.1

It is made clear in *section 73* of the *Insolvency Act 1986* (as modified) that an LLP may be wound up either voluntarily, under *Chapters II to V* inclusive of *Part IV* of the *IA 1986*; or compulsorily by the court, under *Chapter VI* of that Part. Some provisions, i.e. *Chapter I* and *Chapters VII to X* relate to all types of winding up.

Compulsory winding up, and those general provisions, are dealt with in Chapters 16 and 17 of this work. Many of those provisions are unchanged from the original *IA 1986*, save for the incorporation of references to LLPs instead of companies etc. A detailed treatment of the law relating to liquidations is of course beyond the scope of this work, and the intention is therefore not to cover ground which is treated in the main works on the subject, but rather to give an overall picture of the position, and to concentrate on those aspects which are peculiar to

LLPs. References to the *Insolvency Rules* (see 13.1 above) are kept to a minimum.

A determination to wind up   15.2

The terminology used for a decision by an LLP to enter into a voluntary winding up, of either sort, is referred to as a 'determination' that it should be so wound up.

The exact time at which such a determination occurs is important, as it represents the formal commencement of the winding up (*IA 1986, s 86*, as modified), and various time periods within which actions need to be taken start with that determination. Thus, within 15 days, it must deliver a copy of the determination to the Registrar, or it and every designated member in default is liable to a fine (*IA 1986, s 84*, as modified). Similarly, within 14 days, it shall give notice of the determination in the *London Gazette*, or it and the liquidator and every member in default (not, this time, the designated members only) is liable to a fine (*IA 1986, s 85*, as modified). It must cease to carry on its business, except so far as it is needed for the purposes of the winding up, from the moment of commencement (*IA 1986, s 87(1)*, as modified).

The problem is that there is no indication whatever of what constitutes a determination, or by what means it must be reached. The default provisions in *regulation 7* are silent (for discussion of the *Regulations*, see 1.14 above). It is not even clear whether such a determination would be an 'ordinary matter' for the LLP, and hence (if the default provisions apply) requiring only a simple majority under *regulation 7(6)*; or a 'change in the nature of the business' requiring unanimity under that provision.

This is therefore an area which the draftsman of the partnership agreement needs to provide for carefully, in order that there can be no confusion as to e.g. whether a formal members meeting is needed, and what voting requirements there shall be. There is no bar on a determination for a voluntary winding up being made because there is already a voluntary arrangement in force, but the subsequent winding up may not have the effect of terminating the trusts applicable to property in the hands of the arrangements supervisor (see 13.25 above).

Continuation of the corporate entity   15.3

One of the reasons for bringing LLPs into the corporate arena for winding up is that there should continue to be an accountable entity throughout the carrying-out of the liquidation process, so that it only terminates once those procedures are completed.

Section 87(2) of the *IA 1986* (as modified) accordingly provides that the corporate state and corporate powers of the LLP continue, whatever the partnership agreement may say, until the eventual dissolution. The interests of the members within that entity cannot change during that period, and *section 88* of the *IA 1986* (as modified) accordingly provides that any transfer of a member's interest, and any alteration of the member's status (e.g., presumably, changing from designated member to non-designated) is void unless sanctioned by the liquidator.

Declaration of solvency   15.4

The distinguishing feature which determines whether a voluntary winding up is to be a members' or a creditors' winding up (as recognised by *section 90* of the *IA 1986*, as modified) is whether a declaration of solvency has been made, in accordance with *section 89* of the *IA 1986* (as modified).

To be effective, such a declaration must have been made within the five weeks immediately preceding the determination to wind up. Making it on the day of the determination is acceptable, provided it precedes the determination.

The declaration must contain a statement of the LLPs affairs as at the last practical date before the declaration. Once made, it must be delivered to the Registrar within 15 days of the determination to wind up, and if this is not done the LLP, and every member in default, is liable both to a fine and a daily default fine.

Responsibility for the declaration   15.5

It is the designated members' job to deal with the declaration (referred to in 15.4 above), and indeed it is one of the rare occasions when the legislation specifically provides for there to be a meeting of the designated members (though it lays down no mechanism for this). If there are more than two designated members, a majority of them may make the declaration.

The declaration is to the effect that, having made a full enquiry into the LLP's affairs, the declarants have formed the opinion that the LLP will be able to pay all its debts (together with interest) within such period from the determination as they may specify, not exceeding a year.

The responsibility for this is high, and the declarants would be foolish indeed if they did not ensure that they had evidence of proper accountancy support for this opinion, since if a declarant does not have reasonable grounds for the opinion in question he is liable not only to a potential fine but also imprisonment. Further, there is a presumption that he did not have reasonable grounds if, in the events which subsequently happen, it proves that the LLP did not in fact have enough to pay such debts and interest within the chosen period. Any prospective declarant is therefore going to need to be very sure of his ground before making the declaration.

Members' voluntary winding up

Appointment of the liquidator   **15.6**

In a members' voluntary winding up, the members pick their own liquidator(s). Upon that appointment their own normal powers cease, unless their continuance is sanctioned either by the liquidator, or by a specially convened members' meeting. Similarly, a members' meeting may fill any subsequent vacancy in the office of liquidator.

These meetings are to be held in the manner provided for in the *Insolvency Act* (which in practice is silent) or by the partnership agreement, or as the court may determine. That agreement should also spell out what constitutes a quorum, but if it does not the quorum will simply be two. *Sections 91* and *92* of the *IA 1986* apply.

Meetings during the winding up   **15.7**

If the winding up continues for more than a year, the liquidator has to summon a members' meeting at the end of each year, and to lay before the members an account of his acts and dealings, and the conduct of the winding up, during that year (*IA 1986, s 93* as modified).

Once the winding up is concluded, the liquidator shall make up a final account showing how the winding up had gone and how the LLP's property has been disposed of, and shall lay that before a members' meeting (*IA 1986, s 94* as modified). The provisions in 15.8 above as to the calling of meetings apply, and if the liquidator fails to call any requisite meeting he is liable to a fine.

In the case of the final meeting, there is an additional requirement to advertise the meeting at least a month beforehand in the *London Gazette*, and to send a copy of the final account and a report of the meeting to the registrar within a week after the meeting, on pain of a possible fine and daily default fine.

Effect of the LLP's insolvency   **15.8**

It may be that, during the course of the winding up, the liquidator forms the opinion that, contrary to the statutory declaration made by the designated members (see 15.4 and 15.5 above), the LLP will not in fact be able to pay its debts and interest thereon within the specified period.

If the above is the case, the liquidator has to take a number of steps. First, he has to organise a meeting of the creditors (*IA 1986, s 95(2)* as modified). To do this he has to:

- summon a meeting within 28 days of forming the above opinion;

- post notice of that meeting to all creditors at least seven days in advance;

- advertise the meeting in the *London Gazette*;

- advertise the meeting in two local newspapers;

- give creditors (without charge) such information about the LLP's affairs as they may reasonably ask for.

Statement of affairs for the creditors meeting   **15.9**

The liquidator's next task after the steps listed in 15.9 is to prepare a statement of affairs for the meeting, in the prescribed form 4.18, and verified by affidavit (*IA 1986, s 95(3)(4)* as modified). This has to show:

- the LLP's assets, debts, and liabilities;

- the creditors' names and addresses;

- the securities which any of them hold;

- the dates of each such security;

- such other information as the prescribed form may require.

This statement is laid before the creditors at their meeting, which is presided over by the liquidator. As from the time of that meeting, the winding up becomes a creditors voluntary winding up, and this meeting of creditors then fulfils the same function as the meeting referred to in 15.10 below.

Creditors' voluntary winding up

The creditors' meeting   **15.10**

As mentioned above (see 15.11 above), it is possible for what starts off as a members' voluntary winding up to be converted into a creditors' one.

The much more common route, however, is where the declaration of solvency is absent, and so it is intended from the start that it will be a creditors' winding up.

In those circumstances (where there is no declaration of solvency), the LLP has, under *section 98* of the *IA 1986* (as modified), to call a creditors' meeting at the outset, i.e. not more than 14 days after reaching its determination to wind itself up. It must give the creditors at least seven days' notice of the meeting by post; advertise in the *London Gazette*; and advertise it in two local newspapers.

The notice of the meeting must give two pieces of information. The first is the name of a licensed insolvency practitioner (in practice, the LLP's own nominee for liquidator) who will in the run-up to the meeting give creditors such information as to the LLP's affairs as they may reasonably require, without charge. The second is a local address at which, in the last two days of that interim period, a list of the LLP's creditors' names and addresses can be freely inspected. Failure to comply with these requirements renders the LLP (but not, on this occasion, any individual members) liable to a fine.

Statement of affairs   15.11

It is however the role of the designated members to take charge of the arrangements for the creditors' meeting itself, and to appoint one of their number to preside over the meeting.

They must also make out a statement of affairs, covering similar information to that referred to 15.11 above, and lay that before the meeting. Failure to do any of this renders the designated members liable to a fine.

Appointment of liquidator   15.12

A liquidator may, under *section 100* of the *IA 1986* (as modified), be nominated by the LLP itself, or by the creditors at their meeting, or by both.

The creditors will in practice often nominate their own candidate, as they feel uncomfortable with the idea of the LLP choosing its own. Their nominee will prevail in those circumstances. There is however power in those circumstances for any member or creditor, within seven days, to apply to the court for an order that the members' nominee be appointed, either instead of or jointly with the creditors' nominee; or that a new third choice be appointed instead of the creditors' nominee.

Once the liquidator is appointed, all powers of the members cease under the modified *section 103* of the *IA 1986*, save to the extent that the liquidation committee described at 15.13 below (or, if no such committee is appointed, the creditors generally) consent to their continuance. If there is a subsequent vacancy in the office, the creditors may under *section 104* of the *IA 1986* (as modified) make the necessary appointment to fill that vacancy, unless the original appointment was by the court.

Note that if a liquidator is purportedly appointed by the members at their meeting, with the creditors' meeting being some time later, there are restrictions under *section 166* of the *IA 1986* (as modified) as to what steps the possibly temporary appointee may take in that interim period, so that essentially only protective action can be taken.

Liquidation committee   15.13

The creditors also have the option, at their meeting, to appoint, from amongst their own number, up to five people to serve on a liquidation committee, as provided in *section 101* of the *IA 1986*.

If the creditors' meeting does so, then the LLP in turn can at any time appoint up to five members from its own ranks. The LLP's nominees may however be objected to by the creditors and, if so, they are debarred from membership of the committee (unless the court otherwise directs). An application may also be made to the court for substitutes to be appointed in place of those so removed.

Liquidator's reports and meetings   15.14

In the context of a creditors' voluntary winding up, there are obligations on the liquidator similar to those referred to in 15.7 above, to produce annual and closing accounts etc., and to hold annual and final meetings (*IA 1986, ss 105, 106*, as modified).

In this instance, however, the meetings must be of both the creditors and the members of the LLP. There is an exclusion if the winding up has been converted from a members' to a creditors' one, and the necessary meeting of creditors, the calling of which effects the conversion, is within the last three months of the first year, so that no further creditors' meeting is needed for that year.

Provisions applying to all types of voluntary winding up

Appointment or removal of liquidator by the court   **15.15**

The continuity of the office of liquidator is clearly vital to the success of any liquidation. *Section 108* of the *IA 1986* (as modified) thus gives the court the power to appoint a replacement liquidator if, for any reason, there is no liquidator acting, and no limit on who may ask it to exercise this power. This might for instance occur if there is no contributory to make such an application as is referred to in 15.6 above (e.g. if all members have, as suggested in 17.5 below, resisted the temptation to offer to make voluntary contributions to the LLP in the event of its liquidation).

Similarly, the court has power, under the same section, to remove a liquidator and appoint another, and again no limitation is put upon the identity of potential applicants. There must naturally be good cause shown for this to be done.

Notice by the liquidator of his appointment   **15.16**

Any liquidator under a voluntary winding up must, on his appointment, give notice of his appointment, in the prescribed form.

This notice must be sent to the Registrar, and also be advertised in the *London Gazette*. Failure to do so will render the liquidator liable to a fine and a daily default fine. *Section 109* of the *IA 1986* (as modified) applies.

Acts possible prior to appointment   **15.17**

It is possible that the members of the LLP, though they reach a determination to wind up either in members' or creditors' form, may fail to appoint or nominate a liquidator, as the case may require. In such a case, in the interim period, the members may not normally exercise any other powers, without the consent of the court (*section 114* of the *IA 1986*, as modified).

There are however two exceptions to the above limitation. Firstly, they may do so to the extent necessary to call the requisite creditors' meeting and provide it with a statement of affairs. Secondly, they may dispose of goods which either are perishable, or whose value would drop if not immediately sold; and they may also do anything necessary for the preservation of the LLP's assets. If they do anything beyond the scope of these exceptions, they are liable to a fine.

Distribution of the LLP's property   15.18

Having collected in the LLP's property, the liquidator's duty is naturally to distribute it, and *section 107* of the *IA 1986* so provides.

The liquidator's first task is to pay the preferential debts (e.g. VAT, PAYE, some staff payments etc.). Next, he must distribute the remaining assets *pari passu* amongst the ordinary creditors. Lastly, if there are still funds left after all creditors have been paid in full, he is to distribute the assets amongst the LLP's members, according to their interests in the LLP (unless the LLP partnership agreement directs a different method of distribution amongst members).

It may be thought likely to be desirable to distribute the assets of the LLP amongst the members *in specie*, in a situation where the partnership agreement does not provide for this. In such a case, it may be prudent to resolve, at the same time as appointing the liquidator, upon a mechanism for him to achieve this, e.g. by valuing the assets etc, and by giving him such indemnity as may be needed. Note however that all proper expenses of the winding up, including the liquidator's own remuneration, are to be paid in priority to all of the above distributions, in accordance with *section 115* of the *IA 1986*.

Taking shares in consideration of sale of the LLP's property   15.19

It may be the case that the liquidator wants to dispose not just of the LLP's assets, but of a substantial part of the LLP's business or property, in circumstances where the consideration being offered by the potential buyer is not cash, but a part of the ownership of its own business.

The simple example of the above is shares in the buyer if it is a limited company, but it could be other forms of interest in such a company, or it could be the equivalent interests in an LLP acting as buyer (though this would presumably be more complex in view of the more personal involvement expected of a member of an LLP as distinct from a shareholder). In such circumstances, *section 110* of the *IA 1986* (as modified) provides that such a broad range of such transactions, including those where the right to participate in the transferee's profits is or is part of the consideration, can in principle be entered into by the liquidator, but only with the 'requisite consent'.

Obtaining the requisite consent 15.20

In the case of a creditors' voluntary winding up, the 'requisite consent' referred to in 15.19 must come from the liquidation committee, if there is one, or from the court if not (i.e. there is no provision for a meeting of creditors generally, if there is no committee).

In the case of a members' voluntary winding up, however, the liquidator must summon a meeting of the members to determine whether they are prepared either to give the liquidator general authority to enter into transactions of this nature on their behalf, or to authorise a specific transaction. A suitably authorised transaction, once entered into, is binding on the members. The LLP can, if such a situation is anticipated, give such authority before, or at the time of, its initial determination to wind up.

The final subsection of the modified *section 110* of the *IA 1986* (see also 15.19 above) does indicate, however, that if the LLP is subject to a court winding-up order within a year of such a determination, the LLP's authority is not valid unless sanctioned by the court. Presumably this is intended to relate only to any lasting effect of such a consent, i.e. to any still-pending transaction, rather than requiring retrospective consent to an already-implemented deal, but the section is not specific on this.

Dissent from such arrangements 15.21

There may be members of the LLP who are not content with the decision reached at the members' meeting. A right of dissent is thus given by *section 111* of the *IA 1986* (as modified) to any member who did not vote in favour of the transaction at the members' meeting (i.e. not only any member who voted against, but also any one who abstained or was absent).

Such a dissenter has the right to notify the liquidator in writing, within a week of the relevant meeting, of his objection. The liquidator then has a choice. He may simply refrain from entering into the transaction, since the result of the meeting is merely to authorise him to enter into the transaction, not to oblige him to do so. Alternatively, he may decide to go ahead, in which case he must purchase the dissenters' interest in the LLP at a price to be determined by agreement or arbitration. The price for this must be paid prior to the LLP's dissolution. The method of raising the necessary cash is to be determined by the LLP.

Guidance by the court 15.22

The *IA 1986* recognises that a number of questions may arise during the course of a winding up which will require the guidance of the court, and *section 112* (as modified) therefore gives the right to seek such guidance to the liquidator, or to any contributory, or to any creditor.

Surprisingly, although these provisions apply to a members' voluntary winding up as much as to a creditors', no such right is given to a member of the LLP, if not a contributory. The court may not only be invited to determine any question referred, but also to exercise any power which it would have if the winding up was a compulsory one.

The court is given very wide powers to decide how to deal with any such application, provided only that it is satisfied that it would be 'just and beneficial' for it to intervene. It can essentially make what order it thinks fit. If the order is to the effect that the winding up be stayed, then the LLP must forthwith notify the Registrar.

Subsequent compulsory winding up   15.23

The fact that an LLP is being wound up voluntarily does not bar the right of a creditor subsequently to apply to the court to have it compulsorily wound up. Nor does it bar the similar right of a contributory, but in the latter case the contributory must be able to satisfy the court that the interests of contributories generally will be prejudiced by allowing the winding up to continue on a voluntary basis.

Section 116 of the *IA 1986* (as modified), which reserves the above rights, makes no mention of the rights of the members, if not contributories, and it may be the inference is accordingly that their right to petition for a compulsory winding up is lost once a voluntary winding up commences.

16 – Winding Up by the Court

This chapter deals with the processes peculiar to the winding up of LLPs by the court. It looks first at the grounds upon which a petition may be brought, and who may bring it. The position between the presentation of the petition and any eventual order on it is considered.

The process by which the LLP's affairs are then investigated is covered. A key issue is who the liquidator is to be, and the methods by which he may be appointed, as well as his general duties and his role in the conclusion of the winding up, are reviewed.

Introduction   16.1

A winding up by the court is the second of the two overall methods of winding up an LLP (the other method, voluntary winding up, is dealt with in Chapter 15).

This may either be the first exposure of the LLP to any of the range of insolvency measures, or may follow other attempted remedies, such as a failed voluntary arrangement, or the discharge of an administration order.

Choice of court   16.2

There is concurrent jurisdiction for the High Court, and the county court, in relation to compulsory winding up matters, under *section 117* of the *Insolvency Act 1986* (as modified). The county court in question will be that having insolvency jurisdiction for the area in which the LLP has its registered office. If the county court is chosen, it has the same powers as the High Court for winding up purposes.

If the wrong court is inadvertently chosen, anything done before the mistake is discovered remains valid in accordance with *section 118* of the *IA 1986* (as modified), and indeed it may be decided to retain the proceedings in that incorrect court, e.g. if a judge already has experience of the matter and it is deemed sensible to keep the case there for case management reasons.

Further, if a matter is proceeding in the county court, but the opinion of the High Court is desired on a particular aspect, this can be sought by way of a case stated, if so desired either by all the parties, or by one party with the approval of the county court judge, and the proceedings are then temporarily transferred to the High Court. *Section 119* of the *IA 1986* (as modified) refers.

Circumstances leading to compulsory winding up 16.3

There are, under *section 122* of the *IA 1986* (as modified), five sets of circumstances in which an LLP can be compulsorily wound up. These are as follows:

- If the LLP determines it should be wound up by the court. In other words an LLP's members, if they decide that the end of the line has been reached for their business, have the choice of determining to wind up via the voluntary route, or by means of the court's intervention.

- If the LLP does not start its business for a year from incorporation, or suspends its business for a whole year. This shows that the LLP is not intended to be allowed to be a dormant vehicle, as can quite legitimately be the case with a company for many years. (Some professional firms, which registered LLPs when the legislation came into force on 6 April 2001, simply in order to protect their names from being registered by rivals, but without any fixed intention to start to practice as active LLPs, have discovered this to their potential cost.)

- If the number of members of the LLP is reduced below two. Thus, though the incorporated body of the LLP does not automatically cease to exist if membership falls below two (as made clear in other provisions, such as *section 24* of the *CA 1985*, as modified (making a sole member jointly and severally liable with the LLP for debts incurred after six months trading without another member – see 12.2 above), it is nonetheless a reason for an active application for winding up.

- If the LLP is unable to pay its debts (as defined in 16.4 below).

- If the court is of the opinion that it is just and equitable that the LLP should be wound up. This is likely to be the least certain area, and is looked at in more detail in 16.6 *et seq.* below.

Inability to pay debts   16.4

There are in effect four sets of circumstances in which an LLP may be deemed to be unable to pay its debts.

If any one of these prevails, that is sufficient to ground a successful petition, even if the LLP can show that its finances amply pass the tests posed by the other possibilities. The example of the application of these principles to companies has shown on many occasions that failure by a company to observe the requirements of the first of these possibilities, i.e. a statutory demand, has led to a valid petition against an otherwise solvent company and, even if not to an eventual order, then at least to some sudden and intensive negotiation and high cost to the company in order to wriggle out of its predicament.

The possibilities, in accordance with *section 123* of the *IA 1986* (as modified), are as follows:

- if a creditor serves a statutory demand (see 16.5 below) which is not satisfied within three weeks;

- if execution or other court enforcement process is returned wholly or partly unsatisfied;

- if the LLP is unable to pay its debts as they fall due; and

- if the value of the LLP's assets are less than the amount of its liabilities (including those of a contingent and prospective nature).

The last two of these tests require an exercise in judgment and financial analysis by the court, but effectively mean that if the court is satisfied of the LLP's insolvency on either an income approach or a capital approach, that will enable it to grant a winding up order.

Statutory demands   16.5

The first of the reasons described at 16.4 above relates to the 'statutory demand', as it has come to be known, i.e. a demand, framed in the prescribed form, that the LLP should pay a sum due. That sum must be at least £750, or such other amount as may be set by the Secretary of State. In practice, that has been £750 since the inception of the *IA 1986*, and so with the effects of inflation has encompassed progressively more and more debts. The demand must be served on the LLP by leaving it at the LLP's registered office.

The LLP then has three weeks to pay up, or to secure or compound for the sum in question. It may, if it disputes the debt, challenge the demand itself in the court. Where many companies have erred is in not taking such demands sufficiently seriously, either by ignoring them or, even if the debt is genuinely disputed, by choosing to carry on that dispute in correspondence rather than with the court's protection, thus handing to the creditor on a plate the negotiating advantage of being able to petition for winding up.

The area of the statutory demand has been a fertile ground for case law, as a result of which the following principles have emerged.

- Service by post is acceptable (*Re a Company (No 008790 of 1990) [1991] BCLC 561*) but service by fax without consent is risky, as a clear copy may not print out (*Hastie & Jenkerson v McMahon [1991] 1 All ER 255*).

- The fact that a demand may overstate the debt does not invalidate it (*Re a Debtor (No 490 SD 1991), ex parte the Debtor v Printline (Offset) Limited [1992] 2 All ER 664*) so that the recipient should pay the undisputed part.

- The court does have jurisdiction to set aside a demand (despite the lack of a defined procedure to parallel similar applications in the context of individual insolvency) but only if there is a genuine dispute as to the claimed debt, and the setting aside application is not merely tactical (*Re Janeash Limited [1990] BCC 250*).

- Thus a serious cross-claim for an amount exceeding the original debt will normally be enough for a setting aside (*Re Bayoil SA [1999] 1 BCLC 62*).

Just and equitable   16.6

The ability of the court to wind up an LLP on the ground that it is 'just and equitable' to do so gives it an avowedly broad discretion, and it has been held that it should not fetter that discretion by deciding only to follow the lead of other previously accepted instances of unjust and inequitable behaviour (*Ebrahimi v Westbourne Galleries Limited [1973] AC 360*).

Some examples may be fairly straightforward, e.g. fraud on the part of a controlling member. Total deadlock in the management of the LLP may also be sufficient. More difficult however is where there is an exclusion of one or more members from the running of the business, and a breakdown of trust and confidence. Here, the original development of the law was in the context of partnerships, and that was then adopted in company law for those situations where the company was a quasi-partnership, so that the relationship between the participators, and the need for the trust between them, became important.

Interaction with other remedies   16.7

What may be difficult, not only for the petitioner in choosing what to apply for, but also for the court in deciding an appropriate remedy, is the interaction between this provision (*section 122* of the *IA 1986*: see 16.3 above) and the possible availability of other relief under *section 459* of the *Companies Act 1985*, dealing with remedies for unfair prejudice (see discussion in 12.59 et seq).

Section 125(2) of the *Insolvency Act 1986* (as modified) specifically requires the court, on considering a 'just and equitable' petition, to consider this aspect. If the court considers that the petitioners are entitled to relief (either by winding up or otherwise) and that (in the absence of any other remedy) it would be just and equitable for the LLP to be wound up, then it should make a winding up order.

However, the above does not apply if the court also thinks that there is another remedy that is available to the petitioners, and that they are acting unreasonably in seeking a winding up rather than that other order. The court will therefore need to determine whether *section 459* is potentially applicable (bearing in mind that an LLP may exclude its application) and whether, in the light of *O'Neill v Phillips [1999] 2 All ER 961*, there is a real prospect of a petition under that section offering effective relief without a winding up.

Potential petitioners   16.8

A range of people may have the status necessary to present a winding up petition. This may, by *section 124* of the *IA 1986*, include:

- the LLP itself;
- the members;
- any creditor(s) (even if only contingent or prospective);
- any contributory(ies);
- a magistrates' clerk seeking to enforce fines;
- the Secretary of State (see 16.9 below);
- the Official Receiver (where a voluntary winding up is already in progress).

One point to note is that the reference to 'the members' as potential petitioners is plural, whereas in the case of creditors or contributories the alternative of the singular is also offered. Thus the inference is that only the membership acting together by a duly passed resolution may petition, but this seems at odds with the idea of a 'just and equitable' petition being available to remedy wrongdoing on the part of one or more members, and in such circumstances individuals may need to rely on other capacities than mere membership, i.e. their status as creditors and/or contributories.

Petition by the Secretary of State   16.9

The powers of the Secretary of State are to be used, under *section 124A* of the *IA 1986*, where it appears to him to be expedient to do so in the public interest, and where the court consequently considers it just and equitable to agree the winding up.

This may follow (inter alia) an investigation undertaken by the Secretary of State under his powers under the *CA 1985* (see the discussion in 12.35 et seq).

Commencement of a winding up   16.10

It is not just the making of a winding up order which may potentially affect an LLP. There are various provisions which apply in the period from commencement of the winding up to the time when the petition is finally ruled upon by the court.

Commencement, in this context, means (under *section 129* of the *IA 1986*, as modified) either the time of a determination by the LLP for voluntary winding up; or in other cases the presentation of the petition. (Note therefore that if the determination is for the compulsory winding up of the LLP, so that the LLP is to be the petitioner, it is the petition not the determination which is the trigger for commencement.)

Dispositions between commencement and order   16.11

A provision which has tripped up many a company, and has the potential to do so for LLPs, is *section 127* of the *IA 1986*. As modified, this provision states that, after commencement of a winding up, any disposition of an LLP's property is void (without a court order to the contrary).

In the company context it has often been the case that the first the company has known of this is when its bank, having read in the *London Gazette* of the presentation of a winding up petition, shuts the bank accounts, and the company then realises that the creditor (whose statutory demand they have ignored, and whose petition they have regarded as just another debt collecting tactic) has actually achieved the closure of their business before the matter has ever reached the court. A frantic application then follows for what is known as a validation order, i.e. permission to carry on trading if the court can be persuaded that there is not an insolvent situation. Another possibility is an application to restrain the advertising or publicising of the petition, if the danger is spotted in time, and the petition is alleged to be groundless or vexatious.

Protection between commencement and order 16.12

The other side of the coin (from what is discussed at 16.11 above) is that, under *section 128* of the *IA 1986* (as modified), commencement will afford the LLP's property some protection, in that any subsequent process of execution against its property is also void.

Further, under *section 126* of the *IA 1986* (as modified), if other proceedings are in train against the LLP, it can apply for those to be stayed. That application may be to the court in which those proceedings are going on, if that is the High Court or the Court of Appeal; or to the winding up court in other instances. The court hearing the application has discretion as to whether to grant the stay and, if so, upon what terms.

The court's powers   16.13

The court's powers on hearing a winding up petition, under *section 125(1)* of the *IA 1986*, are wide. It may of course simply grant or refuse the application. It may adjourn either conditionally or unconditionally. It may make an interim order, or any other order it thinks fit.

One restriction on its powers is that it must not make a winding up order simply because the LLP has no assets, or because any assets it has have been mortgaged to an amount equal to or in excess of their value. Another is that referred to in 16.7 above (alternative remedy available – *IA 1986, s 125(2)*, as modified). If a winding up order is made, then the LLP (or anyone else so directed by the court) must send a copy to the Registrar (*IA 1986, s 130(1)*, as modified). The court may also, under *section 147* of the *IA 1986* (as modified), make an order to stay the winding up (either altogether or for a limited time) upon such terms and conditions as it thinks fit. Application for this may be made by the Official

Receiver, the liquidator, or any creditor or contributory. Copies of any order so made must be sent to both the LLP itself and the Registrar.

Further, there is a power for the court to order a rescission of the winding up order, but application for this must be made promptly, and the power will be sparingly used. (Both an inherent power and a statutory one under *Rule 7.47* apply.)

The LLP's statement of affairs   16.14

Once a winding up order is made, there is a broad duty placed upon the Official Receiver to investigate, under *section 132* of the *IA 1986* (as modified), the promotion, formation, business, dealings and affairs of the LLP and, if it has failed, the causes of that failure. If he thinks fit, he may report his findings to the court, and that report becomes prima facie evidence of the facts stated in it.

The first routine step in that investigation is to require one or more people to give a statement of affairs as to the LLP. This is to give the same information as referred to in 15.9, and any other information the Official Receiver requires. The categories of people who may be required to make the statement include past and present members of the LLP; anyone who took part in the formation of the LLP within the last year; any employee within that year; or anyone who is or has during that year been a member or employee in an LLP which in turn is a member of the subject LLP. (In this context, 'employee' includes anyone acting under a contract for services, i.e. self-employment status in other contexts is not a bar to the validity of the requirement.)

Once notice of the requirement is given to any such person, they have 21 days to produce the statement, unless the Official Receiver later releases the obligation or extends the period. There is however a power for anyone subject to such a requirement, if they have requested a release or an extension of time which has been refused, to apply to the court for relief. (These requirements for the production of statements of affairs also apply if a winding up order has not yet been made, but a provisional liquidator has been appointed.) Any person subject to a valid requirement who does not comply with it is subject to a fine and a daily default fine.

Public examination of members   16.15

Another weapon in the locker of the Official Receiver (or any subsequently appointed liquidator) is the power to apply to the court for a public examination under *section 133* of the *IA 1986* (as modified). This is within the discretion of the liquidator, save that (unless the court orders otherwise) he may be required to make such an application by creditors representing at least one half of the overall creditors by value, or by contributories representing at least three quarters of the contributories by value.

Those potentially subject to such an order are:

- any past or present member;

- any previous receiver or manager, liquidator or administrator;

- anyone who has been involved in the promotion, formation or management of the LLP.

The court will, if it grants the application, make procedural orders for the holding of the examination, which may range over any aspect of the LLP's affairs, or the conduct or dealings of the examinee. Questions may be posed not only by the Official Receiver or liquidator, but also by any special manager, any proving creditor, or any contributory.

This is a potentially fearsome procedure, and its seriousness is underlined by the fact that not only is failure to comply punishable as a contempt of court, but a court may, if it fears the prospective examinee might abscond, order his arrest and the seizure of any books, papers, records, money or goods in his possession (*IA 1986, s 134*, as modified).

Provisional liquidators   16.16

The court may, at any time before a winding up order is made, appoint a provisional liquidator of an LLP, to carry out such tasks as the court may give him, and subject to such limitations as the order appointing him may contain.

Section 135 of the *IA 1986* (as modified) applies here.

Appointment of a liquidator – the Official Receiver's role   16.17

The starting point is that, under *section 136* of the *IA 1986* (as modified), the Official Receiver is (subject to 16.19 below) the liquidator as from the making of a winding up order, and continues as such until another is appointed. He may also revert to the role in the event of a subsequent vacancy.

In his first twelve weeks of office, he must consider whether he believes it appropriate to invite the creditors and contributories to appoint a liquidator. If he decides it is not, he has to notify the court, the creditors and the contributories accordingly. If he thinks it is appropriate, he has to summon separate meetings of the creditors and the contributories. In any event, he can be required to summon such meetings by not less than a quarter of the LLP's creditors by value.

If the above process is not to be used, the Official Receiver may ask the Secretary of State, in accordance with *section 137* of the *IA 1986*, to appoint a liquidator (and in any event he must consider whether to do so if meetings of creditors and contributories are held but do not result in an appointment). The Secretary of State may make such an appointment (though he is not obliged to) and any liquidator so appointed must notify his appointment to all creditors (or, if the court permits, simply advertise it) and in the notice or advertisement, deal with the question of whether he intends to summon a creditors' meeting to consider appointing a liquidation committee.

Appointment of a liquidator by creditors and contributories   16.18

Each of the creditors and the contributories may, at their separate meetings, nominate a liquidator. Not surprisingly, if they make different choices, the creditors' nominee will prevail (*section 139* of the *IA 1986*, as modified).

That does not mean the making of a choice by the contributories is a waste of time, as if the creditors do not make a choice at all then their candidate will get the job. If there is a real dispute after different nominations, any creditor or contributor can apply to the court to ask it either to appoint the contributories' choice instead of, or jointly with, the creditors' nominee; or to appoint a third candidate not previously chosen by either side.

Appointment of a liquidator after voluntary arrangement or administration   16.19

A final variation on the theme of appointment of a liquidator is that the Official Receiver may never be involved at all.

If the LLP has previously been the subject of a voluntary arrangement, or an administration, then if a winding up order is made during the arrangement, or immediately upon the discharge of the administration, the insolvency practitioner previously acting as supervisor or administrator may be appointed by the court as liquidator, under *section 140* of the *IA 1986* (as modified).

Liquidation committees 16.20

If the possible meetings of creditors and contributories referred to above have been called (see 16.17), then at those meetings they may appoint a liquidation committee (*section 141* of the *IA 1986*, as modified). Alternatively any liquidator (other than the Official Receiver) may if he thinks fit summon such meetings specifically for the purpose of enabling consideration of whether such a committee should be appointed, and, if so, who should be on it; and indeed he must do so if requested by not less than one tenth of the LLP's creditors by value.

The danger of the matter being considered by two separate meetings is that of course they may not agree. The presumption is that there should be such a committee, and so if only one meeting reaches a decision to appoint, whether the other disagrees or is silent, the committee shall be established (unless the court otherwise orders).

Rules 4.151 to 4.178 apply to the establishment process. The committee has certain functions designated for it by the legislation. If however there is no such committee, or if the liquidator at the time is the Official Receiver, those powers are normally vested in the Secretary of State. In the latter case, therefore, the committee's actual involvement is held in suspense until another liquidator is appointed.

The position regarding contributories 16.21

Under *section 148* of the *IA 1986* (as modified), it is the task of the court, as soon as possible after a winding up order is made, to make a list of all contributories, unless it appears to the court that it will not be necessary either to call on contributories to make any payment, or to adjust the rights of the contributories *inter se*.

The court may then call upon any contributory so listed to pay to the liquidator either any monies generally due to the LLP (*IA 1986, s 149*, as modified) or any monies due as calls (bearing in mind that members can only be liable insofar as they have chosen to be). If it needs to distinguish between contributories, it can be practical and consider the likelihood of actual payment being received when adjusting the contributions called for.

The court may also adjust the rights of contributories *inter se*, and in particular rule upon the distribution of any surplus assets (see 16.23 below). If a contributory is seen as likely to abscond, or to remove or conceal property in order to avoid payment of calls, then the court may order his arrest, and the seizure of his books, papers, and movable personal property, under *section 158* of the *IA 1986*.

The liquidator's general duties   16.22

It is not the place of this work to look in detail at the role of liquidators, for that generally will be the same in the LLP context as it is in the company context, but it worth pausing to look at those provisions which may impact upon an LLP, and the anticipation of which may help in the drawing up of the partnership agreement.

The liquidator's general duties are stated in *section 143* of the *IA 1986*, namely to get in, and realise the LLP's assets. By *sections 144* and *145* of the *IA 1986* he is to take over all the LLP's property (including intangibles) and may apply to the court for an order vesting any property held by the LLP (or any trustees for it) in his name. He may bring or defend any proceedings which are necessary in relation to the LLP's property, or generally to effectuate the winding up. At the end of the process, he is to distribute the LLP's property.

Distribution of surplus   16.23

The distribution is of course normally to the creditors, but in the (admittedly perhaps rare) instance where there is a surplus after all expenses and creditors have been paid, there may be a need to distribute that surplus.

The statute simply refers to the distribution being to 'the persons entitled to it'. In the company context, ascertaining who those people are is a comparatively straightforward exercise, as their shareholdings will determine the position. In an LLP context, however, the position is more difficult. Admittedly, the distribution will be to the members, but in what proportions? The most obvious would be the proportions which capital accounts bear to each other, but this may not always represent the wishes of the membership. There seems no reason (other than that it may seem unduly pessimistic to consider such matters when setting up the LLP) why the partnership agreement should not attempt to determine the question, especially if any form of distribution *in specie* is considered both possible and desirable.

Final meeting   16.24

At the end of the process, when all has been collected in, the liquidator's task under *section 146* of the *IA 1986* (as modified) is to summon a final creditors' meeting to consider whether to accept his final report and grant him his release, and he must keep sufficient funds in hand to enable him to do this.

That may be simultaneous with the final payments out but, if before that, must be adjourned until those payments are made.

17 – General Winding Up Provisions

This chapter looks at those provisions which are common to all types of winding up as regards an LLP. It starts by considering the role of contributories in a winding up, and the potential application of that role to members of the LLP. It reviews briefly the powers of a liquidator, and who needs to sanction some of those powers, before moving on to potential removal of a liquidator. A range of matters regarding malpractice in relation to winding up is then covered, including various offences of fraud etc., the summary remedies available to the court for breach of duty, wrongful trading, and the potential clawback of 'withdrawals' taken by members (a provision unique to LLPs).

Sanctions for the improper use of 'phoenix' trading names for LLPs are explained. Following the malpractice theme, the provisions guarding against transactions at an undervalue, and preferences, are examined, together with the convoluted definitions applicable to the concept of being an 'associate' in relation to those provisions.

Introduction   17.1

A substantial number of provisions apply to all sorts of winding up of LLPs, whether the liquidation in question be a members' voluntary, a creditors' voluntary or a compulsory one. These are found in the provisions of the *Insolvency 1986* set out in the table below.

Part of the Act	Sections	Nature
IV (Ch I)	73–82	Members as contributories★
IV (Chs VII to X)	163–219	Liquidators and malpractice★
VI	230–246	Miscellaneous (inc transfers at undervalue & preferences★)
VII	247–251	Interpretation

Part of the Act	Sections	Nature
XII	386–387	Preferential debts
XIII	388–398	Insolvency Practitioners & qualifications
XIV	399–410	Public administration
XV	411–419	Subordinate legislation
XVI	423–425	Debt avoidance
XVII	426–434	Miscellaneous & general
XVIII	435–436	Interpretation (inc 'Associate'★)
XIX	438–444	Final provisions

Limits of presentation   17.2

The point needs making again that this is a book on LLPs, not a treatise on insolvency. For that reason, a large number of the provisions listed above are not touched on at all, since they are not substantively varied by the LLP legislation from their company equivalents, and readers should direct themselves to the standard insolvency texts for detailed discussions of them.

This chapter tries simply to pick out those provisions which either can be predicted as likely to impact in some instances on LLPs, or which are different for, or unique to, LLPs. Those areas are indicated by an asterisk in the above table.

Members as contributories

Agreement to contribute   17.3

It is possible for members of an LLP to agree to between themselves, or with the LLP itself, that in the event of the liquidation of the LLP they will contribute to its assets, in order to help meet the debts and liabilities of the LLP and the expenses of the winding up.

This agreement may relate to liquidation generally, or in specific circumstances. It may be to whatever extent of contribution is agreed. The agreement may provide for adjustment of the rights of the contributories between themselves. Even past members may be included within the agreement, if it made clear that their liability is to survive their ceasing to be members. All this is provided for in *IA 1986, s 74* (as modified).

Reasons for agreeing to contribute   **17.4**

What *section 74* of the *Insolvency Act 1986* (see 17.3 above) does not make clear, however, is why on earth the members would wish to enter into such an agreement in the first place. Since the whole point of seeking the status of a limited liability partnership would seem to be to avail the members of that limitation, what motive could there be for voluntarily assuming even a restricted degree of personal liability?

It is suggested that, for the avoidance of doubt, and subject to the point made in 17.5 below, it may well be prudent for the partnership agreement specifically to state that no such agreement exists, since the section does not specify what form the contribution agreement might take, and it would be as well to avoid any possibility of a later contention that there was some form of implied agreement to that effect.

There seem to be only two possible reasons for agreeing to contribute. One is dealt with in 17.5 below. The other is if such an agreement is necessary to persuade third parties that the LLP is sufficiently financially sound for them to deal with it. Even in such circumstances the agreement to contribute should be limited and precisely defined, or the whole LLP formation will be pointless.

Status as contributories   **17.5**

In the event of there being any such contribution agreement (see 17.4 above), those present and past members of the LLP who have agreed to contribute are referred to as 'contributories', under *IA 1986, s 79* (as modified).

The term also includes anyone alleged to be a contributory. It does not however include anyone whose liability to contribute is the compulsory result of proceedings being taken against him for fraudulent or wrongful trading, or by way of the provisions referred to later in this chapter relating to the 'clawback' of withdrawals (see 17.18 below). The attainment of this status appears to be the only other possible reason for agreeing to make a contribution on a winding up. Thus, if an agreement provided that, in the event of liquidation, each member should contribute, say, five pounds (rather like a member of a company limited by guarantee) this would give all members the position of contributories in a winding up, with consequent rights to e.g. present a petition, or vote in a compulsory winding up for the appointment of a liquidator, or have a say in the appointment of a liquidation committee. If members feel that such a status, in the event of a winding up, would benefit them, then they should include provision for this in the partnership agreement.

Contribution as a debt   17.6

The contributory's liability creates a civil debt payable when called upon. The debt is defined by the modified *section 80* of the *Insolvency Act 1986* as a specialty debt, so the period of limitation applicable will be twelve years (in accordance with *section 8* of the *Limitation Act 1980*).

The debt binds a deceased contributory's estate, and his personal representatives in turn are brought into the definition of contributories, and if they default, the court may order the administration of the estate to be taken over in order to enforce the payment (*IA 1986, s 81*, as modified).

Similarly, if the contributory becomes bankrupt then, under *section 82* of the *IA 1986* (as modified), his trustee represents him and becomes a contributory, with the debt being provable in the bankruptcy, not only for calls already made, but also in an estimated amount for future calls.

Liquidators

General   17.7

A number of provisions relating to the appointment of liquidators have already been dealt with in the previous chapters (see chapters 15 and 16) relating to both voluntary and compulsory winding up.

Sections 163 to *174* of the *Insolvency Act 1986* (as modified) deal more generally with the liquidator's position once appointed.

A liquidator's powers   17.8

The powers attaching to a liquidator are set out in *IA 1986, Sch 4* (as modified). Most of those are vested in him automatically.

Some, however, only vest in him with the requisite consent. In the case of a members' voluntary winding up of an LLP, the consent which is requisite, under *IA 1986, s 165* (as modified), is that of the members of the LLP. The liquidator is accordingly given power to summon a meeting of the members to consider whether to give that consent, and provision is made for the procedures applying to such a summoning.

In relation to a creditors' voluntary winding up, if the LLP is dilatory in calling the necessary creditors' meeting, or if the designated members fail to provide the necessary statement of affairs (under *sections 98* and *99* respectively of the *Insolvency Act 1986*) then the liquidator is given the responsibility of applying to the court for directions, under *IA 1986, s 166(5)* (as modified), if either is more than a week late.

Removal of a liquidator   17.9

In the case of removal of a liquidator, again a members' meeting may have a part to play. If a members' voluntary winding up is proceeding, a meeting of the members summoned specially for the purpose may determine to remove the liquidator from office (*IA 1986, s 171*, as modified). (In the case of a creditors' voluntary winding up, the liquidator may be removed by a meeting of the creditors summoned specially for the purpose.)

If however the liquidator has, notwithstanding that it is a voluntary winding up, been appointed by the court (i.e. acting under *section 108* of the *Insolvency Act 1986* where there has either been an unfilled post, or the court has itself removed the liquidator's predecessor) then its appointee can only be displaced by such a members' meeting (or, as the case may be, creditors' meeting) if its calling is approved by:

- the liquidator himself;

- the court;

- members having not less than half of the total members' voting rights (or, as the case may be, one-half (in value) of the creditors).

In the event of such a removal, notice needs to be given to the Registrar, and the liquidator's release from office, and the discharge of his liability in respect of the winding up, dates from that notification.

Malpractice before and during winding up

Fraud in anticipation of winding up   17.10

The period before the commencement of a winding up is normally one in which the main participators in the business, at least, are painfully aware of its problems. The temptation therefore exists to remove the assets of the business and to put them out of the reach of the liquidator who may be looming on the horizon. The offence therefore exists, under *IA 1986, s 206* (as modified), for past and present members, of committing fraud in anticipation of a winding up, and this is punishable by imprisonment, a fine, or both.

The above offence can be made up of a number of acts, as below, but the key thing is that they all have to have been committed in the year before commencement of the winding up. By way of reminder, this is the determination to wind up in the case of a voluntary winding up, or where the LLP is itself the petitioner for a compulsory winding up, or the presentation of the petition in other compulsory windings up.

The prohibited acts, in broad terms are:

- concealing, or fraudulently removing, any part of the LLP's property worth £500 or more;

- concealing any debt due to or from the LLP;

- concealing, destroying, mutilating, altering or falsifying any of the LLP's books or papers;

- pawning or disposing any of the LLP's property obtained on unpaid credit.

The net can be cast wide, and being privy to one of these acts committed by another can bring liability. Shadow members may offend as well as members. It may however be a defence to show that there was no intent to defraud, or to conceal, as appropriate.

Transactions to defraud creditors 17.11

Similarly, but more broadly in terms of time (see 17.10 above), since here the offence can occur by reason of an act within five years before the commencement of the winding up, there are provisions under *IA 1986, s 207* (as modified) to restrain acts which are against the creditors' interests.

An offence is committed if someone, who was at the time a member has:

- made, or caused to be made:

  ○ any gift or transfer of the LLP's property; or

  ○ any charge on the LLP's property; or

- caused, or connived at, the levying of any execution against the LLP's property; or

- concealed or removed any part of the LLP's property, either after the date of any unsatisfied money judgment or order against the LLP, or within a period of two months before such a judgment or order.

In this context 'member' appears not to include shadow member, perhaps because from a five-year distance the degree of control needed for this status could be particularly difficult to prove. It is a defence to show that there was, at the time of the conduct in question, no intent to defraud the creditors. If an offence is proved, it is again punishable by imprisonment, or fine or both.

Miscellaneous offences in the course of winding up   17.12

It is not however only fraud (see 17.10 and 17.11 above) which can create offences by past and present members in the context of a winding up. A range of offences, mostly punishable by imprisonment or fine, and mostly applicable to shadow members as well as to members, appears in *sections 208* to *211* of the *Insolvency Act 1986* (as modified).

Without offering an exhaustive list, these offences include:

- failure fully to disclose to the liquidator the extent of the LLP's property, or details of disposals of it;

- failure to hand over all the LLP's property, books and papers to the liquidator;

- failure to warn the liquidator if someone is falsely proving for a debt in the liquidation;

- preventing the production of any relevant books or papers;

- falsifying losses or expenses;

- destroying, mutilating, altering or falsifying any books, papers or securities;

- making (or being privy to the making of) any false or fraudulent entry in the LLP's accounts;

- making any material omission in a statement of affairs relating to the LLP;

- making a false representation to persuade the LLP's creditors to agree any particular course of action.

Generally, in the context of such matters, it is a defence to show that there was no intent to defraud, or to conceal etc.

Summary remedies   17.13

The court is given summary powers, by *IA 1986, s 212* (as modified), to examine a person's conduct, and to compel the repayment of money (with interest) or the restoration of property etc; or to require the payment of compensation by way of contribution to the LLP's assets in the winding up.

The jurisdiction can apply to any present or past member; or to anyone who has acted as liquidator, administrator or administrative receiver of the LLP; or to anyone outside those categories who has been involved in the promotion, formation or management of the LLP. This last definition is wide enough to mean that it is not necessary specifically to include shadow members, and indeed it could well be wide enough to catch someone who had been acting informally as a 'company doctor' or 'business turnaround adviser'.

The section applies if such a person has misapplied, retained, or become accountable for the LLP's property, or been guilty of any misfeasance or breach of fiduciary duty 'in relation to' the LLP. (The use of the phrase 'in relation to' is interesting, for it seems to go beyond simply a duty owed 'to' the LLP. If, for instance, duties could be established between the members *inter se*, might a breach of any such duty be sufficient to activate the section? Another reason, perhaps, to state the extent or absence of such duties as clearly as possible in the partnership agreement.) In the case of a liquidator or administrator, such duties do include those arising out of the carrying out of his functions in that office, but the court's powers cannot be invoked against such a person, without leave of the court, after he has received his release.

An application to the court for it to exercise its powers under this section may be made by the Official Receiver, by the liquidator, by any creditor, or by any contributory with the leave of the court.

Fraudulent trading – criminal sanctions 17.14

One aspect of the law in this area does not come from the *Insolvency Act 1986* at all, but is to be found in the modified *section 458* of the *Companies Act 1985*, dealing with fraudulent trading. This applies just as much to LLPs as to companies, and to conduct during a winding up just as before it.

That provision creates a criminal offence punishable by a fine or imprisonment. It may link in to the various offences created by the *IA 1986* and examined here. The offence is very simply described, i.e. that it is made out if any business of an LLP is carried on with intent to defraud creditors (whether of the LLP or any other person) or for a fraudulent purpose. Every person knowingly a party to the carrying on of the business in that manner commits the offence.

Fraudulent trading – civil remedies 17.15

Section 213 of the *Insolvency Act 1986* (as modified) picks up on the wording of *CA 1985, s 458* noted above at 17.14.

This provision adds, to the criminal sanctions which *section 458* offers, the ability of the liquidator in such circumstances to apply to the court for a declaration, to the effect that any persons who were knowingly party to the carrying on of the business in the fraudulent manner shall make such contributions to the LLP's assets as the court thinks fit.

The concept of wrongful trading 17.16

In practice, the concept of wrongful trading will be much more frequently a concern than that of fraudulent trading. Most often, that concern will be in a genuine attempt to avoid the possibility of being accused of wrongful trading, and thus to manage the LLP's affairs, when insolvency threatens, in such a manner that the accusation cannot be levelled at members.

Wrongful trading, under *section 214* of the *Insolvency Act 1986*, can apply to a member (or shadow member) who, before the LLP went into insolvent liquidation, knew or ought to have concluded that there was no reasonable prospect of the LLP avoiding insolvent liquidation. If a member has that awareness, it is incumbent upon him to take all steps necessary to minimise the potential loss to the LLP's creditors. Usually, that will mean shutting the doors and ceasing to trade. However, the question becomes more difficult if the member, whilst aware that such liquidation is likely, genuinely believes that continuing to trade will improve the creditors' lot, e.g. because the problems have resulted from an off-season drain on income and the business is about to enter its good season.

Remedies for wrongful trading 17.17

The liquidator may, if the LLP has gone into insolvent liquidation (i.e. if its assets are insufficient to pay both its debts and other liabilities on the one hand and the expenses of the winding up on the other) and if he considers that there has been wrongful trading (see 17.16 above), apply to the court. (No-one else has the right to apply, e.g. the creditors cannot.)

If the court finds the necessary facts made out, it can order the offender to make such contribution to the LLP's assets in the winding up as it thinks fit. It may be necessary for the court to consider the state of mind of the member at the time of the alleged acts. It is entitled to consider that the facts which the member knew or ought to have known, the conclusions which he ought to have reached, and the steps which he ought to have taken, can be viewed from either of two perspectives.

The first of these perspectives is that the facts, conclusions and steps may be considered from the viewpoint of the general knowledge, skill and experience which may reasonably be expected of a person carrying out the same functions as are carried out by that particular member in relation to the LLP. Secondly, they may be considered from the actual general knowledge, skill and experience of that particular member. Thus, it will not be enough for a member to allege that he should be excused because his is purely an operational and not a financial role (e.g. a junior member in a large legal LLP who plays no part in the firm's day-to-day operational decisions) if he actually does know the position or ought to know it from generally available facts. Further, it does not absolve a member who was required to carry out functions to say that he has not in fact carried them out, e.g. it would be no use for a member given a financial management role to say that he had not actually bothered to look at the accounts recently.

The clawback provision – general   17.18

The one provision in the modified version of the *IA 1986* which is exclusive to LLPs is the new *section 214A*, headed 'Adjustment of withdrawals', but popularly known as the 'clawback' provision.

This has led some observers to wonder whether the Government has been sufficiently serious about the principle of excluding personal liability as to make the adoption of the LLP vehicle worthwhile, but the fact remains that there are at least limitations upon the attacks upon members which can be launched under this section, whereas there are no such limits in an ordinary partnership.

The first point to note is that this an overlay to the existing legislation, and not a substitute for it. It applies in the context of any form of winding up; but not in that of any other form of insolvency proceedings, e.g. a voluntary arrangement or an administration. It potentially affects any member, or shadow member.

The concept of 'withdrawals'   17.19

Section 214A of the *Insolvency Act 1986* (see 17.18 above) can potentially be used by a liquidator to attack any 'withdrawal' made during the relevant period.

A 'withdrawal' is very widely defined concept, and can be anything from normal monthly drawings to loan repayments, and includes any form of withdrawal of property. It does not therefore need to be anything abnormal or outside the normal commercial practice. The relevant period is two years from the commencement of the winding up. Anyone who was a member during this period is vulnerable, whether or not he has continued to be a member up to the commencement of the winding up.

Tests applicable to clawback   17.20

The liquidator has to be able to prove to the court that, at the time of the particular withdrawal (see 17.19 above), the member either knew, or had reasonable ground for believing, one of two things. The first is fairly straightforward, namely that, when the withdrawal was taken, the LLP was unable to pay its debts within the meaning of the legislation (see 16.4 above). That can of course relate either to assets against liabilities, or income against expenditure.

The second thing is markedly more vague. It refers to the possibility that the LLP, though not unable to pay its debts before the withdrawal, would become so after the withdrawal, by means of the depletion of assets caused by that act. In some instances this might be simple, e.g. if there were to be such a major capital withdrawal as to change the picture entirely. Even the second limb of this aspect of the test does not cause too many problems, i.e. that not only the withdrawal by that particular member has to be taken into account, but so also do those taken by the other members. Thus if it is a month's drawings which tip the balance, it is the aggregate change in the LLP's fortunes which count.

The problems come with the last words of the relevant subsection, which say that it is enough for the liquidator to prove that the member knew, or had reasonable cause for believing, that the LLP would become unable to pay its debts as a result of all withdrawals 'in contemplation' at the time of the particular withdrawal which the liquidator seeks to recover. No guidance is offered on how this contemplation is to be approached, and no time limit is indicated. Would it, for instance, be sufficient to enable the liquidator to invoke the section if members were to continue their normal drawings pattern if they recognised that to continue to do so for two years, unless trading conditions altered, would be enough to make the LLP insolvent?

The court's discretion on clawback   17.21

Fortunately, the court's jurisdiction in regard to clawback is discretionary. If it finds the liquidator has proved his point, it 'may' make an order in relation to any particular person. It may therefore decline to do so, and it may differentiate between various members.

The order it can make is for the member to make such contribution to the LLP's assets as the court thinks proper. It cannot however make an order for the contribution of a sum which exceeds the aggregate of the withdrawals made by the individual in question during the relevant two-year period.

The member's state of mind on clawback   17.22

There is also a further test that the court has to pose in regard to clawback. It is confusingly worded, with a double negative (by contrast with the similar provision relating to wrongful trading under *section 214* of the *Insolvency Act 1986* discussed at 17.16 above) but what it seems to say is that the individual has to be considered to have posed to himself, each time he makes a withdrawal, the question whether, having taken that withdrawal, there remained a reasonable prospect that the LLP would be able to avoid insolvent liquidation. (As with *section 214*, insolvent liquidation means one where the LLP's assets are inadequate to pay not only its debts and liabilities, but also all the winding up expenses as well.)

Unless the individual knew that such a prospect did not exist, or unless he should have realised that, the court may not make an order against him. That is a relatively familiar concept, from experience of the operation of *section 214*. The problem, however, is that *IA 1986, s 214A* states that the court's ability to make an order is excluded only if the relevant belief is established at the time of 'each' withdrawal during the two-year period. It does not say that the court shall pose the test in respect of all particular withdrawals (though that may well be what it meant to say). It seems therefore that if there is *any* withdrawal during the two-year period, in respect of which the member cannot say that he neither knew nor ought to have known that insolvent liquidation loomed, that is sufficient to open the court's jurisdiction to attack *all* withdrawals during the period. It is to be hoped that the court will interpret this liberally, and in effect apply the test to each withdrawal separately.

Guidance on the member's state of mind   17.23

Whatever the way the test is to be applied (see 17.22 above), there is at least guidance (similar again to that under *section 214* of the *Insolvency Act 1986*: see 17.16 above) on what aptitude is expected of any individual, when considering what he should have known as to the LLP's future prospects.

He is considered to have been under a duty to know or ascertain relevant facts, and to reach appropriate conclusions from them. That duty is to be applied on an individual basis, given two assumptions for each person. Firstly, he must carry out that duty using the knowledge, skill and experience reasonably expected of someone carrying out his functions within the LLP. Secondly, however, there is the knowledge, skill and experience which that particular member actually has. The example given at the end of 17.16 would thus apply.

Conclusions on the clawback provision   17.24

In practice, *section 214A* of the *Insolvency Act 1986* may not be as easy for a liquidator to apply as it may seem. He has a number of points to prove, and the burden of that proof is firmly upon him. He needs to do that in respect of each and every member or shadow member, and the court will have to consider the position on an individual basis, so that the costs may potentially be substantial.

The work involved in trying to prove what the state of mind of someone ought to have been two years before the liquidation commenced – and hence inevitably several years before the matter reaches court – will be considerable. It may in practice be the case that it is only in fairly clear-cut cases that this weapon will be wielded. It is suggested therefore that – particularly going back to the point that no such right is needed in respect of partnerships because the partners' assets are all at risk anyway – the existence of this section should not be sufficient to put people off the idea of forming an LLP.

Proceedings relating to sections 213, 214 and 214A   17.25

There are a number of procedural provisions, contained in *IA 1986, s 215* (as modified), which are common to proceedings for contribution orders under any of the sections relating to fraudulent trading (see 17.15 above), wrongful trading (see 17.19 above) or clawback (see 17.18 above). The liquidator may, in those proceedings, give evidence himself, or call witnesses.

The court may, to give effect to its contribution orders, give directions and, in particular, may order the amount due from the member to be charged upon:

● any debt or obligation due from the LLP to him;

- any mortgage or charge on the LLP's assets held by or (directly or indirectly) for him.

The court may subsequently make further orders to give effect to any such charge. The charge can bind an assignee of a mortgage or charge on the LLP's assets, but not if that assignee took in good faith, for valuable consideration (other than marriage) and without notice of the problems giving rise to the contribution order.

Further, if the person against whom the contribution order is made is a creditor of the LLP, the court can order that all or part of any debt (and interest) owed to that person shall rank in priority after all the LLP's other debts (and interest).

All of these provisions can apply regardless of the fact that criminal sanctions may also be pursued against the offending person.

Restrictions on re-use of LLP names   17.26

There are considerable restrictions, under *IA 1986, s 216* (as modified), upon the activities of any person (natural or corporate) who has been a member of an LLP which goes into insolvent liquidation (for which the test is the same as in preceding paragraphs) within the year before it went into liquidation. (Curiously, here, the relevant time is not the commencement of the winding up, but the day before the actual liquidation took effect.)

Any name by which the LLP has been known during that final year, and any name which is so similar to it as to suggest an association with the LLP, becomes a 'prohibited name'. This does not have to relate to the official name of the LLP only, but can also relate to any trading name used by it. For five years from the day the LLP goes into liquidation, such a person must not (without the leave of the court) be:

- a member of another LLP known by a prohibited name;

- involved at all in the promotion, formation or management of such an LLP;

- involved at all in any business carried on, under a prohibited name, by a vehicle other than an LLP.

Sanctions for wrongful use of prohibited names   17.27

There are two sanctions for breach of the provisions discussed at 17.26 above.

First, under *section 216* itself (see also 17.26), there is a criminal offence of wrongful use of a prohibited name, punishable by imprisonment, or fine or both. Secondly, under *IA 1986, s 217* (as modified), the offender will be personally liable for the debts of an LLP carrying on business under a prohibited name if he is involved in its management.

Further, if anyone (whether a member of the former LLP or not) who is involved in the management of that new LLP's business, acts or is willing to act upon the instructions of someone he knows to be contravening *section 216*, he acquires such personal liability as well. Anyone who is thus personally liable is jointly and severally liable not only with the LLP itself, but also with any other person who picks up such personal liability under the section. This applies to all debts incurred whilst so involved in the LLP's management. Membership of the new LLP is not necessary for a person to be considered as involved in its management if he is actually so involved, directly or indirectly.

Reporting of apparent offences 17.28

It may well be the case that, during the conduct of a winding up, matters come to the attention of those officials involved which appear to them to constitute criminal behaviour on the part of past or present members of the LLP, in relation to the LLP. *Sections 218* and *219* of the *Insolvency Act 1986* (as modified) deal with this situation.

Firstly, those sections provide reporting lines. Thus, the court on a compulsory winding up may order the liquidator to report such matters to the Secretary of State. If however, in such a winding up, it is the liquidator who discovers the conduct, he must report it to the Official Receiver. In the context of a voluntary winding up, the liquidator must report to the Secretary of State, and give him such information and documents as he may require, as the Secretary of State may then investigate the matter using the powers in *sections 431* and *432* of the *Companies Act 1985* (see 12.36 and 12.37 above).

If no such report has been made by the liquidator, but matters come before the court for some reason and it concludes that he should have made a report, it may order him to do so. If subsequent criminal proceedings are taken then it becomes the duty of a range of people to give the prosecution all assistance they are reasonably able to give. This applies to the liquidator, to every past and present member of the LLP, and to every past and present agent of the LLP, which term includes the LLP's auditors, bankers and solicitors. Neglect or failure to give such assistance can result in a court order for compliance.

Transactions at undervalue and preferences

General 17.29

Continuing the theme of those aspects of a winding up which may involve personal liability, the next area to consider is the linked provisions governing transactions at an undervalue (see 17.30 below), and preferences (see 17.31 below), which are found in *sections 238 to 241* of the *Insolvency Act 1986* (as modified), and *section 435* of the same statute which defines the relevant term of 'associate'.

These provisions apply both in the context of an administration and a liquidation (whether voluntary or compulsory) and so there are various references to the role of the 'office-holder', meaning the liquidator or administrator. Both have the concept of whether events have occurred within a relevant time, and that expression is similarly defined for both sets of circumstances by *section 240* (see 17.32 below). The orders which may be made, if the various circumstances are made out, are likewise similar, and governed by *section 241* (see 17.33 below).

Transactions at an undervalue 17.30

Under *section 238* of the *Insolvency Act 1986*, a transaction made at a relevant time at an undervalue may be the subject of an application by the office-holder to the court for an order to restore the position to what it would have been if the LLP had not entered into the transaction.

A transaction at an undervalue between an LLP and a person is deemed to have occurred if:

- the LLP makes a gift to that person; or

- the LLP enters into a transaction with that person on terms which mean the LLP receives no consideration; or

- the LLP enters into a transaction with that person where the consideration received by the LLP is substantially less than the consideration given by it.

Consideration in this sense can be in money, or money's worth. Even if the transaction is thus at an undervalue, however, the court shall not make an order if it believes that the LLP entered into the transaction in good faith, for the purpose of carrying on its business, and in the reasonable belief that it was for its own benefit.

Preferences 17.31

A preference under *section 239* of the *Insolvency Act 1986* can be given at a relevant time by an LLP to two classes of people. The first is its creditors. The second is any surety or guarantor for its debts or liabilities. It is given if the LLP does anything (or allows anything to happen) which has the effect of putting that person in a better position than they would otherwise have been in, in the event that the LLP later goes into insolvent liquidation.

The fact that an event may thus be a preference is not however, of itself, enough to justify an order being sought. It must also be shown that the LLP was influenced by a desire to produce the effect of thus benefiting the third party. That intention is however presumed in the case of a preference where the beneficiary is a person connected with the LLP (though merely being employed by the LLP is not enough to imply connection). The fact that the act alleged to constitute a preference was actually done in pursuance of a court order does not prevent its being attackable under the section.

Relevant time 17.32

The time periods which are indicated by *section 240* of the *IA 1986* as relevant are calculated by reference to the 'onset of insolvency'. That expression is defined as either the date of presentation of a petition for an administration order (if the LLP is subject either to an administration or to a winding up commencing immediately upon the discharge of an administration order) or the commencement of a winding up.

For a time to be a 'relevant time', it has to be one at which the LLP was unable to pay its debts (on any of the tests set out in *IA 1986, s 123*) or became unable to pay its debts as a result of the event in question. Such an inability is however to be presumed (unless proved otherwise) if the third party benefiting from the event is a connected person.

Subject to those tests, the relevant time limits, outside which the office-holder cannot make application, are two years before the onset of insolvency if the event is either a transaction at an undervalue, or a preference given to a connected person; or six months before the onset if the preference is given to an unconnected person. (In either case, an additional relevant period is that between the presentation of a petition for an administration order and the making of an order on that petition.)

Available orders 17.33

Section 241(1) of the *Insolvency Act 1986* lists a number of types of order which, without prejudice to the breadth of the court's powers, it can make on an application in relation to such events as above.

In broad terms, these orders are:

- to require the re-vesting in the LLP of any property transferred;

- to require the vesting in the LLP of the proceeds of sale of any property transferred;

- to release or discharge any security given by the LLP;

- to require any person to repay any benefits received;

- to provide for the restoration of any released or discharged surety or guarantee;

- to create and give appropriate priority to security required to ensure the performance of the order;

- to provide for the extent to which the person who is to be subjected to the order can prove in the winding up for debts and liabilities due to him.

The effect of orders on third parties   17.34

It is not always the case that the person against whom an order (see 17.33 above) is sought will be the same as the person who actually entered into the original transaction, or was given the original preference. Property may have passed into third-party hands. Such an order may not however, under *section 241(2)* of the *Insolvency Act 1986*, affect property or a benefit acquired by such a third party in good faith and for value.

However, a lack of good faith is presumed (unless otherwise proved) if that third party had notice of both the 'relevant surrounding circumstances' and the 'relevant proceedings'; or if the third party was connected to, or an associate of, the LLP, or the original beneficiary of the transaction or preference. For this purpose the 'relevant surrounding circumstances' are that the third party either knew that the transaction was at an undervalue; or knew of the circumstances which made the event a preference. The 'relevant proceedings' are, in short, the commencement of the particular form of insolvency proceedings which relate to the LLP.

Similar provisions for individuals   17.35

In passing, it should be noted that there are provisions in *sections 423* to *425* of the *Insolvency Act 1986* which are similar to those relating to transactions at an undervalue, but in the context of individuals' bankruptcy. These could thus apply to members as individuals.

They are mentioned here only because the concept of association referred to in 17.36 below includes specific extra definitions for members.

Meaning of 'associate' in relation to the LLP   17.36

Reference was made above to whether a person was an 'associate' of the LLP. This term is defined by the modified *section 435* of the *Insolvency Act 1986*.

Being 'associated' is, incidentally, a two-way concept, so that if A is deemed associated with B they are associates of each other. In the context of an LLP, the idea of association needs to be considered firstly in relation to the LLP itself, and secondly (see 17.35 above) in relation to the members of an LLP as individuals (see also 17.38 below). In the former case, it is provided by *section 435(6)*, that an LLP is an associate of another LLP if:

● the same person has control of both; or

● a person has control of one, and the other is controlled by him and/or his associates;

● the same group of two or more people have control of both; or

● the groups having control of each could be regarded as consisting of the same persons if one or more members of either group were replaced by a person who is his associate.

Further, by *section 435(7)* of the *Insolvency Act 1986*, an LLP is an associate of another person (i.e. not necessarily of another LLP) if he, or he and his associates, together have control of it. Control in this context means the ability to ensure that the LLP is accustomed to act in accordance with the controller's directions or instructions, or the ability to exercise (or control the exercise of) at least a third of the votes at any meeting of the LLP or its parent LLP.

Meaning of 'associate' in relation to members of the LLP   17.37

There is special provision in *section 435(3A)* of the *Insolvency Act 1986* (as modified) for who are to be defined as a member's associates.

These are the LLP itself, every other member of it, and the spouse or relative of every other member of it.

Meaning of 'associate' in relation to individuals 17.38

All the above discussion of association includes, to some extent, consideration of when an individual is an associate of another. That is so if that other is:

- his spouse; or
- his relative; or
- his relative's spouse; or
- his spouse's relative; or
- his spouse's relative's spouse; or
- his partner in a partnership; or
- his partner's spouse or relative; or
- his employee; or
- his employer.

'Relative' is in turn defined to mean any brother, sister, uncle, aunt, nephew, niece, lineal ancestor or lineal descendant. Half-blood relationships are included, as are step-relationships or those deriving from adoption, and illegitimate relationships. A member of an LLP is treated as an employee of it for this purpose.

Matters arising after winding up

Declaring an LLP's dissolution void 17.39

There may be circumstances where, even after an LLP has been wound up and consequently dissolved, it becomes necessary to revive it. In such circumstances, the Court has the power to declare the dissolution to have been void (*CA 1985, s 651*, as modified). This would normally be in order to enable litigation against the LLP to proceed. Application may be made either by the LLP's liquidator, or by any other person the Court believes to have an interest. Application cannot normally be made more than two years after dissolution, but this restriction does not generally apply if the prospective claim would be for personal injuries (including funeral expenses under the *Law Reform (Miscellaneous Provisions) Act 1934, section 1(2)(c)*), or for damages under the *Fatal Accidents Act 1976*). If the Court grants an order the successful applicant must deliver an office copy of the order to the registrar within seven days, or become liable to a fine. The Court may also order that the period between dissolution and restoration shall not count towards any relevant limitation or similar period.

Striking off a defunct LLP by the registrar   17.40

Mention has already been made of the fact that, unlike a company, an LLP is not intended to be a dormant vehicle for long. The Registrar may accordingly, under *CA 1985, s 652*, as modified, take steps to remove a defunct LLP from the register. His first move is to write to the LLP, if he believes that it is not carrying on business or operating, to enquire if that belief is correct. There is no minimum period for which that inactivity must have applied. If no reply is received within a month, he sends a reminder letter by registered post, warning that striking off may follow. If either there is still no answer within a month, or if the LLP confirms that it is inactive, the registrar may issue a notice that, unless cause to the contrary is shown within three months, the LLP will be struck off the register and dissolved.

This notice must be given to the LLP, and published in the *London Gazette*. (Such a notice may alternatively be given in like manner if the LLP is being wound up anyway, and the registrar has reasonable cause to believe that no liquidator is acting, or that the LLP's affairs are fully wound up, or six consecutive months' liquidator's reports have not been received.)

Once such notice expires, unless reasonable cause to the contrary has been shown, the registrar may strike the LLP's name off the register, and publish notice of that fact in the *London Gazette*. Upon publication of that notice, the LLP is dissolved. That dissolution does not affect the potential personal liability of any member of the LLP, in circumstances where they would have been liable had the LLP continued to exist. Nor does it affect the ability of the Court subsequently to order a winding up of the LLP.

Striking off a defunct LLP on application   17.41

Application may also be made, on behalf of the LLP, for a striking off. This application must be made, on Form LLP652a, by two or more designated members, under *CA 1985, s 652A*, as modified. On receipt of such an application, the registrar will publish a notice in the *London Gazette* stating that, after three months, he may exercise his powers to strike off, and inviting any person to show cause why he should not do so. If no such cause is shown, he can then decide to strike off, and publish a notice of that fact in the *Gazette*, upon publication of which the LLP is dissolved (though, as in 17.40 above, this does not affect any potential personal liability of a member, or the ability of the Court to order a winding up).

Such an application may not however be made in certain circumstances, namely:

- if, in the last three months, the LLP has:
  ○ changed its name,
  ○ traded or otherwise carried on business (which will not be connoted simply by paying earlier trading debts),
  ○ sold property or rights which, when active, were part of its normal trade,
  ○ otherwise been active except (broadly) for concluding purposes,
- if an application is currently before the Court in relation to a compromise or arrangement under *CA 1985, s 425*;
- if a voluntary arrangement, administration order or winding up of any sort is still current;
- if a receiver or manager of the LLP's property is still acting.

When such an application is made, it must be served within seven days on all members, employees and creditors of the LLP, and on the manager or trustee of any employees' pension fund. Also, it may be required to be served on any type of person specified by the Secretary of State by regulation, but no such regulations have yet been made.

Members' duties on application   17.42

If, after an application is made for voluntary striking off, any person joins any of the categories of people upon whom the application originally had to be served, a designated member must serve a copy upon him within seven days. Further, a designated member must, under *CA 1985, s 652C*, as modified, serve notice in Form LLP652c to withdraw the application for striking off if, before the application is finally dealt with, any of the circumstances which would have prevented the LLP from launching an application in the first place (see 17.41 above) arises. Thus, if the LLP should, e.g. resume its trade, or have any insolvency procedure commenced against it, the application must be withdrawn.

Supplemental provisions regarding striking off 17.43

The formalities of service of applications, e.g. with regard to the correct addresses etc, are dealt with in *CA 1985, s 652D*, as modified. Enforcement of the duties imposed by the provisions governing striking off applications is in turn dealt with by *CA 1985, s 652E*, as modified.

Anyone breaching or failing to perform a duty imposed on them commits an offence and is liable normally to a fine, but if the breach in question relates to a deliberate failure to serve notice of the application with the intention of concealing it, then imprisonment may also follow. There are various specific defences offered, however, which vary according to the particular nature of the breach, but are all based around the concepts of either being unaware of the breach, or having taken all reasonable steps to perform the duty. Further, there are offences under *CA 1985, s 652F*, as modified of knowingly or recklessly giving false or misleading information in relation to a striking off application, or making an application which purports to be a *s 652A* application but is not.

Objections to striking off   17.44

If an LLP has been struck off by the registrar, acting on his own initiative under the provisions summarised in 17.40 above, then the Court may, on the application of any person aggrieved by the striking off, order the LLP's name to be restored under *CA 1985, s 653*, as modified. It can do so if it considers that either the LLP was actually operative at the time of the striking off, or it is otherwise just to do so. Such a restoration order can be made at any time within twenty years from the striking off. Restoration can also be ordered by the Court if the original striking off resulted from an application on the LLP's behalf, under the procedure in 17.41 above. Here, if application is made less than twenty years from the publication of the appropriate notice in the *London Gazette*, the Court may make a restoration order if it is satisfied that:

- any of the members' duties in relation to an application were not performed;

- any of the circumstances preventing a striking off application being made did in fact prevail at the time;

- it is otherwise just to do so;

- it is (if the restoration application is made by the Secretary of State) in the public interest to do so.

The effect of any such restoration order is that the striking off is deemed never to have happened. The Court may give any necessary directions for putting the clock back, as far as may be possible, to the original position.

Effect of dissolution on property   17.45

When an LLP is dissolved, all its property (except any it holds as trustee for a third party) becomes *bona vacantia*, i.e. vests automatically by virtue of *CA 1985, s 654*, as modified in the Crown (or, depending on its location, in the Duchy of Lancaster or the Duke of Cornwall). The Crown may then dispose of the property. If, however, an order is made either for the dissolution to be declared void (see 17.39 above) or for the restoration of the LLP to the register (see 17.44 above) then it does not affect any disposition which has been made by the Crown, but compensation for the value of the disposed of property must be paid by the Crown to the LLP. The Crown may however disclaim any such property under *CA 1985, s 656*, as modified, either within a year of becoming aware of the vesting, or within three months of a notice from any interested party requiring it to decide whether to disclaim or not. Upon disclaimer, the effect is that the property is deemed by *CA 1985, s 657*, as modified never to have vested in the Crown, and the property is treated as if a liquidator had disclaimed the property immediately before the LLP's dissolution, in accordance with *s 178(4)* and *sections 179–182* of the *Insolvency Act 1986*.

18 – Company Directors Disqualification

> This chapter, finishing off the consideration of insolvency-related topics, looks at the way in which LLPs and their members have been fitted into the regime of the *Company Directors Disqualification Act 1986*.
>
> The interaction between disqualification procedures applying to companies and LLPs is examined. The ways in which, and the reasons for which, disqualification may be brought about are set out. In particular the criteria for making a member 'unfit' to manage are looked at. Lastly, the criminal and civil penalties for contravention of an order or undertaking are discussed.

Introduction

General application 18.1

The *Company Directors Disqualification Act 1986 (CDDA 1986)* is applied to LLPs in general terms by *SI 2001/1090, regulation 4(2)* (see 1.14 above in regard to the *Regulations*). Certain general modifications are provided for in that regulation, so that:

- references to a company include references to an LLP;

- references to a company's memorandum of association include references to an LLP's incorporation document (not, it should be noted, to its partnership agreement);

- references to a director, or an officer, of a company include references to a member of an LLP;

- references to a shadow director include references to a shadow member.

There is also one specific modification found in *Part II* of *Schedule 2* to *SI 2001/1090*, with the insertion of a new *paragraph 8A* in *Part II* of *Schedule I* to the *CDDA 1986*. The *CDDA 1986* as set out is as amended also by the *Insolvency Act 2000*, the relevant provisions of which were brought into effect on the 2 April 2001.

Overall effect 18.2

The effect of the above is to bring LLPs fully into the *CDDA 1986* regime. LLPs are effectively treated as companies, so that orders under the *CDDA 1986*, as applied to LLPs, which are obtainable against members will not only disqualify them from acting as members of an LLP, but also as directors of a company.

There is doubt, however, as to whether existing orders against former directors will, for their duration, suffice to prevent them from becoming members of an LLP. Whittaker & Mitchell (in their book *Limited Liability Partnerships – The New Law* (2000), Jordans) aver that existing orders will not have that effect, since the modifications brought in by *SI 2001/1090, reg 4(2)* only apply to the *CDDA 1986* in the context of LLPs, and do not modify the CDDA's general application. The latter point is correct, but it seems illogical for there to be such a difference, and a preferable view is that, when looking at an LLP, director and member are to be used interchangeably, so that a person banned as a director is likewise banned as a member. *Regulations 4(2)(g)* and *(i)*, stating respectively that the *CDDA 1986* shall be read so that 'references to a director . . . shall include references to a member', and with 'such further modifications as the context requires for the purpose of giving effect to that legislation as applied by these Regulations' seem broad enough to cover this.

Disqualification in the LLP context 18.3

Anyone subject to such a disqualification order as described above may therefore not, in the LLP context, be a member of an LLP; be a receiver of an LLP's property; or in any way (directly or indirectly) be concerned or take part in the promotion, formation or management of an LLP (*CDDA 1986, s 1(1)*).

The court can grant leave to override such restrictions under *CDDA 1986, s 17*. It is worth noting that disqualification proceedings are regarded as civil proceedings, not criminal ones, which affects such issues as the burden of proof, and human rights issues such as the admissibility against an individual of evidence compulsorily required of him (*R v Secretary of State for Trade & Industry, ex parte McCormick [1998] BCC 379*).

Disqualification undertakings **18.4**

Quite commonly, in practice, disqualification issues are dealt with by way of undertakings, i.e. the individual threatened with court proceedings to obtain a disqualification order offers or agrees an undertaking with the Secretary of State that he will be subject to such restrictions as are referred to above.

Statutory force is now given to such arrangements by *CDDA 1986, s 1A*.

Register of disqualifications **18.5**

The Secretary of State keeps, in accordance with *section 18* of the *CDDA 1986*, a register which is open to public inspection, of all disqualification orders and undertakings; of all variations to them or instances of leave being granted in connection with them; and of their termination.

Extracts from this list in the register can now be inspected on the Companies House website (www.companies-house.gov.uk) and details are given there for a hotline for the reporting of conduct which might lead to disqualification. Instances of orders and undertakings are steadily increasing.

Becoming disqualified

Causes of disqualification – indictable offences **18.6**

The cause of disqualification does not have to be criminal behaviour, but not infrequently it will be. The court may therefore, under *section 2* of the *CDDA 1986*, make a disqualification order, upon conviction of any person of an indictable offence, where that offence relates to:

- the promotion, formation or management of an LLP;
- the liquidation or striking-off of an LLP;
- the receivership of an LLP's property;
- his role as administrative receiver of an LLP.

Where the court is one of summary jurisdiction, the maximum length of disqualification is five years; otherwise it is 15 years.

Causes of disqualification – persistent companies legislation breaches   18.7

The legislation is also aimed (in addition to the offences described above at 18.6), however, at those who are habitually in breach of the provisions of company legislation aimed at requiring the public availability of information, i.e. the filing with the Registrar of accounts, returns, notices etc.

Any court having winding up jurisdiction over the LLP may under *section 3* of the *CDDA 1986* make a disqualification order in such a case for up to five years. On an application under this section such habitual breach may (*inter alia*) be proved by a person's having been found guilty (whether in criminal proceedings or by means of default orders under the *CA 1985* or the *IA 1986*) of three or more relevant defaults in the previous five years.

Causes of disqualification – convictions   18.8

Tying into these last provisions (see 18.7 above) is the ability of a court of summary jurisdiction, acting under *section 5* of the *CDDA 1986*, to impose a disqualification order, for up to five years, upon convicting any person of any offence relating to a failure to comply with any requirement to file with the Registrar any return, account, notice or other document.

That failure can include the situation where the default is that of the LLP, as well as that of the individual. Disqualification can however only be imposed if there have been findings of guilt (whether by conviction or default order as in 18.7 above) in respect of three relevant defaults (including the instant one) in the last five years.

Causes of disqualification – fraud in winding up   18.9

Another possible trigger to disqualification proceedings is conviction under *section 458* of the *Companies Act 1985* for fraudulent trading (see 17.14 above), or conviction of a member (including shadow member), liquidator, receiver or administrative receiver of an LLP for fraud in relation to the LLP or breach of duty. *Section 4* of the *CDDA 1986* refers.

Again, jurisdiction is conferred on the same basis as a winding up. Similarly, if a court makes an order in respect of fraudulent or wrongful trading, under *sections 213 and 214* of the *IA 1986*, that a person should make a contribution to the LLP's assets, it may make a disqualification order against that person of its own volition, under *CDDA 1986, s 10*. Note that this does not however apply in the case of an order for contribution following clawback of withdrawals under *section 214A* of the *IA 1986*, notwithstanding that responsibility for such withdrawals is a factor in considering whether an order, triggered by other events, should be made – see 17.18) In any such case the maximum term of the order is 15 years.

The court's duty to disqualify 18.10

Over and above the provisions referred to earlier (see previous paragraphs), there is an overriding duty on the court under *CDDA 1986, s 6* to disqualify a person if, on application, it is satisfied that the conduct of a past or present member of an LLP which has at any time become insolvent makes him unfit to be concerned in the management of an LLP.

This may apply to his conduct whether viewed in respect of the one LLP alone, or collectively in respect of that LLP and others. (If the latter is the case, there has to be sufficient connection with the collateral bodies to show the member's unfitness to manage the subject LLP, but the conduct is not required to be of a similar nature to that in relation to the subject LLP – *Secretary of State for Trade and Industry v Ivens [1997] 2 BCLC 334*.) For this purpose an insolvent LLP is one whose assets are not enough to pay its debts and liabilities, and the expenses of a winding up; or one which has had an administration order made against it or had an administrative receiver of it appointed. Member includes shadow member.

The minimum period of disqualification is two years, and the maximum 15 years. (*Sections 6 and 7* offer the only instances in the *CDDA 1986* of a maximum period within which proceedings have to be commenced, and a minimum period of disqualification if ordered at all.)

Procedures on application 18.11

The decision as to whether or not an application should be made under *CDDA 1986, s 6* is that of the Secretary of State.

In order that he can reach that decision, any relevant office-holder (i.e. the Official Receiver, liquidator, administrator or administrative receiver, as appropriate) who thinks there may be circumstances to justify such an application must report the fact to the Secretary of State, who may then require all necessary information and documentation etc.

The Secretary of State must consider not only that the person, against whom action is to be taken, is unfit to act, but also that it is expedient in the public interest for action to be taken. If he reaches those conclusions, he may either make an application himself or, if the application is against a member of an LLP which is being wound up, he may direct the Official Receiver to do so. Such an application may not be made, however, more than two years after the date upon which the relevant LLP became insolvent, unless the court gives leave otherwise.

An alternative to an application as above is that the Secretary of State may accept a proffered disqualification undertaking, if he thinks it is expedient in the public interest to do so.

Application after investigation 18.12

As noted in various sections of this work, the Secretary of State has powers of investigation under a number of provisions, e.g. those under *section 437* of the *Companies Act 1985* (see 12.39 above). If, as a result of any such investigation, he considers it expedient in the public interest to seek a disqualification order against any past or present member (or shadow member) of an LLP, he may apply to the High Court under *CDDA 1986, s 8* for such an order.

If the court considers that the conduct in question makes the person concerned unfit to be concerned in the management of an LLP, it may make the order, for up to 15 years. Again, however, the Secretary of State may as an alternative accept a disqualification undertaking, rather than taking proceedings, if he considers it expedient.

Variation of undertakings 18.13

In a number of instances above (see 18.11 and 18.12 above), reference has been made to the giving of disqualification undertakings, having the same effect once given as a disqualification order. The person subject to such an undertaking is given the power, by *section 8A* of the *CDDA 1986*, to apply to the court for the undertaking to be reduced in time, or terminated.

The Secretary of State is to appear on any such application to draw the court's attention to all relevant matters, and may give evidence or call witnesses.

Matters for determining unfitness 18.14

A number of the above provisions have referred to a member (or shadow member) being deemed 'unfit' (e.g. see 18.10 and 18.12). What then categorises unfitness?

By *section 9* of the *CDDA 1986*, the court or the Secretary of State, as the case may be, when considering whether to make an order or accept an undertaking, shall have regard in any event to the provisions set out in *Part I* of *Schedule I* to the *CDDA 1986* and, if the LLP in question has become insolvent (see 18.9 above) to the matters in Part II of that Schedule. (The Secretary of State may by order vary the terms of that Schedule.)

The scheduled terms 18.15

In broad terms, the *Schedule 1* to the *CDDA 1986* covers:

Part I:

- misfeasance or breach of fiduciary or other duty;

- misapplication or retention by the member of the LLP's funds or property;

- responsibility for any avoidable transactions of the LLP;

- responsibility for any failure of the LLP relating to certain specific record keeping obligations;

- responsibility for members' failure to comply with accounting requirements

Part II:

- responsibility for the causes of the LLP becoming insolvent;

- responsibility for the LLP's failure to provide goods and services which have been paid for;

- responsibility for any transaction attackable (whether or not so proved) as a:

  - void disposition of the LP's property after commencement of the winding up of the LLP, or a

  - transaction at an undervalue or preference;

- responsibility for any declaration requiring clawback of withdrawals (whether made in his favour or not);

- responsibility for failure to call a creditors' meeting in a voluntary winding up;

- failure to comply with various requirements of members as to cooperation during the course of sundry insolvency proceedings.

Other provisions regarding unfitness 18.16

It should be noted however that *Schedule 1* to the *CDDA 1986* (see 18.14

and 18.15 above) is indicative, not exhaustive, and that regard may be had to other factors considered relevant in any particular case, the primary aim being not to punish the individual, but to protect the public.

Each case must be decided on its merits and, though the courts have on occasions laid down some guidelines, such as in *Re Polly Peck International: Secretary of State for Trade & Industry v Ellis No 2 [1993] BCC 890*, they have also been keen to say that such guidelines should not be given over-inflated status, and indeed they have not always been upheld. There are consequently many, many cases on this subject, and on the appropriate period of disqualification to be imposed. Any practitioner involved in a case on such matters will need to check these in much more detail than can be given here.

Automatic disqualification of undischarged bankrupts   18.17

One set of prohibitions which applies without the need for any specific order or undertaking relates to any undischarged bankrupt. Such a person may not, whether directly or indirectly, take part or be concerned in the promotion, formation or management of an LLP. *Section 11* of the *CDDA 1986* applies.

The only exception to the prohibition is if the leave of the court is given. Anyone seeking such leave has to serve notice of his application upon the Official Receiver, who may attend and oppose it if he thinks it in the public interest to do so.

Consequences of disqualification

Criminal penalties   18.18

In the case of both disqualification orders and undertakings, or in the case of automatic disqualification under *section 11*, it is an offence under *section 13* of the *CDDA 1986* to act in contravention thereof. Such an offence may be tried either on indictment or summarily, and in either case is subject to imprisonment and/or fine, with different maxima applying in each case.

Further, under *section 14*, there may be additional prosecutions if the contravention is actually that of a body corporate, since in such cases not only may that body be liable, but so may any actual or purported member or other officer who consented to or connived at the breach, or facilitated it by his negligence.

Personal liability for debts   **18.19**

Personal liability for an LLP's debts can attach, under *section 15* of the *CDDA 1986*, to two groups. Firstly, it can apply to anyone who, whilst themselves under a disqualification, is involved in the LLP's management. Secondly, it can apply to someone who, though not himself disqualified, acts, or is willing to act, upon the instructions of someone he knows to be a disqualified person.

Either person will be personally liable for all the debts of the LLP incurred whilst the relevant circumstances prevail. Such liability will be joint and several with the LLP and with any other person who, for any reason, is also so liable.

There is no procedure for any order under this section, so it will be for a claimant who believes that anyone is under such liability to satisfy the court hearing the main claim, on the normal balance of civil proof, that the circumstances contemplated by the section were prevailing at the time the debt was incurred.

19 – Mergers and Acquisitions

> This chapter looks briefly at the increased range of options which is offered by the existence of LLPs when it comes to the combining of two or more businesses. Ways of combining businesses whereby the original constituent LLPs either remain in existence or are absorbed by the new venture are considered.
>
> The role of the LLP as a potential participant in either partnerships or companies is also reviewed. The impact of the differing styles of accounting which apply to mergers and acquisitions respectively is touched upon. Finally, the role of the LLP as a potential vehicle for joint ventures is examined.

Introduction   19.1

When putting two partnerships together, in what is normally referred to simply as a merger, the options are fairly limited. Essentially, one business is going to need to be absorbed into the other, with the structure of the latter prevailing.

With LLPs, because of their corporate nature, the possibilities are more varied. Whilst there is nothing to stop the same happening, i.e. one LLP effectively being taken over by another, with just the one entity emerging, it is quite possible for many variations to be played on the theme. Those managing the merger process will need to consider first what shape they want the eventual business(es) to be, and then choose the route that suits them best.

Memberships in common   19.2

One possibility in such a merger (see 19.1 above) would be to use the corporate status of the LLP so as to allow each of the two existing LLPs to continue its separate existence, but with each being a member of the other.

This continuation might, for instance, be of use where each of the two had separate niche businesses and distinct 'brand' value, so that it would be a pity to lose one of those values by killing off one of the names, but there would be synergy to be derived from combining resources. The strength, and rewards, of the respective memberships in each other would not necessarily have to be identical.

A central vehicle   19.3

Conversely, it may be that two businesses perceive that there would be added strength, in marketing terms, by representing themselves as being one dominant business. In reality, however, they do not want to give up their separate financial structures, so that they can remain separate profit centres contributing to central marketing, training and administrative functions. In such a case the existing two LLPs could become the members in a third LLP, which would be the publicly apparent vehicle, using an amalgamated name.

Thus Smith & Co LLP could ostensibly join with Jones & Williams LLP to form Smith Jones Williams LLP, but with the two original bodies in fact continuing to exist. This is of course quite possible (and indeed not uncommon) with a coming-together of partnerships, but it is there a much more cumbersome process, as all individual partners are likely to be involved, whereas with LLPs it is simply the corporate entities, with the underlying memberships left undisturbed.

LLPs as partners   19.4

Yet another variation (see 19.2 and 19.3 above) is that an LLP can be not only a member in another LLP, but also a partner in a conventional partnership.

Previously, if partnership AB as an entity wanted to become a partner in partnership CD, it had to do it through the medium of a nominee partner X. That raised issues as to the indemnities to be offered to X for his personal exposure to the legal liabilities of CD, and as to the tax position of X in respect of the income ostensibly derived by him from his position as a partner in CD. With LLPs, however, that problem disappears, so that even if AB wishes for some reason to remain as a traditional partnership, the entity of AB LLP can simply become a partner in CD.

LLP groups   19.5

Finally it is also possible for LLP groups to be created, with the same form of hierarchical structures as company groups (and similar accounting requirements). Thus LLPs can be parents or subsidiaries.

LLPs cannot however be quite the same, in that they cannot have wholly owned subsidiaries, since a subsidiary LLP will need at least two members in order to pass the test of *section 2(1)(a)* of the *LLPA 2000*, namely the requirement that an LLP must have 'two or more persons associated for carrying on a lawful business with a view to profit'. There are however no rules on how small or large the interests of each member have to be, so to all intents and purposes a group structure can be replicated. Equally, if 100 per cent ownership of the subsidiary is deemed essential, it could be a company (see 19.6 below).

The interface with companies   19.6

A merger may also involve a coming-together of an LLP with a company.

Again, this is easier with an LLP than with a partnership. Depending on the circumstances, the LLP may acquire shares in a company (without the need for nominee arrangements which would apply to a partnership taking shares); or the company can become a member of the LLP.

Accounting on mergers and acquisitions   19.7

In many cases the term 'merger' will be used to refer to combinations of businesses. In accounting terms, however, mergers and other acquisitions are different animals, and subject to different treatments. This is dealt with in Financial Reporting Standard 6, whose avowed aim is to:

> '. . . ensure that merger accounting is used only for those business combinations that are not, in substance, the acquisition of one entity by another but the formation of a new reporting entity as a substantially equal partnership where no party is dominant; [and] to ensure the use of acquisition accounting for all other business combinations . . .'.

In other words, mergers will be the exception rather than the rule.

The five criteria for a merger are that:

- no one portrays either original party as either acquirer or acquired;

- all parties arrive at a selection of a management structure and team by consensus;

- no party dominates by reason of relative size;

- the consideration for the deal is largely equity in the new enterprise, not cash etc;

- no members retain a material interest in the future performance of part only of the new enterprise.

The differences involved 19.8

A detailed examination of the differences between the two types of accounting (see 19.7 above) is well beyond the scope of this work. In broad terms, merger accounting will involve showing an amalgamation of both parties' accounts as though they had always been part of the same reporting entity. Acquisition accounting will show the results of the acquired business being brought into the group accounts only from the date of acquisition onwards.

The nature of the adjustments on the combining of the accounts will be different. The point to be made for present purposes is that these are factors which will shape the public accounting face of the new enterprise, and may well be relevant to the method which, on taking proper accountancy advice, is appropriate for the businesses' combination. In particular the values given to the constituent parts of the consideration, e.g. both tangible assets and intangibles such as goodwill, will need to be carefully examined.

Joint ventures 19.9

Another possible area of business combinations which may involve LLPs is one which is undertaken for a specific and limited purpose, i.e. a joint venture.

In this situation, neither of the original parties will lose their identity, but the LLP will offer a demarcated and incorporated vehicle for the undertaking of a common purpose. Traditionally, companies have been used for this purpose, but LLPs may have advantages over them. The transparency of the tax position may help, for one thing. (The Government is however wary of the use of LLPs solely for tax avoidance reasons. It has already removed the benefit of LLP tax status for certain specific ventures, e.g. in the property field, and is considering further restrictions.)

The informality and privacy of the relevant agreement may also be an advantage, as may the limited disclosure provisions applicable to LLPs. The ability to adjust the capital structure of the venture without needing to jump through all the procedural hoops relating to companies share capital, and the general flexibility of the LLP model, may also be attractive. If however it is envisaged that the joint venture may eventually require a Stock Market flotation then company status is still likely to be the preferred route.

20 – Risk Management and LLPs

> This chapter deals with various elements of the risks which attach to LLPs and their members. It looks firstly at ways of minimising the residual elements of personal risk which attach to members, before it then turns to address particular risk issues which arise in the context of insolvency.
>
> Operational risk issues are then considered, in the context both of the quality assurance management techniques which are available, and the insurance implications for the LLP and its members alike.

LLPs as a risk management tool 20.1

In many instances, an LLP will owe its selection as a business vehicle to a process – albeit perhaps an unconscious one – of risk management. In other words, the whole purpose of creating an LLP is to minimise personal exposure to the present and future risks of the business to be operated by the LLP. Logic dictates therefore that the advantages conferred by the LLP's existence need to be maximised.

To look at in another way, the business needs to be run in such a way that the exceptions which bring back into play the possibility of personal liability need to be minimised. This chapter therefore brings together a number of strands which have appeared elsewhere in this work, and reviews the risks and the ways in which they can be controlled.

Personal liability

Pre-incorporation debts 20.2

Prospective members are potentially personally liable on pre-incorporation debts.

Such members should therefore ensure that use is made of *section 5(2)* of the *LLPA 2000*, which allows a partnership agreement to be made before incorporation, in such a way as to bind the LLP to grant an indemnity for such debts immediately upon incorporation.

Dropping below the two-member level 20.3

Members of particularly small LLPs need to be alive to the consequences of continuing to trade for more than the six months' period of grace allowed if the number of members drops below two.

This is because after that time they will acquire joint and several liability for the debts accrued by the LLP, under the modified *section 24* of the *Companies Act 1985*.

Personal liability for negligence etc. 20.4

It is not possible to exclude altogether the risk of personal liability attaching to an individual member for the tortious consequences of his actions within the context of the LLP's business (see 20.2 and 20.3 above), but it is possible to limit this potential exposure.

Carefully written letters of engagement, and a minimisation of moves whereby an individual can be said to have become so personally identified with the act or omission in question as to make him liable, should be effected. It is worth noting that in *Merrett v Babb [2001] 3 WLR 1* one of the things which went against the hapless Mr. Babb, the employed surveyor found negligent for a report written on behalf of his soon-to-be insolvent employer, was that he had signed the report in his own name.

Anything which helps to build the view that it is the incorporated entity of the LLP which is dealing with the customer or client will help to keep personal risk down.

Compliance with statutory obligations 20.5

Time and time again, throughout this work, reference has been made to instances where, in default of compliance with statutory procedures, members or designated members may be personally liable for fines or daily default fines. Many people becoming members in an LLP will be coming afresh to the world of such procedural requirements, especially if they have come from the relatively informal background of a partnership.

Members should ensure that they take the trouble to inform themselves of what their responsibilities are, and what systems are in place for ensuring that the necessary steps are taken. Systematic management of the compliance requirements – which are not particularly onerous if only they are undertaken in due time – is essential.

Clarifying limits of authority   20.6

The LLP is basically liable for its members' acts or omissions, in their capacity as its agents.

If there are to be restrictions placed upon the authority of any member, the means of communicating those limits to the relevant third parties need to be carefully considered, so that *section 6(2)* of the *LLPA 2000* can be taken advantage of, and the LLP can escape liability for any steps which go beyond those limits.

Insolvency-related risks

The onset of insolvency   20.7

One of the classic mistakes that many businesses make, when the financial tide starts to turn against them, is that they fail to take proper professional advice until the eleventh hour is long past. Their resistance to the idea of acknowledging even the possibility of failure makes them soldier on, in the hope that something will turn up.

Often, this course of action means that they miss out on the possibilities of recovery procedures which might help them, such as a voluntary arrangement. In the LLP context, however, the personal consequences of adopting the ostrich position can go beyond whether the business as an entity survives or not.

Orders for personal contributions   20.8

Even if the traditional traps of the provisions governing wrongful trading, transactions at an undervalue and preferences (see 17.29 *et seq.* above) do not catch the members, the wholly new clawback provisions may (see 17.18 *et seq.* above). It is essential, if members are going to avoid the risks of clawback claims, that they monitor effectively and continually the financial health of the business.

The two key elements in avoiding the above risks are that they must consider whether their withdrawals, or other withdrawals 'in contempla-tion' at the time, risk making the LLP insolvent; and they must be able to show whether it was reasonable for them to conclude that insolvent liquidation could be avoided. 'I didn't see it coming' is not a defence.

Mention has been made above of the ability of members to spread the risk of such contributions, and of the impact of any personal guarantees, by suitable provision in the partnership agreement.

Contributions to a winding up — 20.9

In two ways, members can control in advance what their personal exposure in a winding up is to be.

The first way is that they can avoid any direct obligation to make any contribution, since they will only be liable to the extent they have actively agreed to make a contribution. Even in the (perhaps comparatively rare) circumstances where they have agreed to make such a contribution, either because of a wish to have the status of contributory in a winding up, or because this has been necessary to persuade customers to trade with the LLP, it is possible to control and define the limits of this exposure.

Repayment of members' debts — 20.10

The other point (see 20.9 above) is that it lies in the members' hands to control the nature of their funds within the LLP itself. In this context it should be borne in mind that debts to them owed by the LLP will rank *pari passu* with other creditors in the winding up (and can even, if there has been sufficient foresight, be secured so as to take priority over those unsecured creditors) – in contrast members' capital and 'other interests' will be considered as ranking after all creditors, and so in many cases will be irrecoverable.

Members will therefore want to keep under constant control the balance between showing members' capital in the accounts at a level which will persuade third parties to trade with the LLP in the belief that it is a financially viable enterprise; and transferring monies into the arena of debt, by allocation of undivided profits etc., or by refraining from allocating undivided losses. This should help ensure at least an element of protection if all goes wrong.

Post-insolvency trading — 20.11

Two aspects of post-insolvency trading may also pose personal risks to anyone involved.

The first is if the trading is controlled by a person subject to a disqualification order or undertaking under the *Company Directors Disqualification Act 1986*, where both a disqualified individual and anyone acting under his instructions may be liable. (The *CDDA 1986* is considered in Chapter 18.)

The other aspect is if a new trading enterprise is started with a 'phoenix' name, i.e. one identical to or so similar to the name of the insolvent LLP as to be a prohibited name and to fix the individuals operating it with potential personal liability (see 17.26 above).

Operational risks

Risk management as an operational habit   **20.12**

Whatever the nature of an LLP's business, it will have many operational risks attached to it. Recognition of this, and of the need for the LLP status to be available for businesses to limit the personal impact of potentially catastrophic claims (especially in the professional services sector) was after all one of the Government's avowed reasons for introducing the legislation.

Increasingly there is an awareness that it is for businesses to control those risks in a much more positive and proactive manner than has previously been the case. Essentially, the ability to do this lies in the development of systematic management procedures, designed with a recognition of where problem areas lie, and intended to limit risk exposure wherever possible.

Often, the main practical difficulty is getting acceptance of these procedures at operational level. Businesses transferring into LLPs may be able to use the opportunity of the conversion to demonstrate their commitment to risk management and so more easily embed the concept into the firm's culture. They should also ensure that their management structure takes proper account of the risk management imperative, e.g. by the establishment of a risk management committee at suitably senior level, so that its thinking pervades all aspects of the business's operation.

Risk management and insurance   **20.13**

Insurance is a part of risk management, not something which is separate. It is in effect a recognition that, however good control procedures may be, claims may result and it is prudent to lay off some of that risk by buying insurance. It may also be necessary either to pacify clients, or to fulfil statutory obligations.

Increasingly, however, insurers themselves are focusing on the risk control procedures of their insured. This has, as an illustration, been thrown into sharp relief by the experience of the legal profession. In September 2000, solicitors' professional indemnity insurance was available on the open market (having previously been effected via a mutual fund). In the first two years of the market, it has already become apparent that insurers are looking very carefully at not only firms' claims records, but also their managerial procedures and their consequent ability to restrict future claims. Some insurers are even appointing, at their own expense, risk management consultants to inspect and advise on their insured's procedures.

The link with quality management   20.14

There are strong links between the concepts of so-called 'quality management programmes' and risk management. These may be such generic systems as ISO 9001 (now in a modified and seemingly more user-friendly version), or industry-specific programmes such as the Law Society's 'Lexcel' scheme. There is also the Government's 'Investors in People' programme which, although differently targeted, has a number of risk control advantages.

These various programmes are often combined by firms. All of these have very positive implications for risk management. Some, like Lexcel, have indeed recognised that by specifically increasing the risk management elements of their programmes. Insurers are starting to take account of these qualifications in their premium-setting exercises.

Insurance in the LLP context   20.15

Many LLPs will be in the professional services sphere, and as such will need to carry professional indemnity insurance. That will cover the LLP as an entity.

There remain however, as mentioned earlier in this chapter (see 20.1, 20.2 and the following paragraphs), some personal risks, and members will therefore want to know that their personal exposure is also covered, e.g. if they themselves are vulnerable to claims for negligent acts or omissions by reason of being personally identified with them. Early evidence is that, reassuringly, insurers are willing to cover this risk as well for no extra premium, since from their viewpoint there is only one risk. It is too early to tell what the effect of *Merrett v Babb [2001] 3 WLR 1* (see

20.4 above) will be in this respect, insofar as it exposes employees to residuary risk.

Directors' and officers' insurance   20.16

In addition to the normal professional indemnity cover, however, members of LLPs may well wish to follow their brethren in the company field, and to cover the risks attached to them as managers by taking out the equivalent of directors' and officers' insurance cover.

The above cover relates to wrongful acts or omissions in the course of an individual's duties as an officer of the business, and can cover duties which may be owed to a wide range of people, from creditors and the public generally, through staff, to fellow members and the LLP itself. One possible reason for this might even be to cover actions taken against controlling members for failure to take out a sufficiently high level of insurance cover.

Run-off cover   20.17

One of the most difficult aspects of professional indemnity cover is the issue of run-off, i.e. the continuation of cover for individuals after they have ceased their association with the insured business.

This difficulty has been thrown into sharp perspective by *Brocklesby v Armitage & Guest [2001] 1 All ER 172*. This case, by considerably increasing the range of circumstances where a claimant can assert that there was 'deliberate concealment' of facts so that the limitation clock does not start to run against him until discovery of those facts, has greatly reduced the protection offered to individuals by the concept of statutory limitations of actions, and increased the possibility of claims crawling out of the woodwork long after an individual's retirement.

The mere fact of operating through the medium of an LLP will help to minimise the above risk, since it will be easier for a potential claimant to pursue the identifiable LLP than a long-gone member, and there will be no need for the claimant to establish who the members generally were at the operative time.

Individuals will however still want the reassurance of run-off cover. So long as the LLP continues, this should not be too much of a problem, and can be provided for in the partnership agreement (subject to possible problems if the uninsured excess escalates over the years in a manner which the retired member neither controls or knows of, but which may impact upon him). The difficulty will come if the LLP ceases to trade, and there is no successor practice. Former members may then need to consider taking out insurance in their own right, if they can both procure and afford this.

Appendix 1 – LLP Forms

LLP2	Application for incorporation of an LLP (approved by Registrar of Companies on 5 March 2001).
LLP3	Notice of change of name of an LLP (approved by Registrar of Companies on 5 March 2001).
LLP8	Notice of designated member(s) of an LLP (approved by Registrar of Companies on 5 March 2001).
LLP190	Location of register of debenture holders of an LLP.
LLP225	Change of accounting reference date of an LLP.
LLP225 cym	Change of accounting reference date of an LLP (additional form prescribed by SI 2001/2917).
LLP244	Notice of claim to extension of period allowed for laying and delivering accounts—oversea business or interests of an LLP.
LLP287	Change in situation or address of registered office of an LLP (approved by Registrar of Companies on 5 March 2001).
LLP287a	Notice that the registered office of an LLP is situated in Wales (approved by Registrar of Companies on 5 March 2001).
LLP288a	Appointment of a member to an LLP (approved by Registrar of Companies on 5 March 2001).
LLP288b	Terminating the membership of a member of an LLP (approved by Registrar of Companies on 5 March 2001).
LLP288c	Change of particulars of a member of an LLP (approved by Registrar of Companies on 5 March 2001).
LLP363	Annual return of an LLP.
LLP363 cym	Annual return of an LLP (additional form prescribed by SI 2001/2917).
LLP391	Notice of removal of auditor from an LLP.
LLP395	Particulars of a mortgage or charge in respect of an LLP.
LLP397	Particulars for the registration of a charge to secure a series of debentures in respect of an LLP.
LLP397a	Particulars of an issue of secured debentures in a series in respect of an LLP.
LLP398	LLP: certificate of registration in Scotland or N. Ireland of a charge comprising property situated there.
LLP400	Particulars of a mortgage or charge on a property that has been acquired by an LLP.

LLP401	Register of charges, memoranda of satisfaction and appointments and cessations of receivers.
LLP403a	LLP: declaration of satisfaction in full or in part of mortgage or charge.
LLP403b	Declaration that part of the property or undertaking charged (a) has been released from the charge; (b) no longer forms part of the LLP's property or undertaking.
LLP405(1)	Notice of appointment of receiver or manager in respect of LLP.
LLP405(2)	Notice of ceasing to act as receiver or manager in respect of an LLP.
LLP410(Scot)	Particulars of a charge created by LLP registered in Scotland.
LLP413(Scot)	Particulars for the registration of a charge to secure a series of debentures in respect of an LLP.
LLP413a(Scot)	Particulars of an issue of debentures out of a series of secured debentures in respect of an LLP.
LLP416(Scot)	Particulars of a charge subject to which property has been acquired by an LLP registered in Scotland.
LLP417(Scot)	Register of charges, memoranda of satisfaction and appointments and cessations of receivers.
LLP419a(Scot)	LLP: memorandum of satisfaction in full or in part of a registered charge.
LLP419b(Scot)	LLP: memorandum of fact that part of a property charged (a) has been released from the charge; (b) no longer forms part of the LLP's property.
LLP466(Scot)	Particulars of an instrument of alteration to a floating charge created by an LLP registered in Scotland.
LLP652a	Application for striking off an LLP.
LLP652a cym	Application for striking off an LLP (additional form prescribed by SI 2001/2917).
LLP652c	Withdrawal of application for striking off an LLP.
LLP652c cym	Withdrawal of application for striking off an LLP (additional form prescribed by SI 2001/2917).

Appendix 2 – LLP Fees

Matter in respect of which fee is payable	Amount of fee
For registration of a limited liability partnership on its incorporation under the 2000 Act	£95.00
For registration of an annual return submitted by a limited liability partnership	£35.00
For registration of notification to the registrar of companies of a change of the name of a limited liability partnership	£20.00
For the performance by the registrar of companies of his functions in relation to an application by a limited liability partnership under section 652A of the 1985 Act, as applied to limited liability partnerships, for a limited liability partnership's name to be struck off the register	£10.00
For the registration of a charge under Chapters I and II of Part XII of the 1985 Act as applied to limited liability partnerships Per entry on a register of charges kept by the registrar of companies in respect of a limited liability partnership	£20.00
For a paper copy of a document relating to a limited liability partnership recorded and kept by the registrar of companies and delivered by post: (a) in respect of one document (b) in respect of each further document relating to the same limited liability partnership requested on the same occasion	 £9.00 £2.50
For paper copies of particulars registered by way of an alphabetical index, accessed on the screen of computer terminals, of live and dissolved companies and limited liability partnerships together with their former names: (a) per screen of information on a computer terminal delivered by post (first page) (b) for each additional page	 £4.00 £1.00
For a certified copy of, or extract from, any record kept by the registrar of companies for the purpose of the Companies Acts and relating to a limited liability partnership For a certificate of incorporation of a limited liability partnership (a) for the first certificate supplied on any occasion (b) for each additional certificate supplied on the same occasion	£25.00 £25.00 £10.00

Appendix 3 – Inland Revenue Guidance

Limited Liability Partnerships

This article sets out the Revenue's views on how the members of a Limited Liability Partnership (" LLP"), regulated by the Limited Liability Partnership Act 2000 (" the LLP Act"), which carries on a trade or profession, will be taxed.

In this article the following expressions are used:

"Ordinary Partnership" means a partnership within the meaning of the Partnership Act 1890.

"Limited Partnership" means a partnership regulated by the Limited Partnership Act 1907.

"Old Partnership" includes both an "ordinary" and a "limited partnership".

During the passage of the LLP Act, Ministers announced that the tax treatment would be reviewed for those LLPs used for businesses for which the LLP structure was not originally intended. Legislation would be brought forward in the Finance Bill 2001 after appropriate consultation. This review was prompted by concerns that some businesses, particularly investment businesses, could be motivated to adopt LLP structure for tax reasons rather than to obtain limited liability. Further details of the tax treatment of LLPs were announced by the Chancellor in his Pre Budget Report (PBR) on 8 November 2000. Details and an invitation to comment were given in the PBR Press Release - Inland Revenue 5. An announcement will be made in due course of the further changes to the tax treatment of LLPs (if any) which are required because of points raised during this consultation.

General

LLPs are in law regarded as "bodies corporate" and will be subject to aspects of company law. But for tax they will generally be treated as "partnerships". As mentioned above this guidance covers LLPs carrying on a trade or profession. It does not cover the detailed tax treatment of investment businesses for which the LLP structure was not originally intended.

Section 10 of the LLP Act ensures that where an LLP carries on a "business with a view of profit" the members will be treated for the purposes of income tax, corporation tax and capital gains tax as if they were partners carrying on business in partnership.

That is to say the LLP will be regarded as transparent for tax purposes and each member will be assessed to tax on their share of the LLP's income or gains. For members liable to income tax their share of the partnership's profits to be charged to tax will be calculated in accordance with the rules set out in Section 111 ICTA 1988 and for those members liable to corporation tax in accordance with the rules set out in Section 114 ICTA 1988.

This article deals with the UK tax treatment of LLPs formed under the LLP Act (i. e. UK LLPs as opposed to overseas LLPs). It would be for the tax authorities of other countries to decide how to tax UK LLPs under their own tax codes.

Computation of taxable profits of professional businesses

In Tax Bulletin, Issue 38 (December 1998, page 606) the Revenue set out guidance on what is meant by "true and fair view" for the purposes of calculating the taxable profits of a professional business.

It is confirmed that those rules will apply equally to the computation of the Case II Schedule D profit of a LLP which carries on a professional business for the purposes of calculating the Income Tax liability of the members of the LLP.

Capital Allowances

Where a LLP succeeds to a business previously carried on by an old partnership this will not of itself give rise to a balancing event for the purposes of the Capital Allowance provisions.

Interest Relief

Members of a LLP, who are individuals, will be entitled to claim interest relief on the loans they obtain in order to defray money applied in the circumstances set out in Section 362(1) ICTA 1988; provided that they otherwise meet the conditions of the relief.

ESC A43 covers interest for investments in partnerships. Where an ordinary partnership converts to a LLP, the existing terms of the extra-statutory concession are not appropriate, to preserve existing relief. To rectify this we are currently considering what changes should be made to the text. (A 1907 limited partner would not have been entitled to such relief in the first place, so it would be inappropriate to extend ESC A43 to those circumstances.)

Loss Relief

a. Unlike Section 117 ICTA, the undrawn profits of a member of a LLP cannot normally be added to their subscribed capital in order to calculate the limit of their entitlement to sideways loss relief. This is because, subject to any agreement between them, a member's undrawn profits will normally be regarded as a debt of the LLP. This means that the member ranks, for that sum, alongside the other creditors in the event of liquidation. If however the terms of the agreement between the members specifically provide that the undrawn profit stands as part of a member's capital contribution and that agreement is unconditional then that amount can be taken into account in calculating the limit.

b. The following is an example of how the provisions of Section 118C-D will apply:

Mr A becomes a member of a LLP on 6 April 2003. He introduces capital of £10,000 into the partnership. The LLP carries on a trade. During the year ended 5 April 2006 he makes a further capital contribution of £6,000.

His share of the LLP's Case I loss is as follows and he claims relief under Section 380 ICTA for those losses against his other income.

Ye 5 April 2004	£6,000
Ye 5 April 2005	£6,000
Ye 5 April 2006	£3,000

Mr A is entitled to Section 380 relief as follows:

2003/2004	£6,000 (unrelieved capital contribution £4,000)
2004/2005	£4,000(1) (unrelieved loss £2,000)
2005/2006	£5,000(2) (unrelieved capital contribution £1,000)

1) sideways loss relief is restricted to the unrelieved capital contribution brought forward of £4,000. The balance of the loss of £2,000 (£6,000 – £4,000) is carried forward.

2) sideways loss relief of £5,000 available i. e. loss of year £3000 + unrelieved loss brought forward £2,000. Unrelieved capital contribution carried forward is £1,000 i.e. total contributions £16,000 less total sideways loss relief given £15,000)

Where a member of a LLP makes a capital contribution to a partnership in order to meet a liability for negligence for which they are personally responsible then that amount will be taken into account in determining the amount of their capital contribution to the partnership for the purposes of Section 118ZC ICTA. Provided that the conditions for relief are otherwise met then that partner will be entitled to relief up to a maximum of the amount of that additional contribution either under the normal sideways loss relief provisions, or under Section 109A ICTA if he/she has left the partnership, or the partnership has ceased business.

c. The provisions in Section 118C-D ICTA (restriction of sideways loss relief to members of a LLP) do not apply to a LLP which carries on a profession; only to one which carries on a trade. Provided that the conditions for relief are otherwise met; a member of a LLP, which carries on a profession rather than a trade, will be entitled to loss relief, either under the normal sideways loss relief provisions, or under Section 109 ICTA, if he/ she has left the partnership, or the partnership has ceased business.

Overlap relief

Where a partnership carries on a trade or profession each partner is deemed to carry on a personal trade or profession. The basis period rules are applied to that deemed trade or profession and any overlap profit is personal to each partner.

If, on conversion, a LLP succeeds to the business previously carried by an old partnership then a partner's personal trade or profession will be regarded as continuing. He/ she will be entitled to a deduction for overlap relief at the time they finally retire from the LLP (or perhaps earlier if the LLP changes its accounting date).

Demergers

Where a LLP takes over only part of the old partnership's trade, such an event constitutes a "demerger" to which Statement of Practice 9/ 86 applies. Unless it can be shown that on the demerger the part of the business carried on by the LLP is recognisably "the business" previously carried on by the old partnership then the cessation provisions will apply. In that event each member of the old partnership will be entitled to their personal overlap relief. Equally the commencement provisions will apply to all the members of the LLP.

But if it can be shown that the LLP does carry on "the business" previously carried on by the old partnership then, as it will have succeeded to the old partnership's business, the cessation provisions will not be applied to the old partnership and any overlap relief will be carried forward. Equally the commencement provisions will not be applied to the members of the LLP. But the old partnership will be assumed to have commenced a new business in relation to the part of the trade it retains.

Whether or not the business carried on by the LLP is recognisably "the business" previously carried on by the old partnership is a question of fact.

Cash basis - catching up charge

Again if on conversion the LLP succeeds to the business previously carried on by an old partnership then the spreading rules for the catching up charge will continue to apply as if the conversion had not occurred.

Cessation

Where a LLP succeeds to a business previously carried on by an old partnership this will not of itself involve the cessation of the old partnership's trade or profession.

Tax returns

Where an old partnership incorporates as a LLP during an accounting period then if the partners so wish a single partnership return need only be made for the one tax year. They may do this even if the partnership changes its accounting date. Single PAYE returns may also be made for the tax year in which an old partnership incorporates as a LLP.

UK branches of overseas LLP's

The tax treatment of a UK branch of an overseas Limited Liability Partnership, and the members of such an LLP, will depend on how the foreign entity is regarded for the purposes of the UK taxation provisions. Where the foreign LLP is regarded as a "body corporate" for the purposes of the UK Taxes Acts the profits of the UK branch will be chargeable to corporation tax. On the other hand if it is regarded as a partnership then members will be separately liable to tax on their share of the branch's profits under the existing legislation for partnerships rather than under the LLP Act. The latter act only applies to UK registered LLPs.

Double Taxation Relief

Where an overseas tax authority regards a foreign branch of a UK LLP as a "body corporate" the UK members will be entitled to claim Tax Credit Relief in respect of their proportionate share of the foreign tax paid on the overseas branch's profits.

Dividends

A UK LLP is not itself "liable to tax" in the UK as the LLP tax provisions identify other persons (i. e. the members) as the persons who are to be taxed. Accordingly for the purposes of the Double Taxation Agreements (DTA) the LLP itself is not regarded as being resident in the UK and cannot itself therefore claim relief from foreign taxes under such Agreements. As is now the case with ordinary and limited partnerships the members must make the claim.

Assuming they are UK residents in accordance with the provisions of the relevant DTA the members of an LLP will be entitled to relief for any withholding tax on overseas dividends. Normally a DTA provides for withholding tax of a maximum of 15% to be deducted and relief for that tax will be given. Where a partner is an individual then no relief will be due in respect of the taxes paid (the underlying taxes) on the profits out of which the dividend is paid.

In the very narrow circumstances where the LLP is not treated as transparent, but instead as a body corporate for tax purposes (such as when the LLP is in liquidation or being wound up in circumstances where transparency cannot be retained in the manner explained below under "Capital Gains – Liquidation /Winding Up"), we can confirm the LLP could itself claim relief for foreign taxes, including if appropriate underlying tax.

Partnership Annuities

Where an obligation to pay an annuity is transferred from the old partnership to the LLP then the members of the LLP will be entitled to higher rate income tax relief for their share of the ongoing payments; and incoming LLP members who assume part of that obligation will also be entitled to such relief for their share.

If an obligation to pay an annuity is not transferred to the LLP and the members of the old partnership continue to pay it they will be entitled to higher rate income tax relief for their share of those payments until such time as they cease to be a member of the LLP or until the business originally carried on by the old partnership ceases, whichever is the earlier.

Capital Gains

Partners capital interests

So long as the LLP carries on a trade or profession with a view to profit a partner's capital interest as a member of a LLP will not be regarded as a chargeable asset in its own right. In these circumstances the members of the LLP will be directly taxable on their share of the chargeable gains arising on the disposal of the LLP's assets and there will be no concurrent charge on a non-transparent basis.

Temporary cessation of trading

The transparency of a LLP, for capital gains purposes, is not disturbed by reason of temporary periods of time during which no trade or profession is carried on by it. For example, if the LLP ceases to carry on one business and disposes of its assets in order to realise funds to commence another business then those asset disposals, and any gains or losses arising in consequence, will be treated as those of the members.

Transfer of a business to a LLP

Where a business, previously carried on by an old partnership, is transferred to a LLP then, for the purposes of the Capital Gains legislation, this will not of itself constitute a disposal by the partners in their interests in the old partnership's assets. This applies equally to the members of partnerships in Scotland as it does to those in England and Wales.

Furthermore such a transfer will not affect:

a)   the availability of indexation allowance.

b)   the ownership period for retirement relief.

c)   the holding period for taper relief.

Application of Statement of Practice D12

The rules set out in Statement of Practice D12 apply equally to the members of a LLP as they do to members of an old partnership. When D12 is next updated it will be amended to incorporate this confirmation.

Liquidation/Winding up

Liquidations

Where a LLP ceases to carry on a trade or profession then it will no longer be regarded as a "partnership" for the purposes of the taxation provisions and will instead be regarded as a "body corporate". The LLP will thus cease to be transparent (Section 59A(2) TCGA).

Where a LLP goes into liquidation, chargeable gains on the disposal of the LLP's assets by the liquidator will be computed by reference to the date on which they were first acquired by the LLP and their cost at that date. In the liquidation period, the LLP's capital gains will be treated in precisely the same way for tax purposes as those for any other body corporate (Section 8(6) TCGA).

LLP members will be taxed on any gain (or given relief for any loss) that arises on the disposal of their capital interests in the LLP. The base cost of a partner's capital interest is not equal to the market value of that interest at the time when transparency is lost. The allowable acquisition cost of each partner's interest will be determined according to the historical capital contributions made as if the LLP had never been transparent. This treatment does not affect pre-liquidation asset disposals, which remain undisturbed.

Informal Winding up

Where the members of a LLP proceed to wind up its affairs in an orderly way, without the formal appointment of a liquidator, by settling outstanding liabilities and realising the assets following or in the course of a cessation of commercial activity, then it will be accepted that the transparency of the LLP will be preserved during the period in which the assets are being disposed of provided the conditions set out below are met.

Those conditions are:

- that the LLP is not being wound up for reasons connected in whole or in part with the avoidance of tax, and

- that, following the termination of the LLP's business, the period of winding up is not unduly protracted taking account of the LLP's assets and liabilities.

If these conditions are not met, then the transparency of the LLP may be regarded as coming to an end before the informal winding up process has been completed. It is also emphasised that, whatever the circumstances, transparency cannot continue beyond any date on which a liquidator is formally appointed (whether or not that liquidator is charged for a period with completing any outstanding business transactions).

CGT roll-over relief

Where, as a result of claiming business asset roll-over relief (Sections 152 – 154 TCGA 1992) a LLP member postpones a chargeable gain through their acquisition of a share in a LLP asset, there is the potential for that gain to fall out of charge in the future by reason of the LLP ceasing to be transparent. This could occur, for example, where the LLP asset remains unsold when the LLP goes into liquidation and vests in the liquidator (who will compute the gain arising on the disposal of the asset in the course of liquidation without regard to past roll-over relief claims by any LLP member). Accordingly, there is a tax liability on the member, at the point in time when the LLP ceases to be transparent, which is based on an amount equal to the postponed gain or gains which have not then come back into charge (Section 156A TCGA 1992). Gains which accrue to a member in consequence of this special provision do not attract taper relief.

Annuities

Provided that the rights remain substantially the same then:

- the transfer of a partner's annuity rights and/or
- the transfer of annuity obligations to former members

from an ordinary partnership to a LLP will not be regarded as a chargeable disposal.

Similarly where an annuitant agrees to the substitution of the LLP for the predecessor partnership as the payer of the annuity, and the terms otherwise remain substantially the same, then the annuitant will not be regarded as making a chargeable disposal.

Inheritance tax

Business property relief and agricultural property relief

Where an old partnership incorporates as a LLP a partner's period of ownership for both reliefs will not be regarded as being interrupted.

Deemed transfers by close companies

Because Section 267A(d) IHTA 1984, inserted by Section 11 of the LLP Act, deems transfers of value to be made by the members of the LLP and not by the LLP itself, liability under Section 94 IHTA 1984 cannot arise even if the LLP might otherwise be a close company.

Availability of reliefs

The normal reliefs and exemptions available to partners in an old partnership will equally be available to members of a LLP. In particular Section 10 IHTA 1984, which provides an exemption for dispositions not intended to confer gratuitous benefit, will apply.

Stamp duty

Transfer of property to a LLP

Section 12 of the LLP Act requires that for the stamp duty exemption to apply the proportions of property conveyed or transferred into a LLP must either be unchanged "before" and "after" the transfer, or the proportions must not have been changed for tax avoidance reasons. Strictly under property law the partners' interest in the LLP will replace their interests in the old partnership's assets. In determining whether the stamp duty exemption applies the Revenue will not, however take this point.

The Revenue will accept that any property transferred to the LLP within one year of its incorporation will qualify for relief from stamp duty under Section 12 of the LLP Act, provided that the conditions for that relief are met.

Section 12(2) of the LLP Act prevents stamp duty exemption being available if property is transferred at the time of the LLP's incorporation and also there are retirements of former partners and/ or admission of new partners to the LLP.

Provided that all the other conditions for the exemption are met the Revenue accepts that this charge can be averted by arranging matters so that the change of partners takes place the instant before or after incorporation. To confirm that matters were organised in this way the Stamp Office will need to see all associated documents effecting any change in the membership of the old partnership and of the LLP prior to and/ or after incorporation, as well as evidence that any stamp duty appropriate to those documents has been paid. It may be necessary to call for further information once these documents have been reviewed.

Transfers of interests in a LLP

An interest in a LLP is not a chargeable security for Stamp Duty purposes. So if stamp duty is due on the transfer of such an interest it will be payable at the 1%, 3% or 4% rate, as appropriate, rather than the 0.5% rate applicable to shares. This is in line with the intention behind the LLP Act that the treatment of LLPs should be the same as for partnerships. Since the sale of an interest in any other type of partnership bears duty at the property rates, the sale of an interest in a LLP will be charged in the same way.

General

As with all transactions potentially liable to stamp duty, the Technical Services Unit Manager at any Stamp Office will be happy to assist customers in connection with any enquiries regarding the operation of the stamp duty relief in the Act.

National Insurance Contributions

The National Insurance Contributions (NICs) position of members of a LLP is the same as that of partners in an ordinary partnership. Thus the members of a LLP will be liable to Class 2, Class 3 and Class 4 NICs as appropriate.

Taken from *Tax Bulletin*, December 2000, Issue 50. Each Bulletin contains certain qualifications should be referred to before reliance is placed on an interpretation.

© Crown Copyright. Reproduced with the permission of the Controller of Her Majesty's Stationery Office.

Appendix 4 – Precedents

Limited liability partnership agreement[1]

THIS AGREEMENT is made the . . . . . . day of . . . .

BETWEEN each of the Members and all others of them and the LLP

NOW IT IS AGREED as follows:

1 Definitions and interpretation

For the purposes of this Agreement

1.1 The following expressions have the following meanings:

1.1.1 'the LLP' means the limited liability partnership [to be] incorporated under the Name which the Members [shall seek to register at Companies House *or* have registered at Companies House with number *(number)*]

1.1.2 'the Initial Members' means the persons (whether individuals in limited liability partnerships or limited companies) whose names and addresses appear in Schedule 1

1.1.3 'the Members' means those of the Initial Members and/or such other or additional persons as may from time to time be appointed in accordance with the provisions of this Agreement whose membership of the LLP has not been determined in accordance with those provisions

1.1.4 'the Name' means *(name)* [limited liability partnership *or* LLP *or* llp][2] or such other name as shall from time to time be registered by the LLP at Companies House as its name

1.1.5 ['the Former Partnership' shall mean the partnership known as *(name)* carried on by [certain of] the Members [and others] known as *(name)*]

1.1.6 ['the Transfer Agreement' means an agreement dated *(date)* and made between the partners in the Former Partnership of the one part and the LLP of the other part whereby it was agreed to transfer the assets and liabilities of the Former Partnership to the LLP]

1.1.7 'the Registered Office' means *(address)* or such other address as shall from time to time be registered by the LLP at Companies House as its registered office

1.1.8 'the Designated Members' means [all the Members *or* those Members whose names and addresses appear in Schedule 1, Part 1] or such of the Members for the time being of the LLP as shall be designated in accordance with the provisions of this Agreement[3]

1.1.9 'the Initial Auditors' means *(name and address)*

1.1.10 'the Auditors' means the Initial Auditors or such other auditors as may from time to time be appointed in accordance with the provisions of this Agreement

1.1.11 'the Initial Bank' means *(name and address)*

1.1.12 'the Bank' means the Initial Bank or such other bank as may from time to time be appointed as the lead bank of the LLP in accordance with the provisions of this agreement

1.1.13 'the Business' means the profession trade or business of *(nature of business)* to be carried on by the LLP [in succession to the Former Partnership]

1.1.14 'the Act' means the Limited Liability Partnerships Act 2000

1.1.15 'the Commencement Date' means [*(date)* or the date upon which the transfer of the Business pursuant to the Transfer Agreement [shall be or was] effected][4]

1.1.16 'the Initial Property' means the freehold or leasehold property or properties [to be] owned or occupied by the LLP for the purposes of the Business details of which are set out in Schedule 2

1.1.17 'the Property' means the Initial Property [*and/or* such additional *or* replacement property *or* properties as may from time to time be owned or occupied by the LLP for the purpose of the Business]

1.1.18 'the Intellectual Property' means all industrial and intellectual property rights including without limitation, domain names, patents, trade marks and/or service marks (whether registered or unregistered), registered designs, unregistered designs and copyrights and any applications for any of the same owned by the LLP and used in connection with the Business and all Know-how and confidential information so owned and used

1.1.19 'Know-how' means all information (including that comprised in or derived from data, disks, tapes, manuals, source codes, flowcharts, manuals and instructions) relating to the Business and the services provided by it

1.1.20 'the Year End Date' means *(date)* or such other date as may be determined in accordance with the provisions of this Agreement

1.1.21 'an Accounting Year' means a year ending on a Year End Date

1.1.22 'the Capital' means the net capital of the LLP as shown in any balance sheet prepared in accordance with the provisions of this Agreement as belonging to the Members and being the excess of the assets of the LLP over its liabilities

1.1.23 'a Member's Share' means a Member's share and interest of and in the Capital[5]

1.1.24 'a Contribution' means any money or assets paid into the accounts of or transferred into the ownership of the LLP by a Member (other than by way of a loan for which specific written arrangements between [him] and the LLP shall have been made) less any liabilities attaching to such money or assets which shall be assumed by the LLP in substitution for [him]

1.1.25 "a "Current Account" means the account of a Member with the LLP to which there shall be credited all amounts of profit payable to that Member or against which there shall be debited any loss in respect of that Member in accordance with clause 9 and any Drawings taken by that Member so that any credit balance from time to time on respect of any Current Account shall be a debt due from the LLP to the relevant Member

1.1.26 'Drawings' means sums drawn by any Member on account of any anticipated profits of the LLP and any other sums paid or assets applied for [his] personal benefit by the LLP (other than for any such expenses as shall be provided for in this Agreement) including in particular but without limitation any Tax paid on [his] behalf by the LLP

1.1.27 'the Initial Drawings Amount' means the monthly sum of *(amount)*

1.1.28 'the Interest Rate' shall mean a rate *(specify)* [above the base rate for the time being of the Bank]

1.1.29 'the Primary Percentage' means *(specify)*

1.1.30 'the Weekly Sum' means *(amount)*[6]

1.1.31 'a Payment Date' shall mean *(date)* in each Month or if the same shall not be a Working Day then the Working Day immediately [preceding *or* following] the same

1.1.32 'Tax' means any Income Tax, Capital Gains Tax or National Insurance Contribution payable by any Member in respect of [his] status as a member of the LLP or [his] share of the profits of the LLP or the proceeds from the disposal of any of the assets of the LLP

1.1.33 'the Chairman' means *(name)*

1.1.34 'the Chief Executive' means *(name)*

1.1.35 'the Members' Quorum' means *(number)* Members

1.1.36 'the Designated Members' Quorum' means *(number)* Designated Members

1.1.37 'the Expenditure Limit' means *(amount)*

1.1.38 'the Requisite Number' means *(number)* Members

1.1.39 'the Authority Limit' means *(amount)*

1.1.40 'the Notice Period' means a period of *(number)* months

1.1.41 'the Retirement Age' means the age of *(number)* years

1.1.42 'the Payment Period' means a period of *(number)* years

1.1.43 'the Cessation Date' means in respect of any Member the date of the retirement deemed retirement or expulsion of that Member

1.1.44 'the Radius' means a radius of *(number)* miles

1.1.45 'a Working Day' means any day from Monday to Friday inclusive save for any such day which is a bank or statutory holiday

1.1.46 'Month' means calendar month

1.1.47 'Holiday Weeks' mean *(number)* weeks per year

1.2 Reference to any profits or losses of the LLP includes a reference to profits and losses of a capital nature

1.3 Reference to the death of any Member shall in the case of any Member being a body corporate include reference to the winding up dissolution or striking off the register of that Member unless the context otherwise requires

1.4 Reference to any statute or statutory provision includes a reference to that statute or provision as from time to time amended extended re-enacted or consolidated and to all statutory instruments or orders made under it

1.5 Words denoting the singular number only include the plural and vice versa

1.6 Words denoting any gender include all genders and words denoting persons include firms and corporations and vice versa

1.7 Unless the context otherwise requires reference to any clause, paragraph or Schedule is to a clause, paragraph or Schedule (as the case may be) of or to this Agreement

1.8 The headings in this document are inserted for convenience only and shall not affect the construction or interpretation of this Agreement

2 Incorporation

[2.1 The Members shall complete and deliver to Companies House all such documents and pay all such fees as shall be necessary to lead to the incorporation of the LLP in accordance with the Act][7]

2.2 The certificate of registration of the LLP [to be] issued under the Act shall be kept at the Registered Office

3 Commencement and duration

3.1 The provisions of this Agreement shall [take effect *or* be deemed to have taken effect] on the Commencement Date

3.2 The LLP shall carry on the Business and/or carry on such other or additional trade profession or business as the Members shall from time to time determine

3.3 The LLP shall subsist until wound up in accordance with the provisions of the Act[8]

[3.4 In the event that any Member may be personally liable under any contract entered into by [him] prior to the incorporation of the LLP which was for the benefit of the LLP and with the express or implied consent of the other Members then the LLP shall on incorporation be deemed to ratify that contract and shall indemnify that Member from and against all claims, liabilities and costs in connection with it]

4   Name and registered office

4.1   The [Designated] Members may from time to time determine upon a change in the Name and/or the Registered Office

4.2   Upon any change in the Name and/or the Registered Office it shall be the responsibility of the Designated Members to notify Companies House of any such change in accordance with the Act

5   Property and place of business

5.1   The Business shall be carried on by the LLP from the Property

5.2   In the event that any property from time to time comprised within the Property shall be vested in any one or more of the Members (or any nominees for them) those Members (or nominees):

5.2.1   shall as from the Commencement Date be deemed to have held it in trust for the LLP and the LLP shall indemnify them and their respective estates and effects against all liability in respect of that Property after the Commencement Date

5.2.2   shall upon service upon them of any notice requesting them so to do and on receipt of any necessary mortgagee's and/or landlord's consents permitting them so to do convey, transfer or assign the same to the LLP at the cost of the LLP and upon the LLP indemnifying them and their respective estates and effects against all future liability in respect of that Property after the date of conveyance transfer or assignment

Provided that for the purposes of this clause liability shall include in particular but without limitation all liability in respect of any outgoings payable in respect of the relevant Property, any restrictive covenants relating to it, any rent falling due in respect of it and the performance and observance of any lessees' covenants relating to it

5.3   The Property, the Intellectual Property and all computers and ancillary equipment, office equipment, furniture, books, stationery and other property and equipment in or about the Property and used for the purposes of the Business shall be the property of the LLP

6   Accounts

6.1   It shall be the responsibility of the Members to ensure that proper books of account giving a true and fair view of the Business and the affairs of the LLP shall be kept properly posted

6.2   Such books of account shall be:

6.2.1   kept at the Registered Office or at such other place as the Members may from time to time determine

6.2.2   open to inspection by the Members

6.3   The Designated Members shall (acting where appropriate in accordance with the requirements of the Companies Act 1985):

6.3.1   be deemed to appoint the Initial Auditors as Auditors of the LLP for the next ensuing Accounting Year

6.3.2   each year appoint Auditors

6.3.3   have power to remove the Auditors from office

6.3.4   have power to fix the remuneration of the Auditors

6.4   The Members may from time to time determine to amend the Year End Date

6.5   A profit and loss account shall be taken in every year on the Year End Date and a balance sheet [(taking no account of goodwill)] shall be prepared and the same shall be audited in accordance with all relevant Statements of Standard Accounting Practice and in such format and giving such information notes and disclosure of the interests of the Members in the LLP as may be required by the Companies Act 1985

6.6   The accounts to be prepared in accordance with clause 6.5 shall be:

6.6.1   approved by the Members in accordance with the Companies Act 1985 which approval shall be given at a meeting and shall after that approval become binding on all Members save that any Member may request the rectification of any manifest error discovered in any such accounts within three Months of receipt of the same and

6.6.2   distributed to all Members as required by the Companies Act 1985

7   Banking arrangements

7.1   The bankers shall be the Bank and/or such other bank as the [Designated] Members may from time to time determine [and notify to all Members] as being the lead bank or a subsidiary bank of the LLP

7.2   All money, cheques and drafts received by or on behalf of the LLP solely shall be paid promptly into the bank account of the LLP and all securities for money shall be promptly deposited in the Name of the LLP with the Bank

7.3   In the event that it shall be a normal part of the Business to receive money on behalf of any client or third party the LLP shall open a separate client account or accounts with the Bank and:

7.3.1   all money, cheques and drafts received by or on behalf of such clients or third parties shall be paid promptly into such client account(s) and all securities for money shall be promptly deposited in the name of the clients or third parties with the Bank

7.3.2   any such account or accounts shall at all times be operated by the LLP strictly in accordance with any rules or regulations of any professional or regulatory body which may exercise relevant jurisdiction over the LLP

7.4   All cheques drawn on or instructions for the electronic transfer of money from any such account as is mentioned in this clause 7 shall be in the Name of the LLP and may be drawn or given by any [[Designated] Member *or* two [Designated] Members] and in the case of any instructions for electronic transfer written confirmation of those instructions shall be signed by the authorising Member[s]

[7.5   No Member shall sign any cheque in favour of or give instructions for any transfer of money to [him]self or [his] spouse, child, parent or sibling][9]

8   Members' shares and contributions

8.1   Each of the Initial Members shall acquire as at the Commencement Date a Member's Share equal to [the amount specified in the Transfer Agreement *or* the amount shown as being the value of [his] capital in the Former Partnership in the cessation accounts [to be] prepared in respect of the Former Partnership as at the day before the Commencement Date *or* the amount or value of any Contribution made by [him] on the Commencement Date]

8.2   Any Member making any Contribution at any time after the Commencement Date shall acquire a new Member's Share or augment [his] previous Member's Share by an amount equal to the amount or value of that Contribution

8.3   The [Designated] Members may from time to time require the Members or any of them to make such Contribution as is necessary for the Business and shall in that event specify the time within which such Contribution is to be made

8.4   Any such Contribution as above may be made by the member at [his] discretion by payment to the LLP or by transfer from [his] Current Account insofar as the same may be sufficient for the purpose

[8.5   No Member shall be entitled to any interest on the amount for time being of [his] Member's Share][10]

9   Profits and losses

9.1   References to sums being credited or debited to Members in this clause shall be construed in accordance with the following provisions:-

     9.1.1   all sums to be credited to a Member shall be credited to [his] Current Account

     9.1.2   all sums to be debited against a Member shall be debited against [his] Current Account save insofar as that may be insufficient for the purpose in which case they shall be debited in reduction of [his] Member's Share

     9.1.3   if any sums shall fall to be debited against a Member at any time when [his] Current Account and [his] Member's Share shall both have been exhausted then the same shall be set-off against any other monies owed to [him] by the LLP but if there shall be no such monies or if they shall be insufficient for the purposes of that set-off then they may be set-off against any future credits due from the LLP to the Member but for the avoidance of doubt the Member shall not be required to pay any sums to the LLP in respect of any unsatisfied element of such debits

9.1.4   the [Designated] Members may at any time determine to credit or debit at such time as they may specify all or any part of any profits earned by or losses incurred by the LLP in respect of any Accounting Year

9.1.5   All sums shown in the accounts of the LLP as profits or losses in respect of any Accounting Year shall (save insofar as they may already have been credited or debited in accordance with clause 9.1.4) be deemed to be credited or debited automatically and immediately upon the approval of the accounts for any Accounting Year in accordance with clause 6.6 (unless the [Designated] Members shall at the time of or prior to that approval determine to postpone the operative time of such crediting or debiting either generally or until such time as they may specify)

[9.2   Before the division of the profits of the LLP as set out below interest upon the amounts for the time being of each Member's Share shall be credited to Members as follows:

9.2.1   interest at the Interest Rate in force on the Year End Date on the amount of the Member's Share at the start of the relevant Accounting Year shall be credited to Members

9.2.2   in the event that the aggregate of the amounts of interest to be credited to Members in accordance with clause 9.2.1 shall exceed the profits of the LLP for the year in question then the several amounts of interest to be so credited shall abate rateably

9.2.3   in the event that the accounts of the LLP for any Accounting Year shall show a loss then in respect of that year no such interest shall be credited to any Member]

[9.3   Before the division of any [such] profits of the LLP [after allowing for any amounts to be credited in accordance with clause 9.2] there shall be credited to each of the Members named in Schedule 3 out of such profits the prior share of profit specified in that Schedule for [him] provided that:

9.3.1   in the event that the aggregate of such prior shares of profit to be so credited to Members shall exceed the available profits of the LLP for the Accounting Year in question then such prior shares shall abate rateably

9.3.2   in the event that there shall be no profits so available no such prior shares of profit shall be credited to any Member][11]

9.4   The profits and losses of the LLP [after allowing for any amounts payable in accordance with clause 9.2 *and/or* clause 9.3] shall (as the case may be) be credited to or debited against the members' Current Accounts [in equal shares] *or* [in the proportions set out in Schedule 4] *or* [as follows:

9.4.1   as to the Primary Percentage of any profits or as to the total of any losses in the proportions set out in Schedule 4

9.4.2   as to the residue of any profits as set out in Schedule 5][12]

9.5   Notwithstanding the provisions of clauses 9.3 and 9.4 where during any Accounting Year any Member was prevented by reason of ill-health or accident from devoting [his] full time and attention to the Business (except during Holiday Leave Maternity Leave Parental Leave or Family Leave) for a period of more than 13 successive weeks or for any lesser period commencing within 26 weeks after the Member in question shall have resumed normal duties following a period of such absence exceeding 13 weeks then the share of profits to which such Member is entitled shall after that period be reduced by the Weekly Sum for every complete week of incapacity until [he] shall resume normal duties and the share of the profits of the other Members shall be increased by a like sum and be divided between them [equally] *or* [in the proportions set out in Schedule 4]

10   Drawings

10.1   There shall be paid to each Member on the Payment Date in each Month the Initial Drawings Amount or such other sum as the [Designated] Members may from time to time agree in respect either of all Members or such Members as may thus be determined [and notification of any such change shall be given by the Designated Members to all Members]

10.2   Any further payments to be made to or on behalf of any Member and any assets to be transferred to or for the benefit of any Member shall only be made, transferred or applied with the consent of the [Designated] Members [and notification of any such payment transfer or application shall be given by the Designated Members to all Members]

10.3   The LLP shall on the taking of the annual accounts provided for in clause 6 reserve out of profits before distribution:

[10.3.1 any amounts of Tax estimated by the Auditors to be payable by Members during the next following Accounting Year and each Member shall be charged with [his] due proportion of such Tax[13] and]

10.3.2 such amount as the [Designated] Members shall determine in order to provide further working capital for the Business

[10.4 The LLP shall pay for the benefit of each Member such amounts of Tax as shall be payable by him]

10.5   If on the taking of any such annual accounts they shall show that in the relevant Accounting Year any Member drew pursuant to the provisions of this clause 10 in excess of [his] share of the profits for that Accounting Year then such Member shall repay the excess forthwith together with interest on the excess or such part of the excess as shall from time to time be outstanding at the Interest Rate from a date being one Month after the receipt by [him] of such accounts to the date of repayment

10.6   Subject to clause 10.3 each Member shall be entitled to be paid by the LLP the balance (if any) of [his] actual share of any profits shown in the accounts for any Accounting Year at any time after the same has been approved in accordance with clause 6.6.1

11   Members' obligations and duties

11.1 Each Member shall at all times:

11.1.1 devote [his] whole time and attention to the Business except during Holiday Leave, Maternity Leave, Parental Leave, Family Leave[14] or incapacity due to illness injury or other substantial cause

11.1.2 not without the consent of the [Designated] Members engage in any business other than the Business or accept (otherwise than in a voluntary or honorary capacity) any office or appointment [unless that other Business or the office or appointment is not in competition with the Business] (and in the event of any breach of this clause the Member shall account to the LLP for any profit derived by [him] from the business office or appointment in question)

11.1.3 not without the consent of the [Designated] Members derive any benefit from the use of the Name or the Property or the business connection of the LLP (and in the event of any breach of this clause the Member shall account to the LLP for any profit derived by [him] from the use in question)

11.1.4 conduct himself in a proper and responsible manner and use [his] best skill and endeavour to promote the Business

11.1.5 comply with all statutes, regulations, professional standards and other provisions as may from time to time govern the conduct of the Business [or be determined by the [Designated] Members as standards to be voluntarily applied by the LLP to the Business][15]

[11.2 Each Member shall at all times show the utmost good faith to the LLP

or

For the avoidance of doubt the Members shall not owe fiduciary duties to each other or to the LLP (save for such fiduciary duties to the LLP as are implied by their status as agents of the LLP)][16]

12   Holiday leave

12.1 Each member shall be entitled in each calendar year to a number of weeks' leave equal to the Holiday Weeks in addition to statutory or public holidays

12.2 Not more than two weeks' holiday leave shall be taken consecutively (ignoring statutory or public holidays) without the consent of the [Designated] Members

12.3 Members shall be entitled to carry forward not more than *(number)* week[s] of untaken holiday leave from one calendar year to the next

12.4 Each Member shall give notice to the LLP of [his] intended dates of holiday leave and shall be responsible for ensuring that those dates do not conflict with the dates of any form of leave already notified to the LLP by such other Members or senior employees of the LLP as may be appropriate having regard to the work undertaken by the Member

13   Maternity leave

13.1 Each female Member shall be entitled to such maternity leave as she would be under the Employment Rights Act 1996 if she were an employee of the LLP having more than one year's continuous service with the LLP[17]

13.2 During maternity leave the Member shall be entitled to her normal share of the profits of the LLP

13.3 As soon as reasonably practical a Member who becomes pregnant shall notify the LLP of her expected week of confinement and of the date upon which she expects to commence her maternity leave and as soon as reasonably practical after the commencement of her confinement she shall notify the LLP of the date on which she expects to resume her duties

14   Parental and family leave

14.1 Each member shall be entitled to such parental leave and family leave as [he] would be under the Employment Rights Act 1996 if [he] were an employee of the LLP having more than one year's continuous service with the LLP

14.2 During parental leave and/or family leave the Member shall be entitled to [his] normal share of the profits of the LLP

14.3 Each Member shall give notice to the LLP of [his] intended dates of parental or family leave and shall be responsible so far as possible for ensuring that those dates do not conflict with the dates of any form of leave already notified to the LLP by such other Members or senior employees of the LLP as may be appropriate having regard to the work undertaken by the Member

15   Management[18]

15.1 Meetings of each of the Designated Members and the Members[19] shall be held at least [four times] a year and shall normally be convened by [the Chief Executive but may also be convened by] the Chairman or not less than [three] Designated Members or Members as the case may be (or by any liquidator of the LLP appointed under the Insolvency Act 1986)

15.2 Not less than one Month's notice of any such meeting shall be given to all those entitled to attend the same provided that any resolution passed at a meeting of which shorter notice or no notice has been given shall be deemed to have been duly passed if it is afterwards ratified by the required majority of the Designated Members or the Members as the case may be at a duly convened meeting

15.3 Meetings of either the Designated Members or the Members shall be chaired by the Chairman or in the Chairman's absence [by the Chief Executive or if he shall not be present either then] by such Designated Member or Member as shall be appointed for the purpose by those present at the meeting

15.4 No business shall be conducted at a meeting of the Designated Members or the Members as the case may be unless the Designated Members'

Quorum or the Members' Quorum shall respectively be present in person (or have been present earlier in the meeting) provided that any resolution passed at an inquorate meeting shall be deemed to have been duly passed if it is afterwards ratified by the required majority of the Designated Members or the Members as the case may be at a duly convened and quorate meeting

[15.5 Proxy voting shall not be permitted]

15.6 Any matters which are by reason of the Act or by this Agreement reserved for the decision of the Designated Members shall be determined by them [by a simple majority *or* by unanimous vote] at a duly convened meeting provided that a resolution in writing signed as approved by [a majority *or* all] of the Designated Members shall be as valid as a resolution passed at such a meeting

15.7 Any matters not either:

15.7.1 reserved as above for the decision of the Designated Members (or which have been thus reserved but in respect of which the Designated Members shall have defaulted or shall appear likely to default in exercising their powers or taking any decision or other step required of them by the Act or any other statute within any time limit prescribed)[20] or

15.7.2 delegated as below for the decision of a committee

shall be determined by the Members by their votes at a duly convened meeting (save that any such decision taken in anticipation of any default by the Designated Members in acting as above shall only take effect upon the expiry of the time prescribed by law for that action if the Designated Members shall not in fact have acted appropriately by that time)

15.8 At any meeting of the Members a decision may be taken by a simple majority save that:

15.8.1 a majority of not less than seventy five per cent of the Members present and voting shall be required for any of the following purposes

15.8.1.1 any determination to be made under the Insolvency Act 1986 including in particular but without limitation any determination to propose for a Voluntary Arrangement in respect of or a voluntary winding-up of the LLP

15.8.1.2 any resolution to appoint any Member(s) as delegates empowered on behalf of the LLP to approve or reject under the Insolvency Act 1986 Section 4(5A)[21] any modifications to any proposed Voluntary Arrangement in respect of the LLP

15.8.1.3 any resolution to appoint remove or fill a vacancy in the office of a liquidator of the LLP

15.8.1.4 any resolution to give or withhold any sanction required under the Insolvency Act 1986 including in particular but without limitation any sanction under the Insolvency Act 1986 Sections 110(3), 165(2)[22]

15.8.2 a unanimous vote of the Members present and voting shall be required for any of the following purposes:

15.8.2.1 the opening or closing of any place of business of the LLP

15.8.2.2 the admission or expulsion of any Member or the passing of a resolution authorising the service or revocation of any notice requiring any Member to retire in accordance with clause 20.3

15.8.2.3 the appointment of any Member as a Designated Member or the revocation of any such appointment

15.8.2.4 the appointment of all Members for the time being as Designated Members or any reversal of any such resolution

15.8.2.5 the purchase of any capital item or connected items of equipment having (in the aggregate where appropriate) a cost in excess of the Expenditure Limit

15.8.2.6 the borrowing or lending by the LLP or the giving of any guarantee or undertaking by the LLP of or in respect of any sum or connected sums being (in the aggregate where appropriate) in excess of the Expenditure Limit

15.8.2.7 the delegation (or revocation of such delegation) of powers to a committee in accordance with clause 15.9

15.8.2.8 a change in the nature of the Business

15.8.2.9 any amendment to this Agreement

15.9 The Members may from time to time delegate (or revoke the delegation of) any of their powers of managing or conducting the affairs of the LLP to a committee or committees consisting of such Members [and employees of the LLP] as are appointed in the appropriate resolution provided that such delegation may be made subject to such conditions as the resolution may prescribe

15.10 The procedure for the conduct of any such committee as is formed in accordance with clause 15.9 shall be as prescribed by the resolution establishing it or if the resolution does not do provide shall be as determined by a majority of that committee

15.11 For the avoidance of doubt no member who is at any time within any of the circumstances prescribed by the Limited Liability Partnerships Act 2000 Section 7(1) shall have an entitlement to attend any meeting of the Members or the Designated Members or any committee established as above or have any vote at any such meeting and any reference to a resolution requiring to be signed by Members shall be deemed to exclude reference to signature by any such Member

16   Limitations on members' powers as agents

The following limitations on the powers of any individual Member to act as an agent of the LLP shall apply:

16.1 No Member shall without the consent of at least the Requisite Number of Members

    16.1.1 engage or dismiss any employee of the LLP

    16.1.2 except in the ordinary course of the business of the LLP and for its benefit and if the Authority Limit shall not be exceeded pledge the credit of the LLP or incur any liability or lend any money on behalf of the LLP

    16.1.3 give any guarantee or undertaking on behalf of the LLP in respect of any sum or connected sums exceeding (in the aggregate where appropriate) the Authority Limit

    16.1.4 compromise or compound or (except on payment in full) release or discharge any debt or connected debts due to the LLP where the same exceed (in the aggregate where appropriate) the Authority Limit

16.2 No Member shall

    16.2.1 have any dealings with any person, partnership, limited liability partnership or limited company with whom or which the Members have previously resolved not to deal

    16.2.2 procure that the LLP shall enter into any bond or become bail or surety for any person

    16.2.3 knowingly cause or permit or suffer to be done anything whereby the property of the LLP may be taken in execution or otherwise endangered

    16.2.4 assign, mortgage or charge [his] interest in the Capital

    [16.2.5be entitled to make any application to the Court under the Companies Act 1985 Section 459][23]

17   Indemnity and expenses

17.1 The LLP shall indemnify each Member from and against any claims, costs and demands arising out of payments made by [him] or liabilities incurred by [him] in the performance by [him] of [his] duties as a Member in the normal course of the operation of the Business or in respect of anything necessarily done by [him] for the preservation of the Business or the property of the LLP

17.2 Each Member shall be entitled to charge and be refunded all out-of-pocket expenses properly incurred by [him] in connection with the Business provided that:

    17.2.1 All expenses shall be vouched by an appropriate receipt and VAT invoice where appropriate

17.2.2 If the LLP shall provide a credit card for the use of a Member for such expenses he shall provide to the LLP the original vouchers for all expenditure charged to such card

17.2.3 The Members may from time to time resolve to place upper limits on any category or categories of expenses of which reimbursement may be claimed by Members

18 Cars[24]

18.1 Each Member shall be provided by the LLP with a car of [his] choice which shall be the Property of the LLP

18.2 The [Designated] Members shall from time to time determine:

18.2.1 a limit or limits to be placed upon the cost of such cars (whether in terms of their price or the cost of any financing arrangements to be entered into in respect of them) and

18.2.2 a policy as to the ability of any Member personally to provide any excess of the cost of [his] chosen car over and above such limit as above and as to the consequences thereof with regard to the future ownership of the car and the accounting entries thus required

18.2.3 a policy for the periodic replacement of such cars

18.3 Each Member shall be entitled to be reimbursed for the full running cost of the car acquired for [him] as above including vehicle excise duty, insurance premiums, fuel maintenance and repairs

19 Insurance

19.1 The LLP shall maintain policies of insurance for such respective amounts as the [Designated] Members may from time to time determine in respect of:

19.1.1 the Property

19.1.2 all plant equipment and other chattels belonging to or used by the LLP

19.1.3 all cars and other vehicles belonging to or used by the LLP

19.1.4 employers' liability

19.1.5 public liability

19.1.6 professional negligence

19.1.7 loss of profits consequent upon destruction of or damage to the Property

19.1.8 loss of profits consequent upon destruction of or damage to or theft of any plant equipment, chattels, cars and other vehicles including in the case of any computers or ancillary equipment any virus or corruption or loss of any software or data

19.1.9 permanent health in respect of the Members [and any such employees of the LLP as the [Designated] Members may determine]

19.2 The LLP shall procure at its expense that there shall be in force in respect of each Member a policy of insurance which shall provide that in the event of [his] being incapacitated by illness or injury and prevented from attending to [his] duties as a Member for a period of more than 13 successive weeks (or for any lesser period commencing within 26 weeks after a Member shall have resumed normal duties following an absence of more than 13 weeks by reason of illness or injury) the Weekly Sum shall be paid to [him] for each complete week of incapacity in excess of the said period of 13 weeks

19.3 The LLP shall at its expense effect and maintain for its own benefit such life insurance policies in such sums on the lives of such of the Members as the [Designated] Members shall from time to time determine and Members shall co-operate in the obtaining of such policies and in particular but without limitation shall undergo such medical examination(s) in respect thereof as shall be reasonable

20 Retirement

20.1 A Designated Member may resign [his] designation upon giving notice to the LLP and to the other Members such notice to take effect [forthwith *or* upon the expiry of the Notice Period from the date of the said notice] save that in the event that such resignation would reduce the number of Designated Members of the LLP to one then the notice shall not take effect until the Members shall have appointed a new Designated Member to fill the vacancy to be created by the said notice

20.2 If any Member shall give to the LLP and to the other Members notice of [his] intention to retire from the LLP provided that such notice shall be of a duration not less than the Notice Period then on [the Year End Date next following] the expiry of the notice [he] shall retire from the LLP

20.3 A Member shall be deemed to retire from the LLP:

20.3.1 on the Year End Date next following the birthday upon which [he] attains the Retirement Age [(or if before that birthday the LLP shall have agreed with the Member in question to substitute a later birthday then upon the Year End Date next following that birthday)]

20.3.2 on the expiry of not less than three Months' notice requiring [him] to retire given to [him] by the LLP at a time when by reason of illness, injury or other cause he has been unable to perform [his] duties as a Member and has been so unable throughout the period of at least twelve Months immediately preceding the service of the notice or for an aggregate period of at least twelve Months during the period of twenty-four Months immediately preceding such service provided that:

20.3.2.1 there shall be excepted from the calculation of any such period any period(s) of Maternity Leave, Parental Leave or Family Leave and

20.3.2.2 a notice under this clause shall be of no effect if before it expires the Member upon whom it has been served satisfactorily resumes [his] duties as a Member and the LLP accordingly resolves to withdraw the notice

20.3.3 forthwith on the service upon [him] of notice in writing requiring [him] to retire given by the LLP at any time after he has become a patient within the meaning of the Mental Health Act 1983 Section 94(2) or Section 145(1)

21 Expulsion

21.1 If any Member shall:

21.1.1 commit any grave breach or persistent breaches of this Agreement or

21.1.2 have a bankruptcy order made against [him] or

21.1.3 fail to pay any money owing by [him] to the LLP within 14 days of being requested in writing by the LLP so to do or

21.1.4 be guilty of any conduct likely to have a serious adverse effect upon the Business or

21.1.5 cease to hold any professional qualification or certification required for the normal performance of [his] duties as a member of the LLP

then the LLP may by notice in writing given to [him] be entitled forthwith to expel [him] from membership of the LLP provided that any such notice shall give sufficient details of the alleged breach or breaches to enable the same to be properly identified and provided further that if the Member on whom such notice is served shall within fourteen days of the date of service of that notice serve on the LLP a counter-notice denying the allegations and shall within that period of fourteen days refer the dispute to Arbitration the operation of the said notice shall be suspended until written notice of acceptance by the Member on whom it has been served is served on the LLP or the decision of the appropriate arbitrator and any reference in this Agreement to a date of cessation of membership consequent upon such a notice of dissolution shall be deemed to be a reference to the date of the notice of acceptance or the decision of the arbitrator as the case may be

22 Provisions relating to death retirement or expulsion

22.1 In the event that any Member shall on a date other than an Year End Date die or retire or be deemed to retire or be expelled then

22.1.1 [he] shall not be entitled to receive any share of the profit of the LLP from the date of [his] ceasing to be a Member

22.1.2 the LLP shall not be obliged to prepare any accounts other than the accounts which would normally prepared as at the next Year End Date

22.1.3 for the purpose of ascertaining the amount of the Member's Share of the Member in question the profits of the LLP in such accounts shall be apportioned on a time basis in respect of the periods before and after [his] death retirement or expulsion [provided that interest calculated in accordance with Clause 9.1 shall be credited to the relevant Member's Share]

22.2 In the event of the death, retirement or expulsion of any Member there shall be due to [him] from the LLP the amount of [his] Member's Share as shown in the accounts of the LLP for the Year End Date next following such death, retirement or expulsion or upon which the same shall take effect [(and for the avoidance of doubt there shall be no goodwill payable to [him])]

23 Payments following death retirement or expulsion

23.1 In the event of the death of any Member being an individual the LLP shall:

23.1.1 pay on the first day of each of the three Months next following that Member's death an amount equal to the normal monthly Drawings then applicable in accordance with Clause 10.1 such payments to be made to the deceased Member's personal representatives or widow or to such other person as the LLP shall at its absolute discretion determine (provided that the LLP shall not be concerned as to whether the recipient(s) of such payments shall in due course prove to be the person(s) entitled at law to the deceased Member's estate)

23.1.2 pay the appropriate Member's Share (after allowing for any such payments as are referred to in clause 23.1.1) to the deceased Member's personal representatives as soon as may be reasonably practical but in any event within one year of [his] death (together with interest at the Interest Rate on the resultant amount or such of it as is from time to time unpaid)

23.2 In the event of any retirement deemed retirement or expulsion of any Member or in the event of the dissolution winding up or striking off of any Member being a body corporate then that Member's Share together with interest at the Interest Rate upon the balance of that Member's Share for the time being outstanding shall be paid by the LLP to the retiring or expelled Member or to any liquidator appointed in respect of the Member or to the Secretary of State (as the case may be) by equal half yearly instalments over the Payment Period (the first such payment being due on the Year End Date occurring next after the retirement expulsion dissolution winding up or striking off takes effect) provided that the LLP shall be entitled at any time to make such payments earlier than so required at its absolute discretion

24 Other provisions following death retirement or expulsion

24.1 Any Member who shall have retired or been deemed to retire or been expelled shall:

24.1.1 Not before the [first *or* second] Year End Date following the Cessation Date:

    24.1.1.1 solicit business from canvass or accept instructions to supply goods or services to or for any person, firm, limited liability partnership or limited company which has habitually introduced clients or customers to the LLP or was a client or customer of the LLP during the period of one year preceding the Cessation Date

    24.1.1.2 solicit or induce or endeavour to solicit or induce any person who is at the Cessation Date a Member or an employee in any capacity whatever of the LLP to cease to be a member of, or to work for, or provide services to the LLP whether or not any such person would by such cessation commit a breach of contract

    24.1.1.3 employ or otherwise engage anyone who is at the Cessation Date a Member or an employee in any capacity whatever of the LLP

    24.1.1.4 engage in any business of a nature similar to that of the Business (whether on [his] own account or as a partner, or member in, or an employee of, or consultant to any other person, partnership, limited liability partnership or limited company) within the Radius of any place of business of the LLP at the Cessation Date

Provided that each of the separate paragraphs of this clause 24.1 shall constitute an entirely separate and independent restriction so that if one or more of them are held to be invalid for any reason whatever then the remaining paragraphs shall nonetheless be valid[25]

24.2 Pay into the LLP's bank account all sums due from [him] to the LLP and any sums not so paid shall be recoverable by the LLP from [him] as a debt

24.3 Deliver to the LLP all such books of account, records, letters and other documents in [his] possession relating to the LLP as may be required for the continuing conduct of the Business but during any subsequent period in which there shall still be money owed to [him] by the LLP the retired or expelled Member or [his] duly authorised agents shall be permitted to inspect by appointment the books of account, records, letters and other documents of the LLP insofar as they relate to any period preceding the Cessation Date

24.4 Sign, execute and do all such documents, deeds, acts and things as the LLP may reasonably request for the purpose of conveying, assigning or transferring to it any Property or assets which immediately prior to the Cessation Date were vested in the retired or expelled Member as nominee for or in trust for the LLP

25 Winding up

25.1 For the avoidance of doubt no Member has agreed with the other Members or with the LLP that he shall in the event of the winding up of the LLP contribute in any way to the assets of the LLP in accordance with the Insolvency Act 1986 Section 74[26]

25.2 In the event of the winding up of the LLP then any surplus of assets of the LLP over its liabilities remaining at the conclusion of the winding up after payment of all money due to the creditors of the LLP and all expenses of the winding up shall be payable by the liquidator to the Members in such proportions as their respective Members' Shares shall have borne to each other on the [day *or* the last Year End Date] before the commencement of the winding up

[25.3 In the event that any Court makes a declaration or declarations under the Insolvency Act 1986 Section 214A[27] requiring any Member or Members to make any Contribution to the assets of the LLP then the other Member(s) shall indemnify the Member(s) in respect of whom the said declaration(s) shall have been made in such manner that the amount or aggregate amounts payable in accordance with the said declaration(s) shall be borne by the Members in the proportions set out in Schedule 4][28]

26 Guarantees and Indemnities

26.1 In the event that any Member shall have given any guarantee on behalf of the LLP and (if so required by clause 16.1.3) have obtained the necessary consent for that then:

26.1.1 If any guarantee so given shall be called upon by the person to whom it has been given then upon making any payment properly due under that guarantee the Member in question shall be entitled to be indemnified forthwith by the other Members in such manner that the amount or aggregate amounts payable in accordance with the said guarantee shall be borne by the Members in the proportions set out in Schedule 4

26.1.2 Upon the death, dissolution, retirement, deemed retirement or expulsion of that Member the other Members shall:

26.1.2.1 use their best endeavours to procure that the person having the benefit of the guarantee shall release that Member (or [his] estate) from the guarantee

26.1.2.2 provide a substitute guarantor if required by that person as a condition of release

26.1.2.3 jointly and severally indemnify the Member in question or [his] estate from and against any liability under the guarantee arising after the date of the death or dissolution of or the Cessation Date relating to that Member

26.2 For the avoidance of doubt nothing in this clause 26 shall require any Member to indemnify any other Member against any claim or liability resulting from the negligent act or omission of that other whether such claim is brought by the LLP itself or by any third party and whether the other Member is solely liable or is co-extensively liable with the LLP

27   Notices

27.1   Any notice herein referred to shall be in writing and shall be sufficiently given to or served on the person to whom it is addressed if it is delivered to or sent in a prepaid first class letter by the Recorded Delivery Service addressed (in the case of notice to the LLP) to its Registered Office or (in the case of notice to any Member) to [him] at [his] residential address as registered for the time being with Companies House and shall be deemed to have been delivered in the ordinary course of post

27.2   For the purposes of this Agreement any notice shall be deemed to have been given to the personal representatives of a deceased Member notwithstanding that no grant of representation has been made in respect of [his] estate in England if the notice is addressed to the deceased Member by name or to [his] personal representatives by title and is sent by prepaid letter by the Recorded Delivery Service to the residential address as registered for the time being with Companies House of the deceased at [his] death

28   Arbitration

Any dispute under or arising out of this Agreement shall be referred in accordance with the Arbitration Act 1996 to a single arbitrator to be appointed in default of agreement by the President for the time being of the [Chartered Institute of Arbitrators][29] and the decision of the arbitrator shall be final and binding on all parties

AS WITNESS etc

SCHEDULE 1

(Member's names and residential addresses)

[Part 1: Designated members

Part 2: Other members]

(insert details)

SCHEDULE 2

Initial Property

(insert details)

SCHEDULE 3

Prior shares of profit

(insert details)

SCHEDULE 4

Primary Percentage division of profits and losses

(insert details)

SCHEDULE 5

Secondary profit share principles (if any)

(insert details)

(Signatures of all Members and on behalf of the LLP)

[1] The Limited Liability Partnerships Act 2000 (32 Halsbury's Statutes (4th Edn) PARTNERSHIP) ('the Act') and the regulations made under it (particularly Limited Liability Partnerships Regulations 2001, SI 2001/1090 Regs 8, 9, ('the Regulations')) provide (quite deliberately) only the most basic of default codes for the governance of a Limited Liability Partnership ('LLP') incorporated under the Act. The Act envisages (but does not require) that the majority of LLPs shall enter into a partnership agreement such as this. (Curiously, although in the Act the people who would formerly have been 'partners' are now termed as 'members', such an agreement is nonetheless referred to as a 'partnership' agreement.) The Regulations have their main effect via amendments which they make, in relation to LLPs, of the applicable provisions of the Companies Act 1985 (8 Halsbury's Statutes (4th Edn) COMPANIES), the Insolvency Act 1986 (4 Halsbury's Statutes (4th Edn) INSOLVENCY), and sundry other statutes. The impact of the duties etc which are thus imposed on the LLP and its members are accordingly dealt with in this Agreement. The Agreement is intended to be usable for either professional or trading businesses. Professional partnerships seeking to transfer their businesses to LLPs should be careful to check any additional require-ments that their professional bodies may have, such as the requirement for solicitors' LLPs to gain recognition from the Law Society as approved incorporated bodies before commencing practice as such.

[2] Or their Welsh equivalents 'partneriaeth atebolrwydd cyfyngedig', 'PAC' or 'pac'.

[3] The Limited Liability Partnerships Act 2000 ss 8, 9 create the possibility of having a sub-set of members referred to as 'designated members'. The LLP may either regard all members as designated members, or only certain specified and nominated individuals. Certain tasks (and therefore penalties for failure to perform those tasks) fall only upon the Designated Members. The LLP may wish to delegate other tasks to them. This Agreement therefore provides, in a number of places, options according to the Members' preference.

[4] This gives the option of linking the operational commencement of this Agreement to the transfer to it of an existing business, most likely to be that of an existing partnership. If there is no such predecessor business, or such linking is not desired, a specific date can be given.

[5] The terminology of members' shares is unavoidable, but confusing, raising as it does the (false) analogy of shares in a limited company. There is no equivalent for an LLP of the concept of issuing definable denominated shares – it is simply a term for referring to the proportion of the LLP's overall capital which an individual member may hold.

[6] This concept, and the provisions for abatement of profit which relate to it (see clause 9.4 of this Form), are intended for use in circumstances where the

individual members have the benefit of insurance yielding set sums in the case of long term illness (whether or not the premiums are paid for by the LLP). The periods of absence required before there is abatement of profit share will need to be harmonised with the terms of the policies in question. Clause 19.2 provides for such a scheme.

[7] Omit if already registered. The fee payable on incorporation is £95, in accordance with the Limited Liability Partnerships (Fees) (No 2) Regulations 2001, SI 2001/969.

[8] It is quite possible for an LLP to be formed for a specific duration or venture, but this has not been provided for here.

[9] This fairly basic attempt at prevention of fraud is much less likely to be needed if a system of dual signatures/authorisation is both provided for and properly enforced.

[10] Either this clause, or clause 9.1 and subsequent references to it, should be deleted.

[11] This clause allows for prior profit shares to be paid to particular members where, e.g. some are full-time working members and others are not, so that their time input needs particular recognition.

[12] This latter option allows for a different approach to two tiers of profit. This is only likely to be appropriate where particular bonus arrangements are necessary.

[13] Current Inland Revenue provisions no longer regard tax as a debt of the partnership/LLP, and so there is no legal need for the business to retain funds to pay the tax on behalf of members. Many will, however, still feel it prudent for this to be done, to ensure so far as possible that individual members do not get into arrears, and run the risk of insolvency, with its knock-on effects both on the individual's ability to continue as a member and the reputation of the business as a whole.

[14] These are chiefly benefits which attach to employees, not members. They have been included for two reasons. Firstly, the trend in employment legislation is to confer such benefits on 'workers'—a much more loosely defined concept than 'employees', and one which may well include members. Secondly, it would seem perverse for members to have less favourable terms than their staff.

[15] This would include an obligation not to breach quality assurance standards adopted by the LLP such as Investors in People or ISO 9000.

[16] The question of whether such duties should or should not be owed by members to each other was probably the most contentious single issue during the passage through Parliament of the Limited Liability Partnerships Act 2000.

[17] This therefore includes the right to 'extended' maternity leave.

[18] The details of this clause are merely illustrative of the sort of issues which need to be considered, in the light of the complete absence in the Limited Liability Partnerships Act 2000 of any provisions governing meetings. This is likely to be an area to which the draftsman will have to pay particular attention, as the concept of defining meetings in this manner may be alien to former partners. There is no statutory requirement to do so, but failure to do so will leave a large vacuum, and scope for disagreement, when a meeting is needed in difficult or contentious circumstances.

[19] For larger LLPs in particular, there may need to be totally separate provision for Designated Members' meetings on the one hand, and Members' meetings on the other.

[20] An example of this would be failure on the part of the Designated Members to appoint Auditors within the prescribed time limits, in which case the generality of Members may step in to remedy the default (Companies Act 1985 s 385(4) as modified by SI 2001/1090).

[21] Insolvency Act 1986 s 4(5A) as inserted by SI 2001/1090.

[22] Insolvency Act 1986 ss 110(3), 165(2) as amended by SI 2001/1090.

[23] The Companies Act 1985 s 459 as amended gives an individual Member the right to apply to Court for relief in the event that the LLP's affairs are being or have been carried on in an unfairly prejudicial manner. By the Companies Act 1985 s 459(1A) as inserted by SI 2001/1090, members may agree unanimously to exclude the effect thereof. Agreement to exclude subsists for such period as is agreed. In this Agreement the exclusion would apply until the Agreement itself was altered, which in turn would need unanimous consent. Companies Act 1985, s 459 as amended actions are notoriously costly and complex, and it is intended that the mechanisms in place under this Agreement, particularly with detailed buy-out provisions, are such as to make this unnecessary.

[24] Cars are a traditional source of dispute for partnership agreement drafting. This clause is intended simply to be an enabling one, allowing for policies to be made (and changed) off the face of the agreement itself; rather than being prescriptive and requiring alteration of this agreement if circumstances change.

[25] All constituent parts of this clause should be carefully considered to ensure that they are reasonable and will not be void as being in restraint of trade.

[26] Insolvency Act 1986 s 74 as substituted by SI 2001/1090.

[27] Insolvency Act 1986 s 214A as inserted by SI 2001/1090.

[28] This clause should be omitted if it is felt that the making of any declaration requiring a contribution will necessarily require a degree of culpability against which it is not appropriate for other Members to offer an indemnity.

[29] Substitute a relevant professional body where possible.

Agreement for the transfer of a business from a partnership to a limited liability partnership[1]

THIS AGREEMENT IS MADE the . . . . . . day of . . . . . .

BETWEEN:

(1)   *(insert personal names of transferring partners)* of *(address)* ('the Sellers') and

(2)   *(insert name of transferee Limited Liability Partnership)* whose registered office is [intended to be][2] at *(insert registered office address)* ('the Buyer')

NOW IT IS AGREED as follows:

1   Definitions and interpretation

For the purposes of this Agreement:

1.1   The following expressions shall have the following meanings:

1.1.1   'the Business' means the business carried on by the Sellers of the nature set out in Schedule 1 paragraph 1

1.1.2   'the Name' means the name under which the Business is carried on as set out in Schedule 1 paragraph 2

1.1.3   'the Transfer Date' means the date set out in Schedule 1 paragraph 3

1.1.4   'the Actual Completion Date' shall mean the day upon which the transfers from the Sellers to the Buyer which this Agreement provides for are actually completed

1.1.5   'the Business Premises' means the freehold and leasehold premises brief particulars of which are set out in Schedule 2

1.1.6   'the Work in Progress' means the work in progress of the Business at the Actual Completion Date and the right to render bills for such work and to receive the beneficial interest in all money collected as a consequence thereof

1.1.7   'the Book Debts' means the right to receive the beneficial interest in all money paid after the Actual Completion Date by clients of the Sellers in respect of bills issued by the Sellers prior to the Actual Completion Date

1.1.8   'the Liabilities' means all debts of the Business owing by the Sellers at the Actual Completion Date and all other liabilities of the Business subsisting at that date

1.1.9   'Outstanding Agreements' means agreements entered into prior to the Actual Completion Date by or on behalf of the Sellers in connection with the Business (whether with clients for the supply of services to them by the Business or with suppliers for the purchase of goods by or the provision of services to the Business) which remain wholly or partly to be performed

1.1.10   'the Net Assets Value' means such sum as represents the excess of the value of the assets of the Business over the amount of the

Liabilities as recorded in the books of account of the Sellers as at the Actual Completion Date

1.1.11 'Employees' means all the employees of the Business as at the Actual Completion Date

1.1.12 'Members' Accounts' means the accounts of each of the Sellers with the Buyer which show the interests of those persons in the Buyer in their capacity as members thereof

1.1.13 'Know-how' means all information (including that comprised in or derived from data, disks, tapes, manuals, source codes, flow-charts, manuals and instructions) relating to the Business and the services provided by it

1.1.14 'the Intellectual Property' means all industrial and intellectual property rights of the Sellers including, without limitation, domain names, patents, trade marks and/or service marks (whether registered or unregistered), registered designs, unregistered designs and copyrights and any applications for any of the same owned by the LLP and used in connection with the Business and all Know-how and confidential information so owned and used [save and except . . . .][3]

1.2 Expressions importing the masculine gender shall include the feminine and neuter and those importing the singular number shall include the plural and vice versa

1.3 Any covenants or stipulations entered into by more than one party shall be entered into jointly and severally

1.4 Unless the context otherwise requires reference to any clause, paragraph or Schedule is to a clause, paragraph or Schedule (as the case may be) of or to this Agreement

1.5 The headings in this document are inserted for convenience only and shall not affect the construction or interpretation of this Agreement

2 Recitals

2.1 The Sellers are the members of the Buyer[4]

2.2 The Sellers have agreed to transfer the Business to the Buyer as a going concern with effect from the Transfer Date

3 Sale and purchase

3.1 The Sellers agree to transfer upon the Transfer Date to the Buyer and the Buyer agrees then to accept a transfer of the Business as a going concern[5] comprising the following assets used in the conduct of the Business:

3.1.1 the Business Premises[6]

3.1.2 the goodwill of the Business (which for the avoidance of doubt is agreed to include the right to use the Name and the right to take over the benefit of any Outstanding Agreement)

3.1.3   the tangible assets listed in Schedule 3

3.1.4   the Work in Progress

3.1.5   the Book Debts

3.1.6   the Intellectual Property

4   Standard conditions

The Standard Conditions of Sale (Third Edition) shall apply to this Agreement so far as they relate to the Business Premises and they are applicable to a sale by private treaty and are not either inconsistent with the provisions contained in this Agreement or expressly varied by this Agreement[7]

5   Title

The Buyer accepts such title as the Sellers have to the various assets to be transferred to it and shall not be entitled to make any requisitions or objections in relation to the same

6   Liabilities and outstanding agreements

6.1   The Buyer agrees to take the transfer of the Business subject to the Liabilities and to pay satisfy and discharge all of the same and shall indemnify the Sellers against all proceedings, costs, claims and expenses in respect of the Liabilities

6.2   The Sellers shall at completion assign to the Buyer and the Buyer shall accept an assignment of the Outstanding Agreements provided that if any of them cannot effectively be assigned except with the consent of (or by an agreement of novation with) the third party concerned then:

6.2.1   the Sellers and the Buyer shall each use all reasonable endeavours to procure that each such Outstanding Agreement is novated or assigned at the expense of the Buyer and

6.2.2   unless and until such Outstanding Agreement is so novated or assigned:

6.2.2.1   the Buyer shall (for its own benefit and upon such terms as shall so far as possible give to the Buyer the benefit of any such agreement as if the same had been assigned to the Buyer) perform as the sub-contractor of the Sellers the obligations of the Sellers contained in that agreement and shall indemnify the Sellers in respect of any claims made against the Sellers as a result of any failure by the Buyer in the performance of such agreement and

6.2.2.2   the Sellers shall hold any benefit received under any such agreement upon trust for the Buyer absolutely

7 Consideration

7.1 The consideration for the sale of the Business shall be:

7.2.1 the assumption by the Buyer of the Liabilities and the obligations of the Sellers under any Outstanding Agreements (insofar as the latter are not comprised within the Liabilities) and

7.2.2 the Net Assets Value

7.2 Such part of the said consideration as represents the Net Assets Value shall be satisfied by the crediting by the Buyer to each of the Members' Accounts of a proportion of the Net Assets Value equal to the proportion which they held as partners in the Business immediately prior to the completion of this Agreement

8 Completion

8.1 The sale of the Business shall be completed on the Transfer Date at the offices of the Seller's solicitors when the Sellers shall execute and provide all such deeds and do all things as may be necessary effectively to vest the Business and all items referred to in Clause 3 in the Buyer

8.2 In the event that following completion the Sellers shall receive any money in respect of the Book Debts or the Work In Progress they shall forthwith upon receipt pay the same to the Buyer

8.3 The Sellers shall forthwith after completion give notice in writing pursuant to the Law of Property Act 1925 Section 136 to the relevant debtors of the assignment of the Book Debts and/or of the Buyer's right to render bills in respect of the Work In Progress and to collect the money due under any of the Book Debts or such bills

9 Employees

The Buyer will continue to employ all staff employed by the Sellers in connection with the Business and will indemnify the Sellers against any claims or Liabilities of whatever nature arising from the existing contracts of employment of such staff after the Actual Completion Date or from the transfer of the employment of such staff to the Buyer[8]

10 Value Added Tax

10.1 The Sellers and the Buyer consider that the Business is being transferred as a going concern

10.2 The Buyer warrants that:

10.2.1 it is registered as a taxable person for VAT purposes or will be so registered prior to the Actual Completion Date and

10.2.2 it will immediately after the transfer of the assets of the Business use those assets in the same kind of business as they were used in prior to the transfer

10.3 In the event of HM Customs & Excise refusing to accept that the transfer of the Business is a transfer of a going concern the Buyer shall pay to the

Sellers VAT on the assets transferred as assessed by HM Customs & Excise and the Sellers shall provide the Buyer with a tax invoice to support a claim by the Buyer for a recovery of the tax paid

11 Outstanding Obligations

All obligations which remain to be performed after the Actual Completion Date shall continue in full force and effect notwithstanding completion and shall not merge

12 Rights of other parties

For the avoidance of doubt nothing in this Agreement shall confer or purport to confer upon any person, firm, limited liability partnership or limited company which is not a party to this Agreement any benefit or right to enforce any term of this Agreement pursuant to the Contracts (Rights of Third Parties) Act 1999

AS WITNESS etc

SCHEDULE 1

1 Nature of Sellers' business

(insert brief descriptive details of the nature of the Business)

2 Name of Sellers' Business

(name)

3 Transfer date

(insert intended transfer date, allowing for note 2 [1648] of this Form)

SCHEDULE 2

Business premises

(insert sufficient detail of business premises to enable them to be correctly identified in a subsequent transfer, including title number where appropriate)

THIRD SCHEDULE

Plant and other assets

(insert list in sufficient detail to enable assets to be identified)

(signatures of (or on behalf of) the parties)

[1] I.e. a Limited Liability Partnership ('LLP') formed or to be formed under the Limited Liability Partnerships Act 2000 (32 Halsbury's Statutes (4th Edn) PARTNERSHIP) ('the Act'). This Agreement could also be adapted for the transfer of the business of a sole trader. No Capital Gains Tax will be payable on such a transfer, as the principle of tax transparency which underlies the Act means that assets are still deemed to be held by the members as partners, so

that there is no taxable disposal upon transfer (see Limited Liability Partnerships Act 2000, s 10(3)). Any deferred gains, e.g. as a result of roll-over relief, are thus carried over into the LLP's ownership. This aspect of transparency would not be the case, and therefore this Agreement is not suitable for, the (presumably rare) case of the transfer of the business of a limited company to an LLP.

[2] This Agreement can be entered into before the LLP is actually incorporated, in accordance with the Limited Liability Partnerships Act 2000, s 5(2). In that event its effectiveness will depend upon incorporation actually occurring. It would not be sensible to make it operative from the date of incorporation itself, since this will be the date of issue of the incorporation certificate by Companies House, and that date may not be known for some little while thereafter. A suitable gap should thus be allowed when determining the Transfer Date.

[3] Details can here be inserted of any intellectual property which is not to pass to the LLP for any reason. If a balance sheet value has been attributed to any such which is retained, an adjustment will be needed to assets values.

[4] This assumes that the partners in the selling partnership and the members of the buying LLP are exactly the same people. If there are any differences, i.e. because some partners are retiring and not becoming members, or new people are coming in as members who were not partners, then amendment will be necessary. Where possible, such circumstances should be avoided, in order to maintain clear entitlement to the Stamp Duty exemption offered by the Limited Liability Partnerships Act 2000, s 12.

[5] It is assumed that this will be an outright transfer of the Business in its entirety, i.e. that the transferring partnership will retain neither the benefit of Book Debts and Work in Progress, nor the burden of the Liabilities to existing creditors. It may be that some, perhaps larger, businesses will however wish to keep a skeleton partnership operating during a pre-set run-off period, and would wish to keep these elements out of the transfer. For professional partnerships in particular, one potential disadvantage of so doing is that, if there is a period of parallel operation of the old partnership and the new LLP, the latter may not be regarded for professional indemnity insurance purposes as the 'successor practice' to the partnership, which could cause considerable complications.

[6] This Agreement assumes that all the Business Premises, as currently shown in the accounts of the transferring partnership, are to be transferred to the LLP. If this is not so, e.g. because individuals wish to retain them outside the LLP for reasons of control of their investment, then firstly a reduction in the balance sheet will need to be agreed, and secondly arrangements for the occupation of the property in question by the LLP will need to be implemented. If this tack is to be followed, however, consideration will need to be given as to whether there is a danger of breaching any covenant with a mortgagor or landlord against letting etc. Also, in the case of leasehold property, it is likely that the chances of renewal under the Landlord and Tenant Act 1954 (23 Halsbury's Statutes (4th Edn) LANDLORD AND TENANT) will be adversely affected, since it will be the LLP, not the tenants, which is carrying on the business at the premises.

[7] The transfer of the interest in the Business Premises, from the transferring partners or those holding as nominees or trustees, will require to be perfected

later by a Transfer or Assignment. Any requisite consents, from mortgagees or landlords, should have been obtained in the normal way, and it would be prudent to do so before this Agreement is entered into. In the case of complex properties, it might be desirable to annex a draft Transfer or Assignment to this Agreement. Care should be taken to ensure that the title is passed within the period of twelve months from the date of incorporation of the LLP, so as to gain the benefit of the exemption from Stamp Duty contained in the Limited Liability Partnerships Act 2000, s 12.

[8] This very general and simple clause assumes that the same people will in practice be controlling the staff conditions both before and after transfer, so that it is not necessary to attempt to apportion pre and post transfer liabilities, or to delineate more precisely those employment liabilities which the purchaser of a business at arms length might expect to take on.

Novation agreement for use on transfer of business to a limited liability partnership[1]

THIS NOVATION AGREEMENT is made the . . . . . . day of . . . . . .

BETWEEN:

(1)   *(personal name(s) of transferring sole trader or partners)* trading [together] as *(business name of transferor business)* of *(address)* ('the Transferor')

(2)   *(name of transferee limited liability partnership)* whose registered office is at *(address)* ('the LLP') and

(3)   *(name of other party to contract)* of *(address)* ('the Third Party')

NOW IT IS AGREED as follows:

1   Definitions and interpretation

For the purposes of this Agreement:

1.1   The following expressions shall have the following meanings:

1.1.1   'the Contract Date' means the date appearing in the Schedule paragraph 1

1.1.2   'the Contract' means the contract made upon the Contract Date between the Transferor and the Third Party

1.1.3   'the Purpose' means the purpose for which the Contract was made brief descriptive details of which appear in the Schedule paragraph 2

1.1.4   'the Business' means the business which was at the Contract Date carried on by the Transferor brief descriptive details of which appear in the Schedule paragraph 3

1.1.5   'the Transfer Date' means the date upon which the Business was or is intended to be transferred to the LLP by agreement between the Transferor and the LLP and which appears in the Schedule paragraph 4

1.2   Expressions importing the masculine gender shall include the feminine and neuter and those importing the singular number shall include the plural and vice versa

1.3   Any covenants or stipulations entered into by more than one party shall be entered into jointly and severally

1.4   Unless the context otherwise requires reference to any clause, paragraph or Schedule is to a clause, paragraph or Schedule (as the case may be) of or to this Agreement

1.5   The headings in this document are inserted for convenience only and shall not affect the construction or interpretation of this Agreement

2   Recitals

2.1   The Business [is to be] [was] transferred by the Transferor to the LLP upon the Transfer Date

2.2   The Contract was entered into by the Transferor in the course of the operation of the Business

2.3   The Transferor wishes to be released and discharged from the Contract

2.4   The LLP has asked the Third Party to agree to such a release and discharge

2.5   The Third Party has agreed to release and discharge the Transferor from the Contract in return for the LLP's undertaking contained in Clause 3

3   Limited liability partnership's undertaking

In consideration of the release by the Transferor contained in Clause 4 the LLP undertakes to perform the Contract as from the Transfer Date and after that date to be bound by the terms of the Contract (in lieu of the Transferor) in every way as if it were a party to the Contract

4   Release of the transferor

In consideration of the undertaking on the part of the LLP contained in Clause 3:

4.1   The Third Party releases and discharges the Transferor from all claims and demands whatever in respect of the Contract and accepts in lieu of the Transferor the liability of the LLP under the Contract in respect of all claims, demands and liabilities arising from the Transfer Date onwards

4.2   The Third Party agrees to be bound by the Contract in respect of all obligations accruing from the Transfer Date onwards in every way as if the LLP were named in the Contract as a party in place of the Transferor

5   Rights of other parties

For the avoidance of doubt nothing in this Agreement shall confer or purport to confer upon any person, firm, limited liability partnership or limited company which is not a party to this Agreement any benefit or right to enforce any term of this Agreement or of the Contract pursuant to the Contracts (Rights of Third Parties) Act 1999

AS WITNESS etc

SCHEDULE

1   Contract date

(date upon which the Contract was made)

2   Purpose

(insert brief descriptive details of the purpose for which the Contract was made, for example, the purchase of widgets; the supply of professional services etc)

3 Business

(insert brief descriptive details of the nature of the Business)

4 Transfer date

(date upon which the transfer of the Business was or will become effective)

(signatures of (or on behalf of) the parties)

[1] This agreement is intended to be usable for a variety of novations which will be needed upon the transfer of a business to the entity of a limited liability partnership incorporated under the Limited Liability Partnerships Act 2000 (32 Halsbury's Statutes (4th Edn) PARTNERSHIP). It is suitable for use whether or not the earlier business was that of a sole trader or, as will in practice more usually be the case, a partnership. It is not particularly intended for use in the (presumably rare) circumstances where a limited company is transferring its business to an LLP, though it should be capable of adaptation for that purpose. The agreement for the transfer of the business should provide for the circumstances where it is not possible to obtain a novation, and so the Transferor has to hold the agreement on trust for the LLP in return for an indemnity.

Appendix 5 – Commentary on the Solicitors' Incorporated Practice Rules 2001

Part I – Introduction

A. General issues

What is an LLP?

As from 6 April 2001, it has been possible to form limited liability partnerships (LLPs) under the law of England and Wales.

An LLP is a body corporate, incorporated by being registered with the Registrar of Companies under the Limited Liability Partnerships Act 2000.

An LLP is not a company – it is a new type of body corporate. An LLP does not have shares or shareholders, nor does it have directors – it simply has members.

Unlike a company, an LLP does not have a memorandum and articles, and any members' agreement is a purely private document.

Despite the name "limited liability partnership", an LLP is not a partnership, and its members are not partners. Partnership law does not apply to an LLP.

An oversea LLP cannot at present be registered in England and Wales (unless it is a company, in which case it has an obligation to register under the Companies Act 1985 if the company has a place of business in England and Wales).

Tax – a key issue

LLPs will, in general, be treated like partnerships for tax purposes. The transition from partnership to LLP, if handled correctly, need not give rise to a tax charge. The tax treatment may make an LLP a more attractive vehicle for professional practice than a limited company.

What limitation of liability does an LLP give?

Liability of the LLP

The LLP itself will be fully liable in contract and tort for the acts and defaults of its members and employees.

It is open to the LLP to limit its liability by agreement. However, in respect of the limitation of liability to clients, reference should be made to principle 12.11 in *The Guide to the Professional Conduct of Solicitors* (1999). In particular, this principle provides that there must be no limitation of liability below the compulsory minimum level of insurance cover under the indemnity rules (currently £1,000,000 per claim).

Liability of individuals

One of the potential attractions of LLP status will be the protection it may give to individuals against the risk of a large claim not covered by professional indemnity insurance.

An individual member of the LLP (unlike a partner in a partnership) will not in general be liable in contract or tort, by virtue of being a member of the LLP, for the acts or defaults of fellow members or of employees.

Members of the LLP will not be liable for the debts and obligations of the LLP subject to certain statutory qualifications (in particular sections 214 and 214A of the Insolvency Act 1986). However members will not be protected from liability which they incur in their own right either in contract (e.g. where a member guarantees the contractual obligations of the LLP) or in tort (e.g. for negligent misstatement).

What is not clear is the extent to which an individual member or employee of the LLP will be liable in tort for his or her own misstatements. There are at least two views:

- The House of Lords in *Williams* v. *Natural Life Health Foods Ltd* [1998] 1 WLR 830; [1998] 2 All ER 577 held (in the case of a limited company) that an individual (in that case the director of the company) would only be liable in negligence if (a) he or she assumed personal responsibility for the advice, (b) the claimant relied on this assumption of responsibility, and (c) such reliance was reasonable. One view is that, as implied by the *Williams* judgment, individuals in an LLP will incur liability in tort in exceptional cases only.

● The contrary view, which has been put forward in the past by the Government and the Law Society, is that a negligent solicitor or other fee earner who is a member or employee in an LLP would often, or always, be liable to clients in tort. On this view, the courts would be likely to regard legal advice given in the course of a solicitor-client relationship in a different light from representations made in the course of arm's length negotiations as in *Williams*.

It would therefore be dangerous to assume that LLP status will protect solicitors from the consequences of their own personal negligence, which could sometimes include negligent supervision of staff.

It may sometimes be possible for the LLP to limit by contract the liability of its individual members and employees. However, in respect of the limitation of liability to clients, reference should be made to principle 12.11 in *The Guide to the Professional Conduct of Solicitors* (1999). In particular, this principle provides that there must be no limitation of liability below the compulsory minimum level of insurance cover under the indemnity rules (currently £1,000,000 per claim). This applies to the limitation of individuals' liability as well as that of the practice as a whole.

Whatever limitation of liability may be enjoyed by individuals, it will not apply to the joint and several covenants which all members of the LLP are required to give to the Law Society to cover reimbursement of payments made out of the Compensation Fund in respect of the acts or defaults of the LLP, its members and employees. This requirement in effect puts members of an LLP on the same footing as partners in a partnership so far as the Compensation Fund is concerned.

Which type of business organisation?

As from 6 April 2001, solicitors or registered European lawyers (RELs) who are in joint practice have four basic choices as to the business organisation for their practice – a partnership, an unlimited company, a limited company, or an LLP.

Factors which may influence the choice will include tax considerations, the financial disclosure requirements in the case of a company or an LLP, the disclosure of the home addresses of all directors of a company and all members of an LLP, the effective governance of the practice, the legal and personal relationships between the solicitors (or RELs), the reaction of clients and creditors, and the costs (including any tax and stamp duty costs) of making a change.

In particular, solicitors may be influenced by the requirement that the LLP's accounts, prepared on a true and fair basis and audited, must be filed with the Registrar of Companies (unless turnover is less than £1 million and the balance sheet total is less than £1.4 million) so that they are available for public inspection. This is in addition to the obligation to deliver an annual accountant's report to the Law Society.

Given the sensitive nature of the affairs of many clients, you will need to consider carefully the implications of the requirement to disclose the home addresses of all members of an LLP. The addresses will be available to inspection by the public. A provision in the Criminal Justice and Police Act 2001 will allow directors of companies (and, prospectively, members of LLPs) to apply for a confidentiality order. However it should be borne in mind that, even if this provision eventually becomes available to you in the particular circumstances of your practice, home addresses already on the public register will remain there, as there is no mechanism to remove them.

If a change is being considered, you may also wish to look at the option of a company structure, as an alternative to an LLP.

Business and practice issues on conversion to an LLP

Before converting to an LLP, it will be necessary to review the current partnership agreement, with a view to preparing an appropriate procedure (including financial arrangements for present and former partners) for conversion, and appropriate terms for a members' agreement for the new LLP.

It will also be necessary to examine all the practice's business documentation, including contracts with employees and suppliers, leases, bank facilities, income tax, national insurance and VAT arrangements, pension schemes, etc., in order to ascertain what changes will need to be made or negotiated.

Note that under section 36 of the Companies Act 1985 (as applied by the Limited Liability Partnerships Regulations 2001), a contract may be made (i) by an LLP, by writing under its common seal, or (ii) on behalf of the LLP, by any person acting under its authority, express or implied.

Under section 36A of the Act, a document may be executed by the LLP (i) by the affixing of its common seal, or (ii) by way of a document signed by two members of the LLP and expressed to be executed by the LLP. In either case, if the document makes it clear on its face that it is intended to be a deed, it will have effect, upon delivery, as a deed.

You will need to consider the requirements to inform various legal authorities – e.g. serving a notice of change in ongoing litigation, going on the court record in the name of the LLP in future litigation, informing the Legal Services Commission, the Land Registry, the Information Commissioner (to register under the Data Protection Act 1998), etc.

All precedents will have to be reviewed – especially the appointment of members of the practice as executors or trustees.

Executors and trustees

A particular problem is the terms of appointment of executors or trustees in wills and trust deeds executed prior to the conversion. For instance, an appointment of "the partners for the time being of Smith & Brown or any firm succeeding to the business of Smith & Brown" may (or may not) fail as excluding the members of Smith & Brown LLP.

Consideration will need to be given to approaching each testator to suggest the execution of a codicil.

Alternatively, you may decide to keep the partnership in existence for some time after the incorporation of the LLP. There may of course be tax implications in doing this. There will certainly be regulatory implications – e.g. for insurance, investment business authorisation and client accounts.

The legislative framework for LLPs

The primary legislation is:

- the Limited Liability Partnerships Act 2000, which is available on: http:www.legislation.hmso.gov.uk/acts/acts2000/00012--a.htm

Secondary legislation includes:

- the Limited Liability Partnerships Regulations 2001 (S.I. 2001 no. 1090), available on: http://www.hmso.gov.uk/si/si20011090.htm

- the European Communities (Lawyer's Practice) (Amendment) Regulations 2001 (S.I. 2001 no. 644), available on: http://www.hmso.gov.uk/si/si20010644.htm

- the Solicitors' Incorporated Practices (Amendment) Order 2001 (S.I. 2001 no. 645), available on: http://www.hmso.gov.uk/si/si2001/20010645

B. Regulatory issues

The need to become a recognised body

A solicitors' (or RELs') LLP, incorporated under the Limited Liability Partnerships Act 2000, must not commence practice in England and Wales before it has obtained recognition from the Law Society as a recognised body.

Otherwise all solicitors and RELs who are members of the LLP (as well as solicitors and RELs who are employees of the LLP) would be in breach of the Solicitors' Practice Rules 1990. In the case of a solicitors' LLP (or a mixed LLP of solicitors and foreign lawyers), the LLP itself would also be committing a criminal offence under sections 20-24 of the Solicitors Act 1974.

The new rules

The Solicitors' Incorporated Practice Rules 1988 had to be completely rewritten so as to encompass LLPs in addition to companies. The new rules – the Solicitors' Incorporated Practice Rules 2001 – appear in Part II of this Information Pack. They came into force on 6 April 2001.

The Solicitors' Practice Rules 1990 and all the other rules and codes governing the conduct of solicitors and RELs had to be amended so as to encompass LLPs. Again, these amendments came into force on 6 April 2001. They are highlighted in Part III of this Information Pack.

Application for recognition

Before solicitors (or RELs) can practise through an LLP, the LLP will have to

- first, become incorporated by registration with the Registrar of Companies; and

- secondly, obtain recognition from the Law Society as a recognised body under section 9 of the Administration of Justice Act 1985 and rules 2(1) and 21(1) of the Solicitors' Incorporated Practice Rules 2001.

The application to the Law Society for recognition as a recognised body has to be on Form LLP1, which must be signed by one of the LLP's members on behalf of the LLP, and must be accompanied by:

- a copy of the LLP's certificate of incorporation;

- Compensation Fund covenants under rule 19(5) of the Solicitors' Incorporated Practice Rules 2001 from all the members of the LLP;

- the LLP's application fee (currently £500 for three years); and

- the LLP's Compensation Fund contribution (currently £200 for three years).

The application form includes:

- the provision of evidence that the LLP is covered by insurance under the Solicitors' Indemnity Insurance Rules 2000;

- the provision of evidence that the LLP is covered by top-up insurance under rule 18 of the Solicitors' Incorporated Practice Rules 2001 – £500,000 on an each and every claim basis or £2,000,000 per year on an aggregate basis; and

a declaration of compliance with the Solicitors' Incorporated Practice Rules 2001.

Recognition lasts in the first instance for three years, by which time you will need to apply for renewal of recognition.

Membership of the LLP

Who can be a member of the LLP?

Section 2(1)(a) of the Limited Liability Partnerships Act 2000 requires that there must be at least two members to incorporate an LLP. A member could be either an individual or a body corporate.

Rule 5(1) of the Solicitors' Incorporated Practice Rules 2001 provides that the following (and only the following) can be members of the LLP:

- solicitors with practising certificates;

- RELs;

- registered foreign lawyers (RFLs);

- non-registered European lawyers, as defined by rule 1(1)(l);

- recognised bodies;

- European corporate practices, as defined by rule 1(1)(g).

Who must be a member of the LLP?

Section 24 of the Companies Act 1985, as applied by the Limited Liability Partnerships Regulations 2001, provides that, if an LLP is left with only one member for more than six months, limitation of liability will be lost. The Law Society will therefore not recognise an LLP with only one member.

Rule 5(4) of the Solicitors' Incorporated Practice Rules 2001 provides that:

(i)   at least one of the LLP's members, or

(ii)   a director of a company (a recognised body) which is one of the LLP's members, or

(iii)   a member of another LLP (a recognised body) which is one of the LLP's members,

must be a solicitor or a REL.

Additional requirement under Practice Rule 13

Rule 13(2) of the Solicitors' Practice Rules 1990 requires that, in the practice of an LLP,

(i)   at least one of the LLP's members, or

(ii)   a director of a company (a recognised body) which is one of the LLP's members, or

(iii)   a member of another LLP (a recognised body) which is one of the LLP's members,

must be:

(a)   a solicitor who has held practising certificates for at least 36 months within the last ten years, and has completed the training specified by the Law Society; or

(b)   a REL, or a solicitor who was formerly a REL, who has practised as a lawyer for at least 36 months within the last ten years, and has completed the training specified by the Law Society; or

(c)   if the practice does not exercise or assume responsibility for any right of audience or any right to conduct litigation, an RFL who has practised as a lawyer for at least 36 months within the last ten years, and has completed the training specified by the Law Society.

Change in membership

Any change in the LLP's membership must forthwith be notified to the Law Society (rule 25(1)(a)(v) of the Solicitors' Incorporated Practice Rules 2001). Each new member must submit a Compensation Fund covenant under rule 19(5).

Section 9(1)(a) of the Limited Liability Partnerships Act 2000 requires that any change in the LLP's membership be notified to Companies House within fourteen days.

"Place of registration"

Rule 15(1)(a) of the Solicitors' Incorporated Practice Rules 2001 requires that the LLP be registered in England and Wales – i.e. the LLP will be registered with Companies House in Cardiff (either by filing the incorporation document at the Cardiff headquarters, or at one of the English offices).

Registered office

Like a company, an LLP will have a registered office.

Rule 14(1) of the Solicitors' Incorporated Practice Rules 2001 states that the LLP's registered office shall be:

- in England or in Wales; **and**

- at the practising address or one of the practising addresses of the LLP.

Section 2(2) of the Limited Liability Partnerships Act 2000 provides that the "incorporation document" (in effect the application form for registration at Companies House) has to prescribe whether the LLP's registered office is to be situated "in England and Wales", "in Wales" or "in Scotland". (Scotland is irrelevant for our purposes because of rule 14(1).)

If the incorporation document prescribes a registered office "in England and Wales", the name of the LLP has to include one of the English language forms "LLP," "llp" or "limited liability partnership", even if the LLP's registered office is actually in Wales.

If the incorporation document prescribes a registered office "in Wales", the name of the LLP may **either** include one of the English language forms as above, **or** one of the Welsh language equivalents "PAC," "pac" or "partneriaeth atebolrwydd cyfyngedig".

Name of the LLP

The name of an LLP has to comply with Part I of the Schedule to the Limited Liability Partnerships Act 2000. In particular:

- the name of an LLP whose incorporation document prescribes a registered office "in England and Wales" must end with the abbreviation "LLP" or "llp" or the expression "limited liability partnership";

- the name of an LLP whose incorporation document prescribes a registered office "in Wales" must end **either** with one of the English language forms as above, **or** one of the Welsh language equivalents "PAC", "pac" or "partneriaeth atebolrwydd cyfyngedig".

The name must also comply with rule 11(1) of the Solicitors' Practice Rules 1990 and, if the LLP is also to practise outside England and Wales, rule 10(1) of the Solicitors' Overseas Practice Rules 1990.

Note that it is possible to reserve the name for an LLP by registering a shelf company under, say, the name "Smith & Brown Ltd" to reserve the name "Smith & Brown LLP". The filing of the LLP's incorporation document will then have to be synchronised with a change in the name of the shelf company. To utilise this procedure you will need to contact the LLP Team at Companies House in Cardiff (telephone 029-2038 0744) a few days before filing the incorporation document.

Compensation Fund covenants

Every member of the LLP will have to execute a Compensation Fund covenant in favour of the Law Society under rule 19(5) of the Solicitors' Incorporated Practice Rules 2001. This gives the Society, on behalf of the Compensation Fund, the same rights of recovery against a member of the LLP as against a principal in a partnership.

There are two forms of covenant. Form LLPC1 is to be used for an individual (a solicitor, a REL, an RFL or a non-registered European lawyer) who is a member or proposes to become a member of an LLP. Form LLPC2 is to be used for a body corporate (a recognised body, a body applying for that status, or a European corporate practice) which is a member or proposes to become a member of an LLP.

The specimen forms in Part IV of this pack, or those sent out by the Law Society's Regulation and Information Services, can be freely copied for your use.

The covenants have to name the LLP of which the covenantor is or is to be a member.

Before new members join the LLP, it is important to obtain Compensation Fund covenants from them.

Compensation Fund contributions

On applying for recognition, the LLP will be required to pay a Compensation Fund contribution – currently £200 – to cover the first three years. (The Law Society also has power under paragraph 6 of Schedule 2 to the Administration of Justice Act 1985 to require a further contribution from time to time.)

In addition, solicitor members of an LLP will continue to have to pay their annual Compensation Fund contributions when applying for their practising certificates. If the LLP has held or received client money, each solicitor member will be treated as having held or received client money, and thus will pay the full rate of contribution rather than the reduced rate.

REL members of an LLP will continue to pay annual contributions on the same basis as solicitor members.

If an LLP has held or received client money, RFL members of the LLP will continue to pay annual contributions, the level of which will depend on whether the RFL is based in England and Wales or overseas. If the LLP has not held or received client money, RFL members will not be required to make an annual contribution (in respect of that practice).

Professional indemnity insurance

Compulsory insurance under the Solicitors' Indemnity Insurance Rules

The LLP will have to have qualifying insurance under rule 4 of the Solicitors' Indemnity Insurance Rules 2001 (unless it has one or more REL "principals" and has been granted total exemption under Appendix 4.1 or partial exemption under Appendix 4.2).

The compulsory cover under the rules includes not only the LLP itself, but also its members, employees and consultants.

If the whole of the practice of your partnership is being transferred en bloc to an LLP, the LLP will be a "successor practice" to the partnership and, under the Standard Terms and Conditions, will be automatically covered by the partnership's qualifying insurance. However it is important that you keep your insurers fully informed about the formation of the LLP, and you will need to secure their written confirmation of the LLP's cover before you can complete the LLP's application for recognition as a recognised body.

If your partnership is continuing in practice alongside your new LLP, the LLP will not at that stage be a "successor practice", and you will therefore have to arrange the LLP's own qualifying insurance prior to completing the LLP's application for recognition as a recognised body.

Of course, the LLP cannot actually commence practice until it has been recognised by the Law Society.

Top-up insurance

The LLP will also require compulsory top-up insurance under rule 18 of the Solicitors' Incorporated Practice Rules 2001 – £500,000 on an each and every claim basis or £2,000,000 per year on an aggregate basis. Again, this must be arranged before completing the LLP's application for recognition as a recognised body.

It is important that you keep your top-up insurers (both in respect of compulsory top-up cover and voluntary top-up cover) fully informed as to the setting up of the LLP. It will not necessarily be possible to rely on top-up cover already in place for the partnership.

Policyholders Protection Act 1975

It should be noted that, as a body corporate, an LLP (unlike a partnership) will not have the benefit of the Policyholders Protection Act 1975 in respect of its insurance cover, i.e. if the insurance company fails. However, the whole picture – both as to partnerships and bodies corporate – is likely to change with the coming into force of the Financial Services and Markets Act 2000 on 1 December 2001.

Solicitors' Indemnity Fund

Under Part III of the Solicitors' Indemnity Rules 2001, you will need to inform Solicitors Indemnity Fund Limited as soon as the LLP commences practice. Similarly you will need to inform Solicitors Indemnity Fund Limited if your previous partnership ceases to practice as such.

Under rule 26 of the Solicitors' Indemnity Rules 2001, the LLP will be required to make contributions to the Solicitors' Indemnity Fund in respect of the Indemnity Fund shortfall and retired practitioners' run-off cover under the old Indemnity Fund arrangements. The LLP will be exempt from making contributions if it has no solicitor "principal" who was in practice as a solicitor "principal" before 1 September 1999.

Investment business

If the LLP is to do investment business, it will need authorisation, as an LLP, under the Financial Services Act 1986.

If the LLP is to do investment business under the Law Society's authorisation, it will require an investment business certificate issued in the name of the LLP. The LLP cannot use a certificate issued in the name of a partnership. The application form for recognition as a recognised body includes questions on investment business authorisation.

If all the investment business of your partnership is to be transferred immediately to your new LLP, no fee will be required for the LLP's investment business certificate.

If, on the other hand, your partnership will still be carrying on in practice alongside your new LLP, and both will be doing investment business, two separate certificates will be needed, and payment will be required in full for the LLP's new certificate. The current annual fee is £210, plus £70 per member (reducing quarterly).

If you are authorised by another regulator, it is important to keep the regulator informed, and to comply with its requirements.

The whole picture will change on the coming into force of the Financial Services and Markets Act 2000 on 1 December 2001. The Financial Services Authority (FSA) will be the sole regulator under that Act, and the Law Society will no longer issue investment business certificates. An LLP doing mainstream investment business (currently discrete investment business) will need to be regulated by the FSA, and should complete and return the FSA's "opt-in" form by 31 October 2001 in order to take advantage of the "grandfathering" provisions. An LLP doing non-mainstream investment business (currently non-discrete investment business) only will probably not need to seek regulation by the FSA. Note that all firms, whether regulated by the FSA or not, will continue to be subject to the rules of the Law Society as their professional body.

Notepaper of the LLP

Requirements of the Companies Act 1985

Under sections 349 and 351 of the Companies Act 1985, as applied by the Limited Liability Partnerships Regulations 2001, the notepaper of an LLP has to include:

- the LLP's corporate name;

- the address of the LLP's registered office;

- the fact that the LLP is a "limited liability partnership" (or a "partneriaeth atebolrwydd cyfyngedig"), unless this is spelled out in full in the LLP's name;

- the LLP's "place of registration" – that is:

"registered in England and Wales", "registered in England" or "registered in London" if the LLP's registered office is in England; or

  ○ "registered in England and Wales", "registered in Wales", "registered in Cardiff" or a Welsh equivalent if the LLP's registered office is in Wales; and

- the LLP's registered number.

Requirements of the Law Society's rules

There must also be compliance with:

- rule 11(2) of the Solicitors' Practice Rules 1990;

- paragraphs 6–8 of the Solicitors' Publicity Code 1990;

- rule 10(2) of the Solicitors' Overseas Practice Rules 1990 if the LLP has an office outside England and Wales; and

- rule 21 of the Solicitors' Investment Business Rules 1995 if the LLP is conducting discrete investment business under an investment business certificate – but remember that any statement as to regulation/authorisation by the Law Society in the conduct of investment business must be removed from notepaper immediately upon the coming into force of the Financial Services and Markets Act 2000 on 1 December 2001.

Under rule 27 of the Solicitors' Incorporated Practice Rules 2001, the notepaper must contain **either** the names of all the members, identified as "members", **or** a statement that a list of the members is open to inspection at the registered office and the address of that office. There is a free choice between these two options **unless** the following paragraph applies.

Requirements of the Business Names Act 1985

If an LLP is carrying on business under a style **other than** its corporate name, section 4 of the Business Names Act 1985, as applied by the Limited Liability Partnerships Regulations 2001, requires that the LLP's notepaper must include the LLP's corporate name, the name of every member of the LLP and an address for service. Where there are more than twenty members, the section permits, instead of a list of members and an address for service, a reference to a list of members open to inspection at the principal place of business.

Client care

Where a partnership converts to an LLP, principle 3.11 in *The Guide to the Professional Conduct of Solicitors* (1999) requires that you notify clients for whom the firm is currently acting, or for whom money is being held, either before the change or soon afterwards.

If your practice is on the panel of a mortgage lender or insurance company, you will need to advise them of the transfer of your practice to the LLP.

Paragraph 7(a)(ii) of the Solicitors' Costs Information and Client Care Code 1999 requires that the client of an LLP must be given:

- the name and status of the person dealing with the client's matter; and

- the name of the member of the LLP who is responsible for the overall supervision of the matter.

Client bank accounts

It is important to remember that, under rule 14(3) of the Solicitors' Accounts Rules 1998 the partnership's client accounts at a bank or building society have to be in the partnership name, whereas an LLP's client accounts of an LLP have to be in the name of the LLP. If the entire practice of a partnership is transferred to an LLP, new client accounts will have to be opened in the name of the LLP, and all money transferred.

If, on the other hand, part of the practice of the partnership is to continue, the partnership's client accounts will need to be maintained for that purpose – the partnership and the LLP cannot operate shared client accounts.

Accountant's reports

If the LLP holds or receives client money or controlled trust money, it will in due course have to deliver an accountant's report to the Law Society. This obligation extends to the members of the LLP – in other words, their names, as well as the name of the LLP, must all appear on the accountant's report. In addition, the names of any assistant or consultant solicitor (or REL) who has held or received controlled trust money or operated a client's own account as signatory will also need to appear.

If the LLP is late with its accountant's report, the solicitor members will each be subject to section 12(1)(ee) of the Solicitors Act 1974, making them liable for the additional practising certificate fee (currently £50) under section 12A(1), as well as subjecting them to the inconvenience of having to give notice under section 12(4).

Any REL members of the LLP will be liable for an addition (currently £50) to the annual registration fee in respect of the late accountant's report.

Conveyancing and probate

An LLP must not do reserved conveyancing or probate work unless:

(a)   at least one of the LLP's members, or

(b)   a director of a company (a recognised body) which is one of the LLP's members, or

(c)   a member of another LLP (a recognised body) which is one of the LLP's members,

is **either** a solicitor, **or** a REL qualified to provide that service under regulation 12 or 13 of the European Communities (Lawyer's Practice) Regulations 2000.

Bills of the LLP

Under section 349 of the Companies Act 1985, as applied by the Limited Liability Partnerships Regulations 2001, the bills of an LLP will have to include the LLP's corporate name.

For an LLP to be able to sue on its bills, the bill, or a letter accompanying it, must be signed on behalf of the LLP by a member or employee authorised to do so. One way of doing this might be to sign in the form "John Smith for and on behalf of Smith & Brown LLP". (See section

69(2)(a) of the Solicitors Act 1974 as applied by paragraph 29 of Schedule 2 to the Administration of Justice Act 1985 and Schedule 5 to the Limited Liability Partnerships Regulations 2001.)

Note that if an LLP is carrying on business under a style **other than** its corporate name, section 4 of the Business Names Act 1985, as applied by the Limited Liability Partnerships Regulations 2001, requires that the LLP's bills must include the LLP's corporate name, the name of every member of the LLP and an address for service. Where there are more than twenty members, the section permits, instead of a list of members and an address for service, a reference to a list of members open to inspection at the principal place of business.

C. Look before you leap!

We hope this guidance has been helpful. However, we would stress a number of points:

- It is essential to consult your professional and business advisers if you are contemplating converting your practice to an LLP.

- In particular it is important to seek specialist advice as to the tax consequences of the changeover – there are tax pitfalls if the mechanics of the transfer are not carried out in the right way.

- Do not underestimate the amount of planning which will be needed, or how long the preparatory period will need to be.

- You would be advised to contact the LLP Team at Companies House in Cardiff (telephone 029-2038 0744) at an early stage to discuss the arrangements for registration (and especially the question of securing your choice of name). Information about LLPs is on the Companies House website: www.companieshouse.gov.uk/.

- The Law Society's Regulation and Information Services will do their best to assist you in preparing your application, and will process your application as quickly as they can. Their address is:

- The Law Society, Regulation and Information Services, Ipsley Court, Berrington Close, Redditch, Worcestershire, B98 0TD; telephone: 0870-606 2555; local calls: 01527 517141; fax: 020-7320 5862; DX: 19114 – REDDITCH.

- Further guidance on the rules is available from Professional Ethics – telephone: 0870-606 2577.

Table of Cases

Table of Statutes

Table of Statutory Instruments

Index